The Changing French Political System

Editor

ROBERT ELGIE

(Senior Lecturer, European Politics,
University of Nottingham)

FRANK CASS

LONDON • PORTLAND, OR

First Published in 2000 in Great Britain by
FRANK CASS PUBLISHERS
Newbury House, 900 Eastern Avenue
London, IG2 7HH

and in the United States of America by
FRANK CASS PUBLISHERS
c/o ISBS, 5804 N.E. Hassalo Street
Portland, Oregon, 97213-3644

Website: www.frankcass.com

Copyright © 2000 Frank Cass Publishers

British Library Cataloguing in Publication Data:

The changing French political system
1. France – Politics and government – 20th century
I. Elgie, Robert
320.9'44
ISBN 0-7146-5043 9 (cloth)
ISBN 0-7146-8098 2 (paper)

Library of Congress Cataloging-in-Publication Data:

The changing French political system / editor Robert Elgie.
    p. cm.
Includes bibliographical references and index.
ISBN 0-7146-5043-9 – ISBN 0-7146-8098-2 (paper)
    1. France–Politics and government–1995– 2. France–Social
conditions–1995– I. Elgie, Robert.
JN2594.2.C494 2000
320.944'09'049–dc21   99-058569

This group of studies first appeared in a Special Issue on
'The Changing French Political System' of
West European Politics (ISSN 0140-2382) 22/4 (October 1999)
published by Frank Cass.

*All rights reserved. No part of this publication may be reproduced, stored in or introduced into
a retrieval system, or transmitted, in any form, or by any means, electronic, mechanical,
photocopying, recording, or otherwise, without the prior written permission of
the publisher of this book.*

Printed in Great Britain by Antony Rowe Ltd., Chippenham, Wiltshire

THE CHANGING FRENCH POLITICAL SYSTEM

BOOKS OF RELATED INTEREST

Contents

Incomparable Comparatist

VINCENT WRIGHT, 1937–99

The first issue of *West European Politics* published in February 1978, Vincent's brainchild with Gordon Smith, characteristically did not begin with any pretentious mission statements. Its title reflected the practical research interests of its founder-editors but set the scene for a process of extending and expanding its concerns into a journal of comparative European politics with a strong empirical basis in the countries extending westward from *Mitteleuropa*. It reflected Vincent's approach to comparative politics via the best inductive route: an initial comprehensive grounding in the study of a single country, from bottom to top and then from top to bottom. In his case the country was France but he never remained imprisoned within its frontiers.

Vincent maintained critical detachment from his object of investigation, studying it longitudinally over time and laterally by implicit or explicit comparison. He was, from his doctoral days, inoculated against the propensity to superficial culture-bound generalisation, having immersed himself in the wholly untypical electoral politics of the Basses Pyrénées during the Second Empire – what the advocates of a one and indivisible France might have called the 'extreme south-west'. In the early 1970s he broadened his research into two books, on the Conseil d'Etat and the Prefects in the Second Empire, showing his increasing interest in *government*, particularly administrative justice as well as administration more generally.

Recognition of the quality of these books, published in French, ensured that he enjoyed lifelong links with the contemporary embodiments of these pillars of the French state, affording him privileged insight into the inner workings of French government not accessible to almost all scholars, French or foreign. Vincent earned the, at first, grudging respect of the French he encountered because he understood many aspects of their culture and institutions far better than they did themselves. So although he sadistically applied the principle *qui aime bien châtie bien*, he was always in great demand as lecturer, discussant and contributor to French publications.

Vincent not only put this enviable understanding of France into his writing of *The Government and Politics of France* (1978), whose popularity ensured that he was pressed into preparing drastically revised new editions. He attracted and intellectually inspired, as much by his example as by precept, generations of graduate students, first at the London School of Economics but especially at Nuffield College, Oxford. There emerged a flow of first rate theses whose publication, as articles and books, have immensely enriched our knowledge, first of French government and latterly comparative European politics.

Inimitably, Vincent did not seek disciples. (His doctoral students were frequently encouraged to publish their work in this journal, both ensuring that it was constantly refreshed with the research results of those working at the frontiers of our knowledge, as well as helping them to establish their reputations at an early stage in their careers.) He demonstrated what could be attained by bending all one's intellectual capacities to disentangling intractable interactions and presenting one's findings in accessible and stimulating language, without smoothing away the complexities. Vincent exulted in dissipating confusion by incisive clarification. He excelled at systematically taking problems apart to understand them, giving priority to dismembering over reconstituting. He relished the dialectical clash of thesis and antithesis, not worrying too much about whether a synthesis would ever emerge. The convivial controversialist he was would have regretted ending the argument. Vincent was a lifelong, card-carrying member of the remorseless thinking, pellucid writing and pugnaciously talking classes.

Vincent eschewed solemnity in himself and mercilessly mocked it when others took themselves rather than their subject too seriously. Although Vincent was always hard on the portentous humbug and the hollow rhetoric in which not only French intellectuals are prone to indulge, he liked to be regarded as more turbulent and tough-minded than he was deep down. Vincent had a great sense of fun, enjoying robust – even knockabout – argument. He was a rounded human, not just a workaholic. Fastidious in his tastes, he rejoiced in sharing the good things of life with his chosen friends, especially in conversation.

Vincent was exceptionally unselfish in his intellectual dealings. He helped not merely his own students but many others, often from a great distance, who were attracted by his reputation. With colleagues, he would collaborate in exchanges where he had usually far more to offer than to receive. The multiplier effect of his numerous edited works ensured that his influence was spread far and wide. International political economy increasingly attracted his attention, leading to pioneering comparative work on privatisation and the changing relationship of states and markets in Western Europe. By the 1980s and 1990s, Vincent had developed an in-depth knowledge of Italian and Spanish government and politics, thanks in part to his links with the European University Institute in Florence and the Juan March Institute in Madrid. He also continued to teach frequently in France and in the USA.

Vincent's collaborative activities continued as long as the debilitating effects of cancer allowed him to focus his acute mind on the issues to which he had devoted his life's work. Much will be published in the coming months and years of the research with which he was associated. In Vincent Wright's case, Shakespeare's Mark Antony was wrong: the good he did will live after him, not least in the shape of *West European Politics*, which he would dearly have loved to continue editing from beyond the grave. He died much too soon.

JACK HAYWARD

VINCENT WRIGHT'S BOOKS, 1972–97

Le Conseil d'Etat sous le Second Empire, Travaux de recherches de sciences politiques de la Fondation Nationale des Sciences Politiques, Paris: Armand Colin, 1972.

(with Bernard Le Clère), *Les Préfets du Second Empire*. Cahier de la Fondation Nationale des Sciences Politiques, Paris: Armand Colin, 1973 (awarded the Prix Chaix-d'Etat Anqe de l'Institut de France).

(with Frédéric Marx), *Les Universités Britanniques*, Dossier Themis, Paris: Presses Universitaires de France, 1973.

The Government and Politics of France, London: Hutchinson University Press, 1978. (American edition 1980) (2nd revised and updated version 1982, 3rd revision 1983) (3rd edition 1989).

(with Jacques Lagroye) (eds.), *Local Government in Britain and France, Problems and Prospects*, London: Allen and Unwin, 1979 (French edition 1982).

(editor and contributor), *Continuity and Consensus in France*, London: Frank Cass, 1979.

(editor and contributor), *Continuity and Change in France*, London: Allen and Unwin, 1984.

(with Yves Mény), *La Crise de la sidérurgie européenne 1974–1984*, Paris: Presses Universitaires de France, 1985.

(with Howard Machin) (eds.), *Economic Policy and Policy Making under the Mitterrand Presidency*, London: Frances Pinter & Co. 1985.

(with Yves Mény) (eds.), *The Political Management of Industrial Crisis: The Case of Steel 1974–1984*, Berlin: de Gruyter, 1986.

(with Rod Rhodes) (eds.), *Tensions in the Territorial Politics of Western Europe*, London: Frank Cass, 1987.

(with John Vickers) (eds.), *The Politics of Privatization in Western Europe*, London: Frank Cass, 1989.

(editor and contributor), *The Representativity of Public Administration*, Brussels: IISA, 1991.

(editor), *Les privatisations en Europe: programmes et problèmes*, Paris: Actes-Sud, 1993.

(editor), *Privatization in Western Europe*, London: Pinter Publications, 1994 (revised and updated edition of above 1989 title).

(with Yves Mény) (eds.), *La Riforma Amministrativa in Europa*, Bologna: Il Mulino, 1994.

(with Wolfgang Müller) (eds.), *The State in Western Europe: Retreat or Redefinition?* London: Frank Cass, 1994.

(with Sabino Cassese) (eds.), *La recomposition de l'Etat en Europe*, Paris: La Découverte, 1996.

(with Paul Heywood and Martin Rhodes) (eds.), *Developments in West European Politics*, London: Macmillan, 1997.

FORTHCOMING

(with S. Hazareesingh), *Les Frères en lutte: Le grand-Orient de France à la Veille de la Troisième République*, Geneva: Droz [series of Ecole Pratique des Hautes Etudes, Paris].

(with E. Page) (eds.), *Bureaucratic Elites in West European States: A Comparative Analysis of Top Officials*, Oxford: Oxford University Press.

(with B.G. Peters and R.A.W. Rhodes) (eds.), *Administering the Summit*, London: Macmillan, 1999.

(with Hussein Kassim and B. Guy Peters (eds.), *National Co-ordination of EU Policy Making: The Domestic Level*, Oxford: Oxford University Press.

(with Luisa Perrotti) (eds.), *Privatization and Public Policy*, 2 vols., Aldershot: Edward Elgar, 1999.

(with J.E.S. Hayward), *Governing from the Centre: Core Executive Policy Co-ordination in France, Germany*, London: Macmillan.

Administration et Guerre: les préfets du gouvernement de la défense nationale, Paris: Ecole Pratique des Hautes Etudes.

The Changing French Political System: Introduction

ROBERT ELGIE

France is undergoing a period of social, political and economic change. Entrenched patterns of behaviour are being threatened by alternative forms of political action. Traditional cleavages are being undermined by social and ideological uncertainties. Intellectual paradigms are being replaced by new and more flexible perspectives. In short, like so many of its West European counterparts, France, if not in crisis, is certainly experiencing a profound transformation in the organisation and understanding of its political life.[1]

The aim of this volume is to chart some of the most significant changes in contemporary French politics and the study of it. Each contribution focuses on developments that have occurred in more or less specific aspects of the political system, including party politics, political institutions and the policy-making process generally. Together, these essays clearly illustrate both the breadth and the rates of change in various aspects of the political system. They indicate the variety of political situations that have manifested themselves in recent times. They also demonstrate the utility of new intellectual perspectives as a way of making sense of such change.

By way of introduction, the aim of this essay is to put the theme of change in context. It does so, first, by examining *change in French politics*, outlining the broad areas in which change has taken place and, in so doing, setting the scene for the contributions which follow; second, by considering *change and French politics*, suggesting that change is an ongoing process which has not simply resulted in the transition from one distinct model of politics to another; and, third, by reflecting on *French politics and change*, noting that the process of change raises new and fundamental questions as to the nature of the political process, while at the same time it leaves old and equally fundamental questions still needing to be addressed.

CHANGE IN FRENCH POLITICS

Identifying the areas of change in French politics is a task at which Sisyphus himself might have balked. After all, it is scarcely an exaggeration to say that at least one of the most oft-cited sources of change, Europeanisation, has to a greater or lesser extent affected almost every aspect of the political process. Nevertheless, it is useful to illustrate the variety of change in French politics under three separate headings: political representation, political institutions and politics and policy making. Under each heading there have been several notable developments in recent years.

Political Representation

There have been changes in the context of political representation. Most notably, the system has undergone a period of party political change. Here, there have been important developments in the relationships within and between the more established parties in the system. These developments have affected the parties of the left, the mainstream right and the extreme right equally. At the same time, there have also been developments at the limits of the party system and, indeed, beyond. Most notably, established parties have been challenged by new expressions of political mobilisation.

The main development in the relationship between the various parties on the left has been the constitution of the so-called 'plural' majority government, which since 1997 has enjoyed a slender but comfortable parliamentary majority. The 'plural' majority comprises the Socialist Party (PS) as the dominant partner, the Communist Party, the Greens, the small PS-offshoot Mouvement des Citoyens (MDC) party, and the socialists' traditional allies, the equally small Left-Radical Party. The links between the parties remain loose. Indeed, there were competing left-wing party lists at the 1999 European election and such competition only causes difficulties for the government's political managers.

At the same time, the parties have also been united by the fact that, as a government, as a legislative majority and, conceivably, as a presidential majority in a few years time, their fates are intertwined. At present, each element of the 'plural' majority has an incentive to work together.

Of course, the new-found relationship *between* the parties of the left is itself simply a reflection of one of the most important developments *within* those parties in recent years, namely the rather unexpected outbreak of political realism. In particular, the leadership of the Communist Party, although not necessarily the rank-and-file members or even key elements of the parliamentary party, has decided, for the time being at least, that there is political capital to be gained from working with the socialists in government. As such, the party has finally put behind it the rather unhappy experience of the 1981–84 government.

At the same time, the Greens have taken a similar decision. The politically disastrous *ni gauche-ni droite* strategy of the 1980s and early 1990s has been abandoned. While it is certainly the case that the Greens remain a potentially volatile partner – for many activists power is simply distasteful – it is also the case that in recent times the party has been willing to try to shape policy within the confines of the governmental system.

Finally, not the least important development on the left concerns the PS itself. The party has moved into the post-Mitterrand era. Indeed, it has done so rather more quickly than some might have predicted. True, the former president still has his apologists – Jack Lang and Roland Dumas are perhaps the most noteworthy – yet the key change is that Mitterrand and his governments are no longer the party's main reference points. This has allowed the PS to look forward, rather than back, and to plan for the future, rather than constantly being obliged to apologise for past mistakes, whether perceived or real.

On the right, the situation is difficult. Within the Gaullist Rassemblement pour la République (RPR) the divisions caused by the 1995 presidential election have yet to heal. The President, Jacques Chirac, has still fully to forgive his main opponent, Édouard Balladur, and the others who opposed him at that time. Indeed, only recently have key Balladur supporters, such as Nicolas Sarkozy, been allowed back into the presidential fold.[2] Moreover, the trauma provoked by the President's suicidal dissolution of the National Assembly in 1997 merely increased the party's problems. Most notably, it ruined the standing of the President's main supporter, former Prime Minister Alain Juppé, and fuelled the ambitions of one of the main likely candidates for the 2002 presidential election, Philippe Séguin. To add insult to injury, the party has lost, temporarily or otherwise, one of its old faithfuls, Charles Pasqua, who opposes what he considers to be the party's pro-European stance. In short, the Gaullist Party, which was once so monolithic and which demonstrated a distinct cult of personality, is now a federation of opposing fiefdoms over which Chirac has only limited control.

Even that degree of unity, though, is more than is enjoyed by the RPR's main rivals. In 1978, the parties of the non-Gaullist right were brought together under the banner of the Union pour la Démocratie Française (UDF). The UDF, previously a confederation of separate parties rather than a party in itself, was never much more than a flag of convenience. However, it did allow Christian democrats, liberals, radicals and sundry *groupuscules* not only to manage their basic ideological divisions but also to make the best of their political support.

Following the 1998 regional elections, however, the tensions between the various parties became uncontrollable. In several regions, elements of the UDF agreed to ally, either explicitly or implicitly, with the Front National in order to secure the presidency of the council. This strategy, though, was vehemently opposed by other elements within the movement, mainly the centrist Force Démocrate (FD) party. The result was a split which left the neo-liberal, Démocratie Libérale (DL) party clearly separate from a reconstituted FD-dominated UDF and the non-Gaullist right as a whole much weaker than before.

As if this situation was not bad enough, the divisions within the Gaullist and non-Gaullist right are matched by the problems between them. Over the years there have been many calls for a single right-wing party, but personal and institutional rivalries have always drowned them out. In 1998 another attempt was made to increase the degree of co-operation between the various interests concerned. The rather inappropriately named Alliance was a loose organisation which was designed to bring together the RPR, UDF and DL with a view to co-ordinating the parliamentary and electoral strategies of the right. It is, however, moribund. There has been increased co-operation between the RPR and DL, but this has merely alienated the UDF. At bottom, the Alliance was, and remains, nothing more than the sum of its divided and somewhat demoralised parts.

The third component of the party system to have undergone change is the extreme-right Front National (FN). Since the early 1980s the FN has established itself as a considerable force in the political system. Its influence has been manifested not so much in the institutional context, although it does control a small number of municipal councils and holds the balance of power in several regions, but more in both its ability to shape the political agenda, notably concerning immigration policy, and, as noted above, its capacity to cause trouble for its political opponents. Recently, though, the FN too has been undergoing a period of crisis. The long-standing antagonisms between its 'historic' leader, Jean-Marie Le Pen, and his main rival, Bruno Mégret, have come out into the open. Indeed, the party has split between the *lepéniste* Front National pour l'Unité Française (FNUF) and the *mégretiste* Front National-Mouvement National (FN-MN). Both organisations claim to represent the true FN. Both are currently fighting in the courts over the party's finances, the party logo and so forth.

The main difference between them is that the former adopts the *tous pourris* attitude towards the other parties in the system, whereas the latter is more accommodating, seeing the transformation and subsequent success of the Italian Alleanza Nazionale party as a model to be followed. As a whole, the extreme right aspires to winning the votes of the 20–25 per cent of the population who, when polled, say that they 'share the ideas' of the FN.[3]

There is, however, scarcely room for both the FNUF and the FN-MN in the same policy space and there is even less likelihood that the two main protagonists will bury the metaphorical hatchet except in each other's back. Whatever the outcome of this situation, be it two extreme right-wing parties which collectively are able to increase the support for their ideas within the population as a whole, or be it a weakened movement which is punished by the electorate for its internal divisions, the position of the extreme right in the system has clearly entered a new phase.

At the same time as there have been changes both within and between the established parties in the system, so significant sections of the public are also more and more willing to bypass these organisations altogether in order to promote their aims. With regard to issues as diverse as unemployment policy, school reforms, gay rights, the hunting season, sub-national identities, farming expenditure cuts and a host of other concerns, groups are now organising themselves in ways which increasingly challenge the mainstream expressions of both party and traditional pressure group politics. These new organisations take many different forms. Some operate in traditional policy areas but are little more than quasi-spontaneous *coordinations* over which established interest group organisations have little control. The damage recently caused to the Environment Minister's office by 'rogue' farmers is one example. Others are now somewhat more institutionalised, but are concerned with policy issues that have only come upon the scene more recently. One such group which has managed to maintain a certain media profile is Act Up, the AIDS organisation.

Other groups still have combined traditional pressure group-lobbying with electoral politics. Here, the most notable example is the hunting lobby, which elected representatives to regional councils in 1998 and which won more than 5 per cent at the 1999 European election in the form of the Chasse Pêche Nature et Traditions list. To date, this lobby has been extremely successful in its campaign against the implementation in France of the European directive to shorten the hunting season and at times it has made life extremely uncomfortable for the Green Environment Minister, Dominique Voynet.

Together, these groups threaten the authority of received wisdom, routine procedures and established organisations. In some cases, they can force governments to address their issues in the space of a few weeks of concerted activity. The budgetary success of the protests by anti-unemployment groups in January 1998 is notable in this regard. Alternatively, they can place issues on the agenda which might otherwise be ignored. The action by *sans-papiers* groups is a case in point. Certainly, they all know how to gain the attention of the media and use modern communication techniques. In these ways, such groups certainly provide complementary avenues of political expression, if not alternative forms of mobilisation for those people who feel inadequately represented by traditional political forces.

Political Institutions

Just as there have been changes in the context of representation, so there have also been changes in the organisation of political institutions. Most notably, there has been an increase in institutional pluralism, meaning competition between rival institutional interests. In this context, it is useful to signal the effects of 'cohabitation', the increasing influence of the law in the political process and the changing relationship between central and sub-central government.

Since 1986, 'cohabitation', or the situation where a president from one party coexists with a prime minister from an opposed party, has become a regular feature of French political life. The first two periods (1986–88 and 1993–95) were brought about by mid-term legislative elections which returned a majority hostile to the President. The third (from 1997) was brought about by the President himself, following the premature dissolution of the National Assembly. The effect of 'cohabitation' on the functioning of the institutional system is seen in two ways.

First, during the period of 'cohabitation' itself there is a reorientation of the policy-making process within the executive. In domestic policy matters the president remains a nuisance as far as the government is concerned, but little more. True, in foreign affairs, the EU and defence policy the president is still a privileged actor. However, evidence from the first three periods of 'cohabitation' suggests that presidents can no longer command a monopoly of initiative in these areas either. Instead, during 'cohabitation' presidents tread water, trying best to organise their re-election campaign by making life difficult for political enemies and by building and rebuilding links between political friends.

Second, and more fundamentally, 'cohabitation' has gnawed away at the institutional authority of the presidency *per se*.[4] Of course, presidential infallibility was always a myth, but it was one which had some force especially during the de Gaulle incumbency. 'Cohabitation', though, has thrown into stark relief the fact that the President is, first and foremost, a party political actor like any other. As a result, the President can still sound regal and claim to be the representative of all the French people, but the president-king is now shown to be well and truly bare. All told, the leadership capacity of the chief executive is increasingly restricted not just during periods of 'cohabitation' itself, but outside them as well.

A further development has also limited the power of political leaders, namely the entrenchment of the *État de droit*. The influence of the Constitutional Council is now a well-documented phenomenon. Governmental legislation is not only routinely examined by the Council after it has been passed by the legislature, governments also try to anticipate the Council's decisions before bills are presented to the legislature in the first place.[5] There has, thus, been a constitutionalisation of the policy-making process.

In addition, the Council of State remains a significant institution whose decisions can have profound political consequences. It might be remembered that it was the Council of State which struck down the 1998 election of the president of the Rhône-Alpes regional council. It was when the council set about electing a new president that the divisions between the UDF, on the one hand, and DL and the RPR, on the other, became intolerable. Over and above these institutions and other established actors, notably the Court of Cassation and the Court of Accounts (*Cour des Comptes*), new judicial actors are emerging on the scene.

A notable example, here, is the European Court of Justice. The threat of sanction by the Court is now a powerful force to which domestic actors must respond. Equally, the changing role of local government has meant that regional courts have become significant players in their own right. These courts now have the power to decide whether or not local councils have misused public funds. As such, although their decisions can be appealed, they have become a key player in the process of local governance.

Finally, despite its many and serious shortcomings, the Court of Justice of the Republic (CJR) is also worth mentioning in this regard. The CJR was established in 1993 as the body which judges ministers who are accused of having committed an offence during their official duties. The first, and to date only, sitting of the Court was in February 1999. Here, a former prime minister, Laurent Fabius, and two former ministers, Edmond Hervé and Georgina Dufoix, were tried for their role in the blood contamination scandal, whereby blood transfusions were contaminated with the HIV virus in the mid-1980s. In many respects, the trial was a scandal in itself. And yet, the fact that it happened at all is significant. It was a clear sign that ministers are not above the law and that there are ways, however imperfect, of holding them accountable. (Indeed, one former minister, Edmond Hervé, was found guilty). As such, it showed, along with many other examples, that the law is increasingly encroaching on the political realm, that it is constraining the freedom of action that political leaders enjoy.

Another example of institutional pluralism worth noting concerns centre-periphery relations. There has been tremendous change in this area over the last 20 years. Indeed, it would scarcely be misleading to suggest that there is now a system of multi-level governance in France. According to this line of thought, it is misconceived to examine policy making in this area simply in terms of the relations between the central state and local administrative bodies. Instead, it is necessary to factor in the influence of the EU in shaping the regional policy-making space, the role of private actors in the creation of local policy networks and the horizontal links between local authorities themselves (*intercommunalité*). There is no doubt that old problems remain, albeit sometimes in new forms. For example, there is still a propensity towards *suradministration*, or multiple layers of administrative responsibilities, which has merely been exacerbated by the reforms of the last 20 years.[6] However, new opportunities have also been created. So, Le Galès, for one, has stressed the increasing importance of urban governance.[7]

In this context, a new political cleavage has emerged. On the one hand, there are those, such as Jean-Pierre Chevènement, whose focus is a traditional one – the state, the department and the commune. On the other, there are those, such as Dominique Voynet, who place the emphasis on new arenas of influence – Europe, the region and *intercommunalité*. This cleavage is important not only because it will shape the future of centre–periphery relations, but also because it is a reflection of wider ideological concerns, namely the relationship between the nation-state and Europe, the role of the state as either a provider of services or the regulator of those who provide those services on its behalf and, finally, the status of the individual as either a subject of the state's authority or a citizen with the capacity to shape the decisions which affect her.

Policy Change

There is policy change. Political leaders have faced an evolving policy-making environment in which established policy routines have been undermined and traditional solutions have been shown to be deficient. The result is that some problems, such as the problem of long-term unemployment, inner-city violence and drugs, seem impossible to resolve, whereas others, such as monetary and interest rate policy, seem too remote to shape. And yet, the public still demands results, while candidates – presidential, parliamentary and local – continue to create the expectation that these demands will be met.

Against this background, it is useful to identify three areas of policy change. The first concerns a reappraisal of the traditional role of the state. Political leaders have shown a willingness to disengage the state from certain policy domains. The second, somewhat paradoxically, relates to a reaffirmation of the traditional role of the state. Just as political leaders have been willing to disengage the state, so they have also shown a keenness to increase the level of state intervention in specific policy areas if the situation is right. The third concerns the Europeanisation of the policy process. The impact of Europe is now demonstrated in a series of domains.

Over the last decade or so, there has been a reappraisal of the traditional parameters of policy making. For example, there has been a shift from the state as both decider and overseer to the state as a simple parameter-setter. Decision-makers have been willing to shift the responsibility for the supervision of policy in certain domains from the state to independent administrative authorities. Here, the most high-profile example is the Higher Council of Broadcasting (Conseil Supérieur de l'Audiovisuel – CSA). The CSA has the sometimes unenviable task of policing the day-to-day operation of the broadcasting sector. Of course, the state is still closely linked to the process of policy making in this domain. After all, it sets the boundaries of policy within which the CSA operates, not to mention the fact that there is still a considerable number of public-sector broadcasting institutions. However, the CSA is now a key player in its own right with the power to shape the French broadcasting sector over and above the demands of state actors.

In addition to this particular change in the role of the state, there has also been a shift from the state to the market *tout court*. The most significant change concerns the privatisation of public sector companies. Here, what is perhaps most significant is not so much the zeal with which the 1986–88 and 1993–97 right-wing governments sold off the state's assets, but the extent to which the left-wing 'plural' majority government has done the same. Indeed, in the space of less than two years in office the government had authorised the sale of shares in France Télécom, Aerospatiale, Air France and Thomson to name but a few! In most cases, but not Aerospatiale, the state retained more than a 50 per cent stake of the shareholding.

However, that a government which included communist representation should even contemplate, never mind approve, such a policy and in such a wide variety of cases is worthy of note. Indeed, the contrast with the policy of the 1981 administration could hardly be more striking. Thus, we see the boundaries of state intervention being redefined in a series of key industrial and cultural domains.

At the same time, we have also seen a reaffirmation of the state's traditional role. In this context, it is clear that policy makers still believe that the state can play a social function, meaning that its resources should be mobilised in order to address pressing social issues. This belief, like the previous one, is shared by both sides of the political divide, at least in general terms. For example, in 1993 the right-wing Balladur government declared a moratorium on the closure of public-sector organisations in local areas. Of course, there were good political and electoral reasons at the time for so doing, but it was also a signal that the French right (or at least some elements of it) is not as dogmatic in its liberalism as some of its counterparts elsewhere. The state still enjoys a privileged role for at least some of the main policy-makers who belong to this camp.

That said, the reaffirmation of state intervention corresponds mainly to the arrival of the left in government in 1997. In this regard, one of the government's first measures was to announce a plan to create 350,000 new state-sector jobs mainly for young unemployed people. For the most part, these people would carry out only basic functions, such as security guards in schools, but they would at least have a job and they would be in public sector employment. This was a clear indication that the state was still seen as a vehicle by which social and economic problems could be addressed.

A further example concerns the desire to introduce a 35-hour working week. This reform was significant not so much in its practical impact – the success of the measure remains very limited – but because the government was willing to go ahead with the scheme without the support of the main employers' confederation. This demonstrated that decision-makers were ready to impose a state-centred policy, even if one of the main social groups affected by it disapproved.

Finally, an equally significant example concerns the decision to make law and order the government's second most important policy priority after the economy.[8] The left has apparently been converted to the idea, which was once the exclusive property of the right, that the state's resources should be mobilised in a clear and unequivocal fashion in order to address the law and order issue.

Over and above the changing parameters of purely domestic policy making the policy process has increasingly adopted a European dimension as well.[9] The impact of the European Union (EU) can be illustrated very neatly in the context of both budgetary and monetary policy. So, for example, in terms of the former the convergence criteria for Economic and Monetary Union (EMU) have clearly influenced budgetary policy since 1994. Since this time, budgetary decisions have been shaped by the desire to meet the 3 per cent budget deficit criterion. Paradoxically, this constraint has actually strengthened the hand of senior decision-makers – the Budget and Finance Ministers, the Prime Minister and, outside 'cohabitation', the President – in their negotiations with spending ministers, because the former could claim that they were responding to an overriding imperative and the latter simply had no choice but to reduce their expenditure demands. At the same time, of course, the EU still imposed a general constraint on the government and set strict parameters within which decision makers had to operate.

In terms of monetary policy the need to establish an independent Bank of France and then the decision to take part in EMU meant that the French government was obliged to lose the power to control interest rate policy. The fact that governments had manipulated this policy tool to suit their own ends for hundreds of years merely underlines the significance of this change.[10] In the future, the French may have to live with high interest rates even if domestic demand is low.

That said, whatever the impact of the EU, and it has been considerable, it would be wrong to suggest that the French government is now powerless both in these domains and others. In economic policy, for example, key decisions will still have to be made even within the confines of EMU. These decisions will concern budgetary priorities and the most appropriate level of the budget deficit up to the 3 per cent ceiling. Similarly, in monetary policy the government will almost certainly try to act in collaboration with its European partners in order to put pressure, albeit indirectly, on the European Central Bank (ECB) with regard to interest rate cuts. The French have long championed the idea of an 'economic government' which would act as a political counterweight to the ECB and the so-called Euro-XI group of finance ministers may yet provide such a forum. Thus, there is no doubt that the policy process has been Europeanised and that the extent of EU influence will only increase in the foreseeable future. However, the French government does still retain at least a certain strategic decision-making capacity in this regard.

CHANGE AND FRENCH POLITICS

It is clear from the above that French politics has been experiencing a period of change. As such, one of the key academic tasks is to identify the various areas of change and to account for them. This is the basic aim of most of the contributions to this volume. At the same time, though, it is also necessary to place the current period of change in context. It is necessary to examine not just the issue of change in French politics, but also the problem of change and French politics. How should we contextualise the current period of change? What is the significance of recent changes in terms of the French political system more broadly? Here, two key observations can be made: first, that France has experienced not just a discrete period of change, but change as an ongoing process; and, second, that the result of the recent period of change is not simply the move from one discrete type of political system to another, but a series of multi-speed, multi-level and multi-directional moves within an already confused and highly complex system.

The first point to note is that change is not simply a recent phenomenon. On the contrary, change, be it economic, social or political, should be viewed as an ongoing process. It is noticeable, for example, that in his illuminating study of crises in France, Michel Winock concludes that the key characteristic of the French system of government is its 'extreme *instability*'.[11] Indeed, in the period 1871–1968 Winock calculates that France experienced eight separate crises, or an average of one every 12 years. To the extent that crises usually either reflect or instigate a period of change, then these figures suggest that change is endemic to French political life.

Even then, it might be argued that this approach actually underestimates the turbulent nature of the French political system. This is because Winock defines a crisis as a period of 'major disturbances which place the republican system of government in danger'.[12] Change, though, is not simply confined to periods of such extreme stress. After all, Winock suggests, and quite correctly according to his definition, that the years from 1898 to 1934 correspond to a period of stability. And yet, this period encompasses the First World War which, over and above any upheaval during the conflict, was clearly associated with profound economic and social change in the years immediately thereafter. All in all, even leaving aside the period prior to 1871, evidence suggests that change is an ongoing feature of French political life.

The same point can be made with regard to the Fifth Republic itself. The early years of the regime coincided with profound institutional and political reform. The institutions of the Fifth Republic, combined with the direct election of the President after 1962, brought about a complete reorientation of the political system. There were new rules of the game which parties endeavoured to master. At the same time, there was the resolution of the Algerian question. This removed one of the most problematic of political issues and allowed a transformation of the political debate. Thereafter, even though the basic contours of the Fifth Republic had been set in place, institutional and political change continued to occur. Highly familiar examples include the rise of the Gaullist Party, the establishment of the PS, the union and disunion of the left, the end of the Gaullist presidency, the federation of the non-Gaullist right and the alternation in power in 1981.

Furthermore, in addition to the institutional and political changes that occurred after 1958 there was social change too. In his study of French society, Mendras argues that there was, in effect, a second French revolution in the 1960s and 1970s.[13] He points out that the period 1944–65 was marked by economic growth, a rising population, the decline of the peasantry and rural life in general and the rise of the salariat. After 1965 the birth rate fell, immigration and unemployment rose, the Catholic Church modernised and there was an Americanisation of French cultural life. For Mendras, these changes, and others, coincided with a decline in the revolutionary tradition, the end of the clerical/anti-clerical division and an increasing focus on both economic and lifestyle issues, rather than broader social and political questions. All in all, while in Winock's terms there may only have been one threat to the republican system of government during this time (in 1968), it would be wrong, as before, to suggest that regime stability necessarily corresponds to social and political stability.

Against this background, we can perhaps better understand the implications of the current period of change. There is no doubt that change in this period demonstrates particular characteristics. As we have suggested, and as the subsequent contributions to the volume will confirm, the change is multi-speed. That is to say, the pace of change is greater in some areas (Europeanisation) than others (new public management). The change is multi-level. It affects not just political life at the centre, but also the sub-central and supranational level as well. The change is multi-directional. There are countervailing developments (the retreat of the state in some areas and the reaffirmation of the state in others).

At the same time, though, the current period of change should not be considered in isolation. The changes that have undoubtedly occurred during this period merely mingle in with a broader flow of change that predates this time. Indeed, there is nothing to suggest that previous periods of change in both the recent and more distant past were themselves anything other than multi-speed, multi-level and multi-directional in nature as well.

This is not to say, of course, that there are no continuities in the French political system. On the contrary, there may be deep-rooted cultural features which transcend epiphenomenal developments and, certainly, the nature of political institutions is such that there can be regularities in the distribution of power resources which structure the behaviour of political actors over a not inconsiderable period of time. It is simply to say that it is necessary not just to identify and account for the contemporary manifestations of change, but also to contextualise these changes as well.

This is not the place to embark on a full-scale examination of 200 years of change in French politics. There is merely room to assert that the current period of change must be placed in the appropriate context if its significance is to be properly understood. And yet, this point is essential. After all, if we were to try to place the current period in context, then what may emerge is not so much the picture of a political process which has undergone a complete transformation in the last few years and which has induced a move from one type of political system to another, but one which is characterised by ongoing developments affecting an already diffuse and highly complex political process. So, for example, there is no doubt that 'cohabitation' has weakened the presidency, but there were always constraints on the president's powers, despite the political rhetoric and academic commentary which sometimes suggested the opposite. Similarly, at present there are elements of division and unity within both the left and the right, and yet to a greater or lesser degree there always have been. Likewise, certain policy problems may now seem impossible to resolve, but this was no less the case in the 1890s, 1930s, 1950s and no doubt other periods as well. Finally, it is undeniable that domestic decision-makers are now constrained by external forces, but was there ever a time when they were not? Thus, the current period is no doubt one of change in French politics. However, the developments associated with this period should not disguise the nature of change and its place in the French political system more generally.

FRENCH POLITICS AND CHANGE

By examining the recent period of change and by placing it in context, we can build up a broader picture of the French political process. At the same time, we also need to reflect, albeit briefly, on the nature of French politics and change. What questions are raised by the experience of change, both ongoing and current? More specifically, what is new about French politics in the light of recent developments and what remains pertinent about more established debates in this regard?

In the first place, it is clear that the current period of change raises important new questions and establishes new lines of cleavage. The most obvious example concerns Europe. It is still unlikely that there will be a fundamental party political realignment between pro- and anti-European forces. For example, the *jacobin* left in the form of the Mouvement des Citoyens (MDC) has consistently rejected the overtures of the republican right represented by Charles Pasqua and his supporters.

That said, the European question continues both to divide parties internally and to hinder the process of alliance-building more generally. For example, Europe is one of the main sources of difference between the PS, on the one hand, and the communists, Greens and the MDC, on the other.[14] There is no doubt that the cohesion of the 'plural' majority is rendered more fragile by the conflicting reactions within the government to developments at this level.

Similarly, the European issue bedevils the right. Indeed, it was one of the main reasons why the pro-European UDF refused to unite behind a single right-wing list dominated by the once and perhaps future Eurosceptic RPR at the 1999 European election. In these ways, and many others, the European dimension has rendered party politics more unpredictable.

Further examples reflect the changing nature of society itself. The first concerns the so-called *pacte civil de solidarité* (PACS). This measure was designed to give legal protection to non-married couples. In particular, it would give such couples formal rights in areas such as tax policy and inheritance issues. However, the debate quickly centred on the question of whether it would amount to a form of surrogate marriage for homosexual couples. Formally, the left proposed the reform and the right opposed it. However, there were barely disguised divisions within both camps, particularly in the PS itself. These divisions reflected a basic cleavage between what might be called the 'traditionalists', those promoting the established family unit, and the 'progressives', those who were open to other forms of conjugal relationships. Needless to say, there was no risk of the PACS issue splitting the parties, but it was an example of the difficulties parties face in responding to changing social norms.

The second example concerns the *parité* issue. Both the right-wing president and the left-wing government supported a constitutional amendment designed to promote the representation of women in political life. However, they were opposed by the right in Senate, whose support was needed for the reform to be passed and which rejected the wording of the amendment that had been passed unanimously by the National Assembly.[15]

Again, this situation threw into stark relief the cleavage between those willing to reform the political system in line with social expectations and those who were opposed to the reform on the grounds that it was either anti-republican or that it was simply an unnecessary intrusion into the established organisation of political life. In this case, the debate also illustrated the gap between the directly accountable and at least somewhat more socially sensitive National Assembly and the indirectly accountable and 'democratically anomalous' Senate.[16] All told, the likelihood is that as society changes further other issues of this nature will emerge causing additional problems for established political forces, both institutional and party political.

These examples aside, the current period of change also reaffirms more traditional questions about the nature of French politics. One such question concerns the pertinence of the left/right divide. The last special edition of *West European Politics* to be dedicated to France included an essay by Douglas Johnson about *les deux Frances*.[17] Drawing mainly on the work of André Siegfried, François Goguel, René Rémond and Maurice Duverger, Johnson suggested that, although the manifestation of the left/right division may have changed over time, a 'persistent, nagging and unsatisfactory notion that there are, in fact, *les deux Frances*' has persisted.[18] More than twenty years on, this point remains valid.

During this period, the meaning of what it is to be on the left or on the right has changed. Most notably, the left has reevaluated traditional values such as *laicité* and has certainly reexamined the balance between state and market. Still, though, there remains a basic division between the two camps such that they continue to make enemies of each other. Indeed, nothing more neatly illustrates this point than the position of the centrists.

In 1988, they were tempted to move over to the left and work with the socialists, but basic ideological differences, and not a small degree of political conniving, kept them apart.

In 1998, the centrists were again at loggerheads with their right-wing partners, but the likelihood that they will cross the divide and ally with the left is still only a remote possibility. Thus, despite divisions within the left and the right, there remain deep-seated loyalties which continue to structure political debate and which supervene on short-term political developments that superficially at least appear to threaten the basic contours of the left/right divide.

Another example concerns the old debate about French exceptionalism. There is no doubt that French politics is no longer what it was.[19] As a result, there are many writers who believe that French politics has lost its originality (*s'est banalisé*). According to this line of argument, the impact of globalisation, Europeanisation and domestic change means that French politics now manifests itself in the same ways as politics in other countries. At the same time, though, there are many other writers who suggest that, despite the changes that the country has clearly undergone, France maintains important elements of specificity. For example, the state, it might be argued, is still stronger than its counterparts elsewhere. Equally, French society, some say, is still unable to govern itself.[20] It is still beset by special interests. It still lacks a flourishing civil society from which change, other than the state-directed variety, can spring. It is clear, therefore, that the current period of change has not ended this debate. There is no consensus either that France has become simply *un pays comme les autres*, or that it remains socially and politically unique. Instead, the developments of the last few years have simply provided new examples upon which proponents of both sides of the argument have seized in order to make their case.

In these ways, the current period of change raises new problems, both social and political, which are materially different to ones which were present in the past. Thus, political leaders are faced with new challenges and political scientists are encouraged to find new paradigms so as to explain these challenges. Equally, though, the changes that have occurred during this period fail to render obsolete some of the more established elements of the political process. Therefore, decision-makers still operate within a context in which long-standing aspects of the political system remain salient and academics should still continue to ask the basic questions about the fundamental nature of French political life.

THE CHANGING FRENCH POLITICAL SYSTEM

As noted at the outset, the aim of this volume is to chart some of the most significant changes in contemporary French politics and to make sense of them. To this end, the contributions are organised in three separate sections. The first concerns the politics of representation. Three contributions to this volume explicitly address this issue. Joseph Szarka examines the left and the rise of the plural majority; Paul Hainsworth puts the right in perspective, identifying the difficulties that have been faced by the Gaullists, the non-Gaullist right and the extreme right equally; while Andrew Appleton considers the rise of new social movements, suggesting that alternative forms of political participation have become established.

The second addresses challenges to the institutional politics. What is the constitutional basis of good government? This is the issue examined by Guy Carcassonne in his contribution. What is the relationship between law and politics? Vincent Wright tackles this question. What is the relationship between central and local authorities? This is the focus of Emmanuel Négrier's piece. Together, these essays explore the new boundaries of institutional politics and their effect on the wider political game.

Third, three contributions focus on the policy-making process. The first, by Vivien Schmidt, is a wide-ranging survey of the changing relationship between the state and society in Fifth Republic France. The second, by Alistair Cole, considers the role of the public service more specifically. What is the proper role for the *service public* in the contemporary context of policy making? The third, by Steve Griggs, focuses on health policy and the emergence of a new policy network of hospital managers with the capacity to shape outcomes to suit their own ends.

Finally, by way of providing an overview of all of these areas – representation, institutions and policy making – Jill Lovecy considers whether the challenges that France is facing and the changes that it is undergoing mean that the country is now simply one among many, facing the same problems as any other developed system, or whether it still maintains its own particular forms of political uniqueness.

Together, these contributions explore the changing French political system and provide the foundations for future explorations of the politics of this most fascinating of countries.

NOTES

This manuscript was completed before Vincent Wright's untimely death in July 1999. As ever, Vincent supported the project from its inception and as late as March 1999 participated in a conference on the theme of 'The Changing French Political System' at the Maison Française in Oxford. Then, as always, he was a valued contributor, colleague and friend. This special edition of *West European Politics* is dedicated to his memory.

1. This journal has itself provided ample evidence of the extent of change in West European politics in the last few years. Examples can be found in the special editions on Austria, 'Politics in Austria. Still a Case of Consociationalism?', *WEP* 15/4 (Oct. 1992); Italy, 'Crisis and Transition in Italian Politics', *WEP* 20/1 (Jan. 1997); and Spain, 'Politics and Policy in Democratic Spain. No Longer Different?', *WEP* 21/4 (Oct. 1998).
2. Sarkozy was appointed as head of the party and leader of the RPR-DL list at the European election when in April 1999 Séguin unexpectedly stood down claiming that his election campaign was being undermined by both the president himself and other leading RPR figures.
3. See the article by Jérôme Jaffré in *Le Monde*, 24 Feb. 1999.
4. For an interesting account of the changing role of the presidency in French society, see Jean-Marie Donegani and Marc Sadoun, *La Ve République. Naissance et mort* (Paris: Calmann-Lévy 1998).
5. See John T.S. Keeler and Alec Stone, 'Judicial-political Confrontation in Mitterrand's France. The Emergence of the Constitutional Council as a Major Actor in the Policy-making Process', in George Ross, Stanley Hoffman and Sylvia Malzacher (eds.) *The Mitterrand Experiment. Continuity and Change in Modern France* (Cambridge: Polity Press 1987) pp.161–81.
6. I am grateful to Seán Loughlin for underlining this point to me.
7. Patrick Le Galès, 'Du gouvernement des villes à la gouvernance urbaine', *Revue Française*

de Science Politique 45 (1995) pp.57–95.

8. This was signalled in an interview with Lionel Jospin in *Le Monde*, 7 Jan. 1999.
9. A recent overview can be found in Alain Guyomarch, Howard Machin and Ella Ritchie (eds.) *France in the European Union* (London: Macmillan 1998).
10. A discussion of the relationship between the government and the Bank of France can be found in Robert Elgie and Helen Thompson, *The Politics of Central Banks* (London: Routledge 1998).
11. Michel Winock, *La fièvre hexagonale. Les grandes crises politiques 1871–1968* (Paris: Calmann-Lévy 1986) p.376. Emphasis in the original. All translations by the author.
12. Ibid. p.10.
13. Henri Mendras, *La seconde révolution française 1965–1984* (Paris: Gallimard 1994).
14. It might be remembered that one of the main reasons why the MDC split from the PS in the first place was because it opposed the party's pro-European policy.
15. The former left-wing justice minister and senator, Robert Badinter, was also opposed to the reform. Indeed, so was his wife, Elisabeth Badinter, herself a well-known public figure.
16. Lionel Jospin caused a stir when he said that the French Senate was an anomaly among democratic legislatures.
17. Douglas Johnson, 'The Two Frances: The Historical Debate', *West European Politics* 1/3 (Oct. 1978) pp.3–10.
18. Ibid. p.10.
19. See René Rémond, *La politique n'est plus ce qu'elle était* (Paris: Calmann-Lévy 1993).
20. This is thesis proposed by Stanley Hoffmann in 'Les Français sont-il gouvernables?', *Pouvoirs* 68 (1994) pp.7–14.

The Parties of the French 'Plural Left': An Uneasy Complementarity

JOSEPH SZARKA

When President Chirac called early parliamentary elections in April 1997, the right-wing Juppé government was deeply unpopular. The 'cut and run' strategy failed, and in a surprise victory the left was returned with a working majority of 319 seats (out of 577) in the lower house.[1] The left's return to office was enabled by the formation of a multipartite coalition – the *gauche plurielle* ('plural left') – which brought together socialists, communists, left-wing radicals and republicans, as well as political ecologists.[2] It thereby garnered the widest vote possible. Moreover, the socialists' agreement to stand down in certain constituencies in favour of smaller allies provided the opening for victories otherwise impossible under the majoritarian system.

Not only did ecologists enter parliament for the first time (with eight seats in all), but the electoral pact extended to the distribution of ministerial portfolios. Once socialist Lionel Jospin was nominated as Prime Minister on 2 June 1997, the ecologist, Dominique Voynet, and the communist leader, Robert Hue, both former presidential candidates, negotiated the political capital accrued in the 1995 election for ministerial posts for their respective stances. Voynet became Minister for the Regions and the Environment, one of four women appointed to key posts.[3] Of the 27 members of the government, 19 were drawn from the Socialist Party (PS), three from the Communist Party (PCF), 3 from the Left-Radical Party (PRG) and 1 each from the Greens and the Mouvement des Citoyens (MDC).[4] All of these allies had been in government with the PS previously, with the exception of the Greens. The new government included a mix of seasoned personalities and new appointments to ministerial office, but with the more prominent socialists of the Mitterrand era (the so-called *éléphants*) being conspicuous by their absence, Jospin signalled an inclusive recruitment strategy aimed at cementing relations within his heterogeneous majority.

The existence of the 'plural left' as a governing force raises questions about recent developments in French political life. What kind of change occurred at the level of the party system? To what extent did developments reveal the decline or the renewal of particular parties of the left? And did broader consequences emerge for the polity as a whole, such as a political realignment of the left? To explore these issues in the period between June 1997 and April 1999, this essay will first review ways of assessing party system change. The second section studies trends towards renewal within the individual parties of the *gauche plurielle*, while the third analyses relationships between them.

ASSESSING PARTY SYSTEM CHANGE

Although comprehensive analysis of party system change would entail coverage of the parties of the right (and go beyond the remit of the present discussion), recent developments on the left inevitably have wider repercussions. Two ways of assessing change will be presented: first, in terms of stages of development and, second, in terms of levels of change.

Reviewing the evolution of the French party system, Machin took as his baseline the well-known *quadrille bipolaire* of the 1970s when the major parties of the left (PS, PCF) had been roughly equal in size to those of the right (RPR, UDF). He discerned four subsequent stages.[5] The first transition in 1981 was to a party system dominated by the PS, with its ally the PCF in tow. A second stage was precipitated by the PCF's exit from government in 1984, leaving a PS one-party majority. A swing to the right in 1986 constituted a further development, bringing about a two-year period of power-sharing between left and right. Mitterrand's re-election in 1988 and the follow-on parliamentary elections produced the fourth stage, a PS 'minority' parliament and government.

Guyomarch argued that a fifth stage developed during 1992–94, characterised by the re-emergence of the right as the dominant force (evident in the landslide in seats at the 1993 parliamentary elections).[6] At the same time, a steep decline occurred in the aggregate vote of parties of government (PS, PCF, RPR, UDF).[7]

In addition, European integration emerged as a major electoral issue. Following this approach, a further stage can be discerned during 1995–98, marked by progressive improvement in the electoral fortunes of the left. In the 1995 presidential election Jospin emerged as the first-round candidate with the most votes, the *gauche plurielle* won the 1997 parliamentary elections, and in 1998 the left achieved its best results to date at regional elections. Thus a 'sixth' stage, characterised by the emergence of the 'plural left', can provide a mnemonic for the identification of recent developments.

However the stages model has its drawbacks. Party system change conceptualised as a series of adjustments in the relative strength of individual parties captures only one dimension of renewal. This approach stresses electoral gains, and the ability to dominate elected assemblies and form executives. It dwells on the logic of competition, conceived as a process of marginalisation of opponents. This squares with France's rapid-fire electoral cycle encouraging voter reactivity to performance in office, a cycle which has produced several instances of unexpected victory as well as sudden death.[8] It also reflects a significant component of the competitive strategy of parties.[9]

However, the stress on the logic of elimination ignores the logic of co-operation: the governments of the Fifth Republic have generally been formed by coalitions, rather than being drawn from a single-party (with comparable tendencies operating at sub-national levels). Moreover, analysis in terms of individual party strength runs the risk of ignoring continuities within political families along dimensions such as kindred ideologies, policy preferences, and the socio-economic composition of electoral bases. In this respect, a key question that arises in the French context is whether or not the 'plural left' merely represents a return to the *status quo ante* of the 'union of the left' in the 1970s. A conceptualisation in terms of unidirectional modulation would foreclose investigation of this issue. A more comprehensive analysis therefore needs both to account for changes within parties and consider the development of relationships within political families.

The approach proposed by Kitschelt in terms of levels of change goes some way to meeting these needs.[10] He defined three levels of change. Level 1 change is characterised by parties adapting their messages and organisations to new voter expectations. Level 2 change involves new party organisations replacing discredited old parties but with no changes in ideological blocs. Level 3 change is signalled by the appearance of new parties based on changes in cleavage structures and competitive dimensions. These levels of change can usefully 'map' the parties of the *gauche plurielle*, their interactions and the agendas they promote.

THE RENEWAL OF FRENCH LEFT-WING PARTIES

The situation of the French left in the early 1990s was dire. Reaction against the socialists' performance in office led to a crushing defeat in the 1993 parliamentary elections where the PS retained 65 seats, down from 282 in 1988. Other parties of the left likewise suffered, exacerbating internal divisions and exposing a crisis that had been brewing for some years. The 1993 outcome precipitated a period of forced renewal and regrouping. All of the parties forming the *gauche plurielle* have since pulled back from the brink by repositioning themselves in response to electoral demands and to European and international developments. This process of decline and renewal will be explored in relation to each.

Socialist Party

Though the initial conversion of the Section Française de l'Internationale Ouvrière into the French Socialist Party (PS) took place in 1969, the 1971 Epinay conference – and the emergence of François Mitterrand as leader – initiated its transformation into France's leading political party. Yet, if Mitterrand's victories in the presidential elections of 1981 and 1988 orchestrated its rise, he also precipitated its fall. Already in the mid-1980s many voters 'disillusioned' by the socialist performance in office (particularly the recourse to austerity policies in 1983–84) had deserted the left, leading to defeat in the 1986 parliamentary elections. This transpired to be a mere hiccup compared to the 1993 defeat, where the PS-Left Radical vote dropped to 18.6 per cent, having been 39.5 per cent in 1981 and 37 per cent in 1988.

A confluence of factors explains this outcome. The reformist, market-oriented turn adopted by the socialist governments, with its stress on economic orthodoxy, budgetary restraint and the reduction of inflation, no doubt proved unexpected for voters who in 1981 had been promised a 'break with capitalism'. Yet it cannot fully explain their desertion to the right, who proposed the same with interest. However, the phenomenon of structural unemployment, with increases to a new record high in almost every year between 1981 and 1993, speaks of a failure of socialist governments which their voters were unable to forgive.[11] In its wake, unemployment had exacerbated social stresses, notably racism, social exclusion and increased inequality, outcomes which contradicted the core principles of the left.

In addition, the closing years of the Mitterrand era were marked by 'court politics', by a round of disputes between favourites and clans, of corruption in the president's entourage, controversies over the president's activities in the 1930s and 1940s and questions over his later choice of friends.[12]

Scandals over the financing of the PS and the distribution of AIDS contaminated blood to haemophiliacs led to the incrimination of the socialist hierarchy, notably the party leader, Henri Emmanuelli, in the first affair and the former prime minister, Laurent Fabius, in the second.

The image problems of the PS were aggravated by vitriolic in-fighting among the Jospin, Fabius and Rocard factions at the 1990 Rennes conference where no majority emerged. Changes in the leadership of the PS writ these disputes large. After Lionel Jospin resigned from the post of first secretary in 1988, he was replaced by the die-hard Pierre Mauroy, to be succeeded in 1992 by Laurent Fabius (once Mitterrand's heir apparent) and in 1993 by Michel Rocard (Mitterrand's enemy). None was able to broker agreement on a common direction within the party and turn the tide running against the socialists.

The designation of Jospin as presidential candidate in 1995 led to an unexpectedly successful campaign in which he drew the largest number of first-round votes. Though beaten by Chirac in the run-off, Jospin emerged as undisputed party leader, with the opportunity to consolidate the PS and the divided left. Already in 1993 Jean-Christophe Cambadélis, one of Jospin's close collaborators, attempted to organise meetings between the PS, PCF and the Greens. By 1996, these three parties were taking turns to host meetings. Preliminary discussions over electoral programmes were underway in January 1997.

Ironically the surprise dissolution of the Assemblée Nationale by President Chirac on 21 April 1997 caught the right napping, but accelerated the regrouping of the left. On 22 April, the PS and the MDC each agreed not to contest the sitting candidates of the other. The day after, the PS agreed to stand down in favour of the Greens in 30 constituencies. On 29 April, the PCF and MDC drew up a list of joint candidates in 48 seats. The PS and PCF made a joint statement the same day, though each would put forward candidates independently. In consequence, the *gauche plurielle* was able put forward the left's most united front for two decades.[13]

The formation of the 'plural left' corresponds surprisingly closely to the 'big bang' view of French politics outlined by Rocard in 1993, according to which the new role of the PS was to federate the most innovative members of the ecology, communist and centrist parties.[14] Yet Rocard seemed unaware that restructuring of the left required the implosion of the PS, a process to which he contributed by the party's poor showing in the 1994 European elections (which destroyed his presidential hopes). Renewal had required two rounds of ideological and programmatic change. In the mid-1980s, the PS abandoned its Marxist baggage, gave up the temptation of a mixed economy dominated by nationalised firms and accepted the rigours of the internationalised market economy. The transformation was seen as a process of modernisation by some and as a lurch to the right by others. The requirement in the late-1990s was for the PS to be anchored within the left.

François Hollande, the current first secretary, stressed the necessity of this (re)positioning: 'if the PS chose to occupy the centre and desert the left, it would run the risk of electoral sanction'.[15] Implementation of this stance has been threefold. In their discourse, the socialists have returned to stressing the traditional left-wing principles of social justice and equality. In terms of a strategy of government, Prime Minister Jospin avoided the opening to the centre deployed by Rocard in 1988–91 and offered the plurality of his cabinet and parliamentary majority as guarantee of a left-wing orientation. In terms of legislative and policy programme, the left sought to reduce unemployment and social exclusion, to promote equality between the sexes and reinforce minority rights.

These features indicate that the renewal of the PS constituted a species of Level 1 change in that the party adapted it messages and policies to a changing social and political climate. However, as indicated in the electoral survey conducted by Mossuz-Lavau, in 1997 the confidence of voters in the PS as a party of the left was still faltering and in need of consolidation.[16] An ambiguity persisted as to whether the PS remained a 'catch-all', mass party or whether it would complete its transformation to a 'specialist' party of the left, akin to its coalition partners.

Mouvement des Citoyens (MDC)

Jean-Pierre Chevènement, the founder of the MDC, formerly led the CERES current in the PS. Like Jospin, he supported Mitterrand for party leader in 1971. With Jospin, he was among the first of the PS barons to distance himself from Mitterrand as president. In 1991, he resigned his post of Defence Minister in protest against the Gulf War and broke with the PS in 1992. The MDC contested the 1993 elections and the 1994 European elections with little success. Though the party's second in command, Georges Sarre, is becoming more widely know, the MDC remains strongly identified with Chevènement and his views.

Although once Marxist in orientation, Chevènement now represents a strain of traditionalist republicanism, stressing Jacobin centralisation within the nation-state. He campaigned for a 'no' vote in the 1992 Maastricht referendum and pursued the anti-Maastricht line in 1994.[17] In 1995, Chevènement supported Jospin's bid for the presidency, reopening a dialogue which brought the MDC into the 'plural left', and led in 1997 to the winning of eight parliamentary seats and his nomination as Interior Minister. The MDC provides an example of Level 2 party system change. Chevènement understood fairly early the discredit attached to an overtly Marxist stance, but the MDC remains bound to long-standing ideological blocs and attracted to far-left positions. In practice it operates as an external current of the PS, is numerically weak and has limited prospects.

Left-Radical Party (PRG)

The Radicals formed the major party of the Third Republic, but experienced decline and division during the Fourth and Fifth Republics. In 1973, its left-wingers set up the Mouvement des radicaux de gauche and immediately entered into alliance with the PS. They have largely depended upon the latter for survival, though retaining traditional bastions in the south-west. The PRG has a hybrid character. On the one hand are stalwarts such as Jean-Michel Baylet, the party leader. On the other is the phenomenon of new recruits sponsored by the socialists and searching for a party base. These include politicians preferring an arms-length relation with the PS – such as Bernard Kouchner – or who were unwelcome in PS ranks – such as Bernard Tapie. The latter led a Left-Radical list (including ex-socialists such as Catherine Lalumière and the ex-Génération Ecologie member, Noel Mamère) in the 1994 elections which won 12 per cent of the vote, returned eight MEPs, and humiliated Rocard.

However, the party's hopes of expansion were crushed once Tapie was imprisoned on fraud charges. In the 1995 presidential campaign, its putative candidate, Jean-François Hory, was persuaded to pull out in favour of Jospin. The long-standing complicity with the PS earned it government portfolios in 1997. Baylet remains a staunch supporter of Jospin whom he has described as 'déterminé, consensuel, réaliste'.[18]

However, as an instance of party decline and dependence on the PS, the PRG presents a counter-model that other components of the *gauche plurielle* avoid. Given these characteristics, the PRG represents an instance of Level 2 change: it is a new organisation replacing a discredited old party, but is characterised by limited ideological renewal, unclear identity and a weak electoral base.

Communist Party (PCF)

Though the PCF was the largest political party in France during the 1950s, the fall of the Berlin wall in 1989 and the collapse of communism in Eastern Europe appeared to signal its demise. In reality, the process of decline was already marked in the 1970s and 1980s, due to the leadership's inability to adapt to new circumstances.[19] The party failed to come to terms with the presidentialisation of the Fifth Republic, while its rigid support for the Soviet Union's policies raised perennial questions about its integrity. At the same time, its bases were sapped by the numerical decline of its 'natural' electorate, the industrial working classes, and by their progressive desertion to the PS, the Trotskyist left and the far right. Faced with these chronic problems, it took faltering steps to better integration within the French polity.

The PCF repeatedly displayed ambivalence over alliances with the PS. Though both parties signed a 'Common Programme of Government' in 1972, whose stress on nationalisation and redistribution was redolent of a planned rather than a market economy, the PCF came to realise that the agreement increased the electoral reach of the PS at its own expense. In a sudden about-turn in 1978, it split the 'union of the left' by taking a maximalist position on policy objectives, provoking the incomprehension of a part of its electorate and triggering the left's defeat in the parliamentary elections of that year.[20] After the landslide to the left in 1981, the PS held an overwhelming majority while the PCF was demoted to a junior partner.[21] To contain it within his orbit, President Mitterrand appointed four communist ministers.

The new government embarked on a programme of nationalisation which, though resembling the 'Common Programme', was motivated as much by recession and company losses as ideological leaning. Once nationalisation accompanied by Keynesian reflation revealed their limits, the lurch to an austerity policy prompted the resignation of the communist ministers in 1984. Their departure showed the inability of the PCF to influence the course of government and the victory of hard-liners hostile to the PS.

The about-turns accelerated the PCF's electoral decline: between the parliamentary elections of 1973 and 1986, its poll collapsed from 21.4 per cent to 9.7 per cent. It hit a record low of 6.8 per cent with Lajoinie's 1988 presidential campaign. Yet the reformists in the party were unable to seize the upper hand. Under Georges Marchais' leadership, the late 1980s and early 1990s were marked by crisis due to the haemorrhage of dissident members (such as Pierre Juquin, Charles Fiterman and Philippe Herzog) and the inability to recruit young blood.

Robert Hue's accession to party leadership in 1994 signalled the opportunity to reconstruct the party. In 1996, the PCF's 29th Congress ratified a strategy of mutation (party transformation). In his congress address, Hue stressed that the party has long stood for a 'French-style socialism, based on democracy and self-management'[22] and that the party's ideology should be renewed without abandoning its identity. This process has involved an adjustment of PCF terminology. The core theme of economic transformation is now expressed as a *dépassement du capitalisme*

– the aim is to 'overtake' capitalism rather than abolish it. Class war has been redefined in terms of 'citizens' action'. Ideals formerly considered 'bourgeois', such as representative democracy and the rights of the individual, have been embraced. Themes that came into prominence in the late 1980s – unemployment, *précarité*, social exclusion, the fight against racism and the Front National – have retained their currency in the 1990s.

Yet many aspects of the party remain familiar. In terms of policy measures, the PCF proposed Keynesian reflation by increases in the minimum wage and social allowances, hikes in corporate taxation and inheritance tax, a 35-hour week, employment creation for the young, and expansion of public sector services, while being opposed to privatisation.[23] It was hostile to the Maastricht Treaty, though now favouring some other form of (undefined) European integration. The PCF's organisation remains characterised by tightly controlled 'cells' and federations, while national meetings put forward a single text which is duly voted by all, leading Urvoas to conclude that PCF culture was as *'ontologiquement unanimiste'*[24] as ever. The leadership periodically reverts to attacks on 'ultraliberalism' in the purest communist style,[25] with a view to forming the radical wing of the *gauche plurielle*.[26] The mixture of left authoritarian conservatism and timid reform draws attention to the divergent tendencies in the party. The decision to participate in government was the one major sign of a new pragmatism. Fears of being swamped by the socialists remained.[27]

Overall, and in comparison with cognate parties in other countries, claims of a 'transformation' of the French Communist Party were exaggerated. However, a limited instance of Level 1 change did occur: although the party's ideology and organisation barely altered, it adapted some of its messages, sought to renew its electoral base and tentatively searched for its way forward as a 'party of government'.

The Greens

The Greens formed the newest component of the 'plural left', but political ecology in France had led a chequered history at the polls. The breakthrough came in the 1989 European elections where the Greens polled nearly two million voters (10.6 per cent of votes cast) and returned nine MEPs. The steep decline in popularity of the PS benefited ecologists in the regional elections of 1992, where they attained their best result of nearly 3.5 million electors (15 per cent of votes cast). Both these elections were contested under PR providing the opening elsewhere denied in the electoral system. The surge was helped by the presence of two ecology parties the Greens and Génération Ecologie (GE), respectively offering a radical and a reformist stance.[28] In multi-constituency regional elections, the presence of two parties did not split the green vote, but enlarged the reach of political ecology in qualitative and quantitative terms.

These factors encouraged the 1993 alliance between the Greens and GE. Although only 7.6 per cent of votes went to their Entente Écologiste, the total green vote reached 10.8 per cent if smaller formations are included. The ecology vote in a 'first-order' election had more than doubled on previous best and had held up well in relation to the 'second-order' elections of 1989–92. Nevertheless the ecologists were bitterly disappointed as voting forecasts suggested an out-turn of 15–20 per cent. Explanatory factors for the shortfall included over-confidence due to high opinion polls, inexperience in national elections, poor communication of policy objectives, ambiguity over political positioning (with contradictory statements made by the party leaders, Lalonde and Waechter), voter confusion caused by large numbers of 'independent' ecology candidates, and, of course, the large swing to the right.

The disappointment led to a power struggle within the Greens and a change in political positioning, but also to electoral decline. Between 1986 and 1993, with Antoine Waechter as *de facto* leader, the Greens had campaigned on a ticket of being 'neither left nor right'. During 1993–94, Dominique Voynet's current (*les Verts au pluriel*) attained dominance and swung the party away from political isolation to a strategy of alliance with small 'red-green' groups. In reaction the Waechter group seceded to form the 'non-aligned' Mouvement des Écologistes Indépendants. Further, the Greens and GE put forward separate lists at the 1994 European elections (contested on a single national constituency basis). In this unfavourable context and with a large selection of dissident lists on offer, the green vote was split and fell to 4.96 per cent. No European Parliament seats were won: infighting had squandered the political capital of French ecologists.

The climate of division continued in the 1995 presidential campaign where Lalonde, Waechter and Voynet all initially proposed to stand. Only Voynet could collect the necessary 500 endorsements from elected politicians, giving her the opportunity to unite the Green electorate behind her. She combined familiar environmentalist themes – such as improved rail-links, ending reliance on nuclear power, containing nuclear proliferation – with broad-left arguments for a 35-hour working week, better opportunities for women and more aid to developing countries. However, in a context where the electorate was more concerned with employment than the environment, her campaign lacked distinctiveness. Her poll of 3.32 per cent was the lowest for a Green presidential candidate since 1974. Yet Voynet scored two political victories which allowed the revival of a comatose party. First, in side-lining Waechter and Lalonde, she undermined their already ailing parties. During 1995–99 the Greens were once again the only political ecology party of significance in France.

Second, the campaign opened a dialogue with the socialists. The new strategy grew from the conversion to political realism of the party leadership.[29] The left turn of winter 1993 had yet to be properly exploited. An alliance with the PS was no longer the poisoned chalice refused in 1993, when the popularity of the socialists reached its nadir. In bringing the Greens into the French parliament and government, the 1997 coalition gave them their first opportunity to make a national policy impact.

The mixed fortunes of French political ecologists lend support to the thesis of an 'issue-attention cycle',[30] in which public interest in the environment waxes and wanes. The presence of the Greens within a broad left alliance is a pragmatic response to their electoral roller-coaster. Though prone to tumultuous outbursts, the Greens accepted that compromises in government were an acceptable price for ensuring survival in inclement times. Despite their integration into the mainstream left, the Greens represent a unique example of Level 3 change: political ecology's stress on the environment and post-materialist values introduces new cleavage structures and competitive dimensions into the French polity.

A REMAKE OF THE *UNION DE LA GAUCHE*?

Renewal within the 'plural left' was achieved within a context of significant party persistence. Of its five constituents, two old parties (PS, PCF) modified their issue appeal, while two (MDC, PRG) were instances of new parties occupying old slots. Only one party – the Greens – was both a new organisation and based on novel cleavage structures, yet it was also the party which most struggled to survive and remained the target of considerable hostility. Conversely, even when severely weakened, old parties did not disappear. These factors indicate that traditional competitive dimensions, though attenuated, remained crucial. The French party system had again demonstrated not so much a transformational potential as an 'absorptive capacity'.[31]

Yet the *gauche plurielle* differed on several measures from the *union de la gauche* of the 1970s. First, its composition was more heterogeneous, due to the presence of the Greens. Second, in ideological and programmatic terms, the Marxist left ceded to a social market orientation in which the stress was on the management of the economy rather than its transformation, and on the easing of social strains rather than their removal. Third, the aggregate level of support in first round voting for the coalition members in 1997 (44.5 per cent) was much lower than in 1981 (55.6 per cent) and its distribution was significantly different. In 1981, the PS was overwhelmingly dominant. But in 1997 the PS received only 23.5 per cent of the first-round poll, amounting to half the votes of the *gauche plurielle*, and barely 5 per cent up on 1993. While the result in parliamentary seats was substantially more favourable due to the majoritarian system, the PS could not retain popular opinion if it ignored its partners. Though it faced no challenger, it remained dependent on its allies for support in parliament and government and even for credibility as a party of the left. Thus, plurality gave small parties the assurance that their collective participation was essential.

Finally, the policy perspective characterising the 1970s and early 1980s was still national, whereas in the late 1990s – with monetary integration a reality – it was overwhelmingly European.[32] For these reasons, the *gauche plurielle* was not a remake of the *union de la gauche*. Although renewal within the individual components of the left has been modest, the dynamics of the *gauche plurielle* as a coalition confirm the thesis of a significant measure of party system change. Consideration of the relations within the French left will corroborate this thesis.

RELATIONSHIPS WITHIN THE *GAUCHE PLURIELLE*

What held the *gauche plurielle* together? Mutual dependence born of political necessity were the ties which bound the parties to each other. Despite perennial complaints regarding the hegemonic tendencies of the PS, the socialists could not govern alone. Conversely, the smaller parties recognised the 1997 victory as an exit from the wilderness. The left's accession to government provided an unexpected opportunity to respond to the hopes of a disorientated electorate. Were the government to fall due to internal divisions, their electorate would be unlikely to forgive them. Moreover, a substantial level of agreement existed on core policies. At the same time, this consensus was moderated by divergences on the 'pace' and 'audacity' of reform, with each party campaigning for its policy preferences. The 'plural left' demonstrated a pragmatic level of cohesion, even though each component tried to preserve its identity and progress its agenda. Overall, their coalition was characterised by an uneasy complementarity.

In particular, employment policy cemented the parties of the left together. Governments under the Mitterrand presidencies were severely criticised for their record on unemployment. The Jospin government made employment promotion a policy priority, notably with the 1997 Aubry initiative to create 700,000 jobs for young people over a five-year period and the 1998 legislation on a 35-hour working week.[33] Although the PCF and the Greens criticised the exclusion of public sector jobs from reductions in the working week and pushed for more ambitious targets (with further legislation anticipated in 1999), the 'plural left' was united in its emphasis on the need to increase employment. It was also agreed on reducing inequalities and social exclusion, with the 1998 Aubry law on social exclusion, and the 1999 act on public health care for all as major policy initiatives.

The stress on social measures facilitated a truce on economic policy between the pro- and anti-Maastricht components of the French government. In the 1997 parliamentary campaign, Jospin criticised the stability pact as a form of 'super Maastricht' treaty liable to perpetuate austerity policies. After accession to office he accepted its terms, once a section on employment was included at French insistence. Though a largely symbolic measure, it allowed the Jospin government to maintain France's stance to European integration, with phase three of Economic and Monetary Union introduced on 1 January 1999.

Due to global economic integration and market liberalisation within the EU, it was impossible to return to the economic and industrial policy of the PS-PCF government of 1981. In selling off part of the share capital of France Télécom, Air France and Thomson, the Jospin government accepted the consequences of internationalisation. Yet the PCF continued to favour Keynesianism in one country and was opposed to privatisation. On tax policy, in line with its traditional views, the PCF argued in 1998 for an extension of the *impôt de solidarité sur les grandes fortunes*, which Jospin resisted. Due to these tensions, the PCF blew hot and cold, wishing to preserve its room for manoeuvre while seeking to rebuild credibility by being a reliable partner in government.

The differences between policy orientation of the left in the 1970s and in the 1990s emerged strongly in the prominence assumed by 'post-materialist' issues, including sexual politics ('parity' between men and women in political life, gay rights), civil rights for immigrants and environmental questions. In each case, a measure of consensus emerged during 1998–99 over the promotion of new agendas, although differences in enthusiasm among components of the 'plural left' was discernible on specific issues.

Achieving equality between men and women was a core objective of all of the parties of the left. The bill on *parité* put forward by Justice Minister,

Elisabeth Guigou, aimed to incorporate into the constitution a right of equal access of men and women to elected office. The bill was approved in its first reading by the lower house, but rejected by the Senate – where the right retained its majority – on the grounds that it implied an extension of proportional representation and a policy of gender quotas. Although the support of President Chirac for the bill was influential in swinging senators round to acceptance in March 1999, it was too late to prevent a further deterioration of the Senate's image. The *parité* bill was able to create political capital not only by uniting the left, but also by wrong-footing the right.

Conversely, the enhancement of minority rights remained a slippery terrain. Measures to improve the legal protection of non-married couples – including those of the same sex – were put forward in a private members' bill known as the *pacte civil de solidarité* (PACS). Initially, the Jospin government was outpaced. In October 1998 the bill suffered an embarrassing collapse on its first reading since the benches of the left-wing majority were largely empty. In a second reading in early 1999, the government rallied behind the bill, with strong support from left libertarians among the socialists and the Greens.

Immigration policy proved typically fraught. In the first semester of 1998, the PS and MDC proposed to resolve the situation of illegal immigrants – the so-called *sans papiers* – on the case-by-case approach enshrined in the *loi Chevènement*. The Greens, however, favoured wholesale *régularisation*, as did the PCF though it later changed position. In November 1998, after Voynet's criticism of government policy on the *sans papiers* issue, she was rebuked by Jospin in a speech before the lower house. The MDC were prompt to quote Chevènement's famous statement on cabinet solidarity *'un ministre, ça ferme sa gueule ou ça s'en va'* (ministers should button their lip or resign). He, however, stressed that plurality in government required a diversity of views.[34] On this issue, an underlying consensus within the government was stretched to breaking point by calls for a radicalisation of policy.

Environmental issues likewise strained government cohesion. A moratorium on the construction of the Rhône–Rhine canal and the closure of the Superphénix reactor were crucial to the participation of the Greens in the coalition. The PCF in contrast remained pro-nuclear and opposed to closures of nuclear installations. In line with their traditional orientation, the communists refused support to the transposition of the 1996 European directive on the opening of energy markets, wishing to preserve the national monopoly of the state-sector utility, Electricité de France. Voynet, meanwhile, pushed for greater accountability of the nuclear industry and improved safety measures, notably at the Hague processing plant. In late 1998 she was forced to accept plans for underground storage of nuclear waste and the reopening of the Phénix reactor to continue experiments with nuclear recycling, but made public her disavowal of government decisions on nuclear policy. This reinforced the image of the Greens as 'undisciplined' partners in government.

Tensions surfaced over other aspects of environmental policy. The Greens argued for abolishing tax advantages enjoyed by diesel, while the PS preferred a phased reduction to European levels. On nature conservation, Environment Minister Voynet sought to fully implement the 1979 Birds directive. However, under pressure from the hunting lobby, a private members' bill was passed in June 1998 (with socialist votes) to legalise the inclusion of February in the open season for hunting birds (in defiance of the European directive). In early 1999, violent marches were orchestrated against the Greens by hunters and farmers, culminating in the ransacking of Voynet's office. These outbursts constituted a reminder that the management of relations with the *gauche plurielle* could not be divorced from the evolution of public opinion.

Unlike the PRG who, as the 'natural' allies of the PS, had developed the habit of suppressing public criticisms, the Greens and the MDC constituted the main sources of turbulence – separately and in opposition to each other. After a lengthy hospitalisation, Chevènement marked his return to office in January 1999 by a tough stance on law and order, particularly with regard to juvenile delinquency. Prime Minister Jospin intervened to temper Chevènement's more repressive proposals (after protests from Justice Minister Guigou), but seemed to appreciate the Interior Minister's appeal to voters with authoritarian values. Conversely, this trait led to conflict with the Greens. Chevènement resisted Voynet not only on the *sans papiers* but also on her regionalising agenda; in contrast he put stress on *départements* and the central state.[35] The faultline between the MDC, situated to the right of the 'plural left', and the Greens was flagrant. Following the well-worn tradition, complementarity proved to be a combat.

CONCLUSIONS

Knowing that their nation is prey to conflict, the French are attracted by displays of unity. During 1997–99 the *gauche plurielle* benefited from its apparent cohesion, while disunity devastated the right. Power-sharing (*cohabitation*) between a right-wing president and left-wing government was itself the sign of a soft consensus, producing minor disagreements but no major traumas, even though the government pushed through a contentious legislative programme. Its way was smoothed by the favourable climate of 1998, with 350,000 new jobs created and a fall in the unemployment rate to 11.5 per cent (from 12.6 per cent in June 1997). An increase in the 'feel-good' factor and improved national confidence (the 'World Cup effect') resulted in high levels of popularity for Prime Minister Jospin and President Chirac.[36]

The government of the 'plural left' succeeded in harnessing the complementarity between its components by developing co-operation and limiting competition. Thereby it largely overcame its internal divisions. However, the stumbling block for the French left continued to be the problematic aggregation of electoral demand. The hybrid composition of the *gauche plurielle* – an old far-left party, a mainstream social-democrat party, one splinter party, one rump party and a new politics party – accumulated discrete electorates, rather than integrating them. Party leaders totted up the electoral arithmetic, with the spectre of division peering over their shoulder. In France's heterogeneous society they have no other option if they are to form political executives.

However, electorates and parties are conscious of their ideological blocs and the faultlines that separate them. Greens used to refuse aggregation with the left.[37] The idea of federating the 'plural left' within a 'broad-church' party was dismissed by its constituents. This attachment to fading identities narrowed the scope for party system change, producing a distinct evolutionary 'stage', but not a radically new configuration. At a moment of economic and political transition, the *gauche plurielle* represented an attempt to stabilise a crumbling electoral base, rather than a realignment of the French left.

NOTES

1. For detailed analysis of the 1997 election, see Pascal Perrineau and Colette Ysmal (eds.) *Le vote surprise: les élections législatives des 25 mai et 1 juin 1997* (Paris: Presses de Sciences Po 1998).
2. In 1997, socialist deputies in the Assemblée Nationale totalled 251 and communists 35. The political ecologists, left-radicals, republicans and allies formed the Radical-Citoyen-Vert group (RCV), numbering 33 in all.
3. By order of ministerial protocol, Martine Aubry (Employment Minister) and Elisabeth Guigou (Justice Minister) rank second and third after the Prime Minister. In the first Juppé government of 1995, there were more women (12), but all in low-ranking office and eight were dismissed after six months.
4. For details on the composition of the Jospin government, see Bernard Dolez, 'Le gouvernement Jospin', *Regards sur l'Actualité* (July–Aug. 1997) pp.3–11.
5. Howard Machin, 'Stages and dynamics in the evolution of the French party system', in Peter

Mair and Gordon Smith (eds.) *Understanding Party System Change in Western Europe* (London: Frank Cass 1990) pp.59–81.

6. Alain Guyomarch, 'The European dynamics of evolving party competition in France', *Parliamentary Affairs* 48/1 (1995) pp.100–24. In 1993 the UPF (a coalition of the RPR and UDF) won 485 of 577 seats.

7. The share of first-round votes going to the four major parties fell in the presidential elections from 87.5 per cent in 1981 to 70.9 per cent in 1995; and in parliamentary elections it fell from 95 per cent in 1981 to 63 per cent in 1997.

8. In the parliamentary elections of 1981, 1986, 1988, 1993 and 1997, the incumbents have in each case been ousted.

9. To limit examples to the parties of the left, the PS under Mitterrand in the 1970s and 1980s pursued an active strategy of seeking socialist gains at communist expense, and sought variously to recuperate or marginalise political ecology parties. See Guillaume Sainteny, 'Le parti socialiste face à l'écologisme', *Revue Française de Science Politique* 44/3 (1994) pp.424–61.

10. Herbert Kitschelt, 'European party systems: continuity and change', in Martin Rhodes, Paul Heywood and Vincent Wright (eds) *Developments in West European Politics* (London, Macmillan 1997) pp.131–50.

11. In June 1980, there were 1.4 million unemployed; by Oct. 1982 the figure was over 2 million. Numbers rose steadily until May 1987 to reach 2.6 million. With growth rates of around 4 per cent at the end of the 1980s, the figure fell to 2.4 million by May 1990. Thereafter it again rose steadily and was 3.4 million in June 1994, dropping back to 3.1 million by July 1995.

12. Criticisms of Mitterrand by socialists remained muted. Rocard's Nov. 1998 description of Mitterrand as not being an 'honest man' constituted an exception, but was met by embarrassed silence and disavowals from socialist ranks.

13. For details on how the 'plural left' was formed, see Anne-Sophie Mercier and Béatrice Jérôme, *Les 700 jours de Jospin. Histoire d'une prise de pouvoir* (Paris: Plon 1997) pp.125–58.

14. See *Le Monde*, 19 Feb. 1993.

15. Ibid., 4 Aug. 1998.

16. Janine Mossuz-Lavau, *Que veut la gauche plurielle?* (Paris: Editions Odile Jacob 1998) pp.247–62.

17. Already in 1983, after the failure of the Mauroy reflation, Chevènement had urged French withdrawal from the European Monetary System. The argument was won by those who wished to maintain European integration as the priority even at the price of a U-turn to austerity, notably Finance Minister Delors.

18. See *Le Monde*, 8 Sept. 1998.

19. This point has been repeatedly made in the literature: see, for example, François Platone and Jean Ranger, 'L'échec électoral du Parti communiste', in Alain Lancelot (ed.) *1981: Les élections de l'alternance* (Paris: Presses de la Fondation Nationale des Sciences Politiques 1986) pp.69–133; Jean Baudoin, 'Le déclin du PCF', *Regards sur l'Actualité* (April 1991) pp.35–43, and Stéphane Courtois and Marc Lazar, *L'Histoire du parti communiste français* (Paris: PUF 1995) pp.381–418.

20. Ross and Jenson noted that 'Blame fell overwhelmingly, and understandably, on the PCF. ... Within the next three years it lost a quarter of its voters and a third of its members'. See George Ross and Jane Jenson, 'France: triumph and tragedy', in Perry Anderson and Patrick Camiller (eds.) *Mapping the West European Left* (London: Verso 1994) p.168.

21. PCF deputies numbered 86 in 1978, 44 in 1981.

22. Robert Hue, 'Être à la hauteur des exigences de notre peuple et des attentes de la France', *Cahiers du communisme* 1–2 (1997) p.29.

23. See PCF, 'Cinq axes d'initiatives', ibid. 5 (1997) pp.49–58.

24. Jean-Jacques Urvouas, 'La mutation du PCF: fiction ou veilléité?', *Regards sur l'Actualité* (March 1997) p.7.

25. Thus, in his address to the Fête de l'Humanité, 13 Sept. 1998, Hue inveighed against 'la totale liberté laissée aux capitaux financiers de piller la planète et de se rentabiliser au détriment des êtres humains'.

26. Hue speaks of forming 'un pôle de radicalité à la gauche du Parti socialiste', in idem (note 22) p.34.

27. The PCF regularly asserts its independence from the PS, refusing to be a 'courant du PS', *Le Monde*, 8 Sept. 1998, and dismissing the 'synthèse politique nouvelle' proposed by Jospin, ibid. 13 Sept. 1998.

28. Shull discussed the political strategy differences between the parties in terms of a technocratic, managerial approach to the environment (GE) versus a grassroots movement approach (Greens). See Tadd Shull, 'The ecologists in the regional elections: strategies behind the split', *French Politics and Society* 10/2 (1992) pp.13–29.

29. For a discussion of this conversion, see Bruno Villalba, 'L'ordalie parlementaire des écologistes', *Ecologie et politique* 21 (1997) pp.127–37.

30. Anthony Downs, 'Up and down with ecology – the 'issue attention cycle'', *Public Interest* 28 (1972) pp.38–50.

31. David Hanley, 'France: living with instability', in David Broughton and Mark Donovan (eds.) *Changing Party Systems in Western Europe* (London: Pinter 1999) pp.48–70.

32. However this strengthened the hand of the pro-Maastricht PS, since the Eurosceptics in the PCF and the MDC were held hostage during 1997–99 (as were the planned economy stalwarts of the PCF in 1981–84).

33. For details see René Haby, *La vie publique en France avril 1997–juillet 1998* (Paris: Documentation française 1998).

34. *Le Monde*, 19 Nov. 1998.

35. Both came from Franche-Comté where they had led a history of electoral skirmishes and personal animosity.

36. For details, see Olivier Duhamel, 'La cohabitation institutionalisée', in idem and Philippe Méchet (eds.) *L'État de l'opinion 1999* (Paris: Seuil 1999) pp.71–83; and idem, 'La gauche du possible à l'épreuve du pouvoir', in the same volume pp.46–70.

37. Conversely voters of the mainstream right refuse aggregation with the FN.

The Right: Divisions and Cleavages in *fin de siècle* France

PAUL HAINSWORTH

In the beginning there was the right. The French right monopolised the French Fifth Republic for its first 23 years (1958–81). First, Charles de Gaulle (1958–69) and then his Gaullist (Georges Pompidou, 1969–74) and non-Gaullist (Valéry Giscard d'Estaing, 1974–81) successors occupied the presidency. At the same time, Gaullist and non-Gaullist political parties won parliamentary after parliamentary election, ensuring therefore a comprehensive stranglehold on the highest political offices. As is well known, the left – under François Mitterrand's leadership – eventually displaced the right in 1981, and the next two decades were notable for a more even distribution of power in France.

In fact, the left overall was more successful than the right, winning the seven-year, renewable presidency in 1981 and 1988 and succeeding at three parliamentary elections too: thus enjoying government during 1981–86, 1988–93 and most recently in 1997 (in theory, until 2002). This meant that the right won parliamentary elections (and thus government office) in 1986(–88) and 1993(–97) and the presidency (Jacques Chirac) in 1995 (until at least the next election which is scheduled for 2002). Significantly, and in contrast to the left's experience here, neither of the right's most recent parliamentary successes was followed by a parliament that ran its natural five-year course. This suggests that the right has had some difficulty defending its successes.

The Fifth Republic in the two recent decades may be said, therefore, to have leaned to the left, without toppling over. The previously hegemonic right has struggled to come to terms with this state of affairs. Several factors have influenced the changing fortunes of the right and, without professing to be exhaustive, they have included the process of coming to terms with post-Gaullism (since the mid-1970s); the rise of an increasingly professional, market-friendly and successful Socialist Party (PS); the decline of communism, both globally and domestically (in the form of the once-powerful Communist Party – PCF); the emergence of a national-populist, extremist threat in the shape of the Front National (FN); globalisation trends, which – together with accelerated European integration – have had implications for national economic policy formulation, and also for how the question of the nation is presented.

Divisive-prone questions of leadership, personal and party rivalry, strategy and tactics have also characterised the French right in recent years, and this study assesses these variables, in attempting to gauge the health and standing of the right in the changing political context of contemporary France.

Essentially, the time-span concentrated upon here is the period from the 1995 presidential election up to the spring of 1999. Electorally, the period includes presidential, local, parliamentary, cantonal and regional elections and leads into the pre-campaign for the 1999 European elections. It also signals the mid-term point of the Chirac presidency. One of the key points to emerge from the following analysis of these years is that the focus on winning (and retaining) the presidency has served to divide the right as much as unite it. The presidency, the jewel in the crown of de Gaulle's Fifth Republic, and therefore a revered institution as far as Gaullists are concerned, has become, in the mid-to-late 1990s, the site of damaging personal rivalry, unfulfilled policy ambition and leadership decisions, that have resulted in weakening the electoral performance and potential of right-wing political parties.

Paradoxically, though, at a personal level, the right-wing presidential incumbent (the neo-Gaullist leader, Chirac) survived an initially difficult early presidency (1995–97) to bask in much more favourable opinion ratings subsequently.

In the first section below, we assess the foremost party on the French right, the neo-Gaullist Rassemblement pour la République (RPR), founded by Chirac in 1976. The discussion concentrates on the rivalry at the top of the Gaullist movement.

This is followed by a section that focuses on the non-Gaullist right, notably the RPR's main rival and partner, the Union pour la Démocratie Française (UDF), created by Giscard d'Estaing in 1978, ostensibly to balance the RPR's influence, assist his re-election as French president and equilibriate the right-wing political 'family'.

A third section examines what, until very recently, at least, has been seen as the third significant component of the French right, albeit of a different political family: the FN, born in 1972. In particular, we highlight the impact of the ascendant FN upon the RPR-UDF. However, a political bombshell of the past year or so has been the implosion of the FN, a by-product of the personal rivalry between its long-time president, Jean-Marie Le Pen, and his ex-number two, Bruno Mégret. This development is bound to have repercussions for the French right as a whole, although it is too early (at time of writing) to specify these with any accuracy. It will depend upon who wins the struggle for dominance on the extreme right and what are the margins of victory.

GAULLISTS (RPR)

Gaullism or neo-Gaullism has been, in some form or other, the most successfully enduring force of the Fifth Republic. General de Gaulle founded and piloted the regime and, as France approaches the millennium, a (neo-)Gaullist president is again at the helm. Nevertheless, the General's successors have faced considerable problems in conjugating post-de Gaulle France to their advantage. Undoubtedly, the key figure here is Chirac (premier in 1974–76 and 1986–88) and the pinnacle of his success was the 1995 presidential election victory. The 1995 contest also revealed the divisions within the RPR and on the right in general. Significantly, the Chirac victory, while obviously welcome on the right, led directly to difficulties in the years ahead.

As related elsewhere,[1] the 1995 presidential election pitted two Gaullists against each other: Chirac and the ruling premier (1993–95), Édouard Balladur. Initially, comfortably ahead in the polls and well supported by UDF and some RPR notables (including Charles Pasqua and Nicolas Sarkozy), the latter candidate saw his lead decisively whittled away by a combatant and energetic Chirac. Besides his loyal supporters, such as RPR president, Alain Juppé, Chirac managed to attract *inter alia* the backing of the prominent UDF pro-European and ultra-economic liberal politician, Alain Madelin, and the heavyweight, Gaullist, populist politician, Philippe Séguin, who in 1992 had been (alongside Pasqua and Philippe de Villiers) the most influential voice in almost delivering a 'No' vote for France against the Maastricht Treaty on European Union.[2] Séguin, in particular, was an important influence on Chirac's electoral platform, successfully managing to infuse it with a strong dose of social Gaullism. Indeed, as Machin explains, 'social solidarity', 'sharing' and 'changing priorities' were all part of Chirac's campaign discourse.[3] The socially excluded, the homeless and the unemployed were all prioritised by Chirac, as he stressed the need to heal France's 'social fracture'.

Chirac also had the benefit of the RPR to help organise his campaign. As Hanley suggests, he 'was able to use the party machine to weaken his rival and at the same time present a more combative, socially aware image that contrasted favourably with Balladur's complacency'.[4]

Chirac's policy emphasis, including reassuring noises on wages and public expenditure (and taxation), was especially important in winning over a good proportion of young voters and blue-collar workers to his side. Indeed, according to Guyomarch, the 16-point gain in blue-collar support (compared to the same candidate's unsuccessful presidential bid in 1988) appeared 'to be the single most important contribution to Chirac's victory'.[5]

However, such was the nature of Chirac's promise-laden campaign that, it would have been difficult subsequently to satisfy all expectations and, at the same time, preside over the quest to get the French economy in shape to meet the strict (Maastricht) convergence criteria for participation in the first stage of the single European currency in 1999. European integration had not figured prominently in the 1995 presidential campaigns of the principal three contenders, largely because there was a broad enough consensus between them on the necessity of pushing ahead with the European project. Also, none of them wanted to rerun the 1992 Maastricht referendum debate, which had seen France so clearly divided on the issue of deeper integration.

Fortunately, for Chirac, Séguin had evolved towards a less Eurosceptic position and did not threaten to undermine the presidential campaign from the inside. On the contrary, his 'Europe of nations' stance could help Chirac to present a somewhat critical, but essentially committed, attitude to Europe. Ultimately, candidate Chirac (defeated in 1981 and 1988) was not going to let the divisive issue of Europe sabotage his campaign and a certain ambiguity suited his purposes at election time.

In the aftermath of victory, though, some difficult choices had to be made on the French right. Significantly, there was no premiership for Séguin, as Chirac duly appointed Juppé to form a new right-wing government. Other key figures loyal to Chirac in the presidential contest were rewarded with government posts, while Balladur was sidelined for his 'treacherous', insider challenge to Chirac. However, Séguin returned to his prestigious post as president of the National Assembly, a coveted and strategic position. As Cole explains, Séguin 'transformed the presidency of the National Assembly into a public platform from which to criticise the Juppé government that he in theory supported'.[6] Certainly, the high profile office kept Séguin in the public and political eye, and he would enjoy 'revenge' later. In the meantime, his dissatisfaction with the style and substance of Juppé's government was well-aired.

As regard to policy-making after May 1995, Cole again sums up the broad picture: 'Initially responsive to his first-round electoral clientele,

President Chirac attempted to navigate a delicate path between the various contradictory promises that he had made during the election campaign'.[7]

By Autumn 1995, the government was becoming increasingly preoccupied with tuning the French economy to meet the Maastricht criteria, and this meant budgetary restraint and austerity measures. The public sector strikes of late 1995, which were the biggest in France since May 1968, revealed the regime's lack of success in addressing the 'social fracture'. As Parsons notes, Chirac then promised that his government would listen to grievances and genuinely try to tackle social exclusion and unemployment.[8]

However, the reform and cost of the social security system had proved to be a particularly contentious issue throughout the lifespan of the Juppé government (1995–97), while unemployment reached a post-war high (12.6 per cent) in August 1996, going even higher later on in the year. Parsons contends that the president himself:

> could not escape blame for the government's poor economic record ...
> In particular, the priority accorded to the reduction of budget deficits, while the rate of unemployment rose by more than one percentage over the year [i.e. 1996], was seen by many to be in direct contradiction to the promises he made during the election campaign.[9]

A consequence of the government's social and economic problems was the highly unfavourable personal opinion polls for Chirac and Juppé. Certainly, both leaders benefited initially from the customary honeymoon period that tends to follow electoral success. In May 1995, polls showed a 59 per cent satisfaction response (with 22 per cent dissatisfied) for Chirac and a 63 per cent positive rating (against 19 per cent) for Juppé.

However, the *état de grace* for the RPR tandem was the shortest-lived in the Fifth Republic and the president's and prime minister's personal ratings plummeted to record lows. In November 1995, the president's satisfaction rating was 27 per cent (positive) against 64 per cent (negative), whilst the prime minister fared no better at 26 per cent (positive) against 65 per cent (negative). A year later, the figures were almost identical. The most damaging and unpopular policies were seen to be the resumption of French nuclear tests (Chirac) and the reform of the social security system (Juppé).[10] Collectively, these two policies helped to squander the young and 'popular' support won over by Chirac in 1995.

Also damaging for the government were the divisions on the right between those economic liberals – such as Balladur and Madelin[11] – who wanted to accelerate the movement towards a more free market, less 'statist' economy and others – such as Séguin – who called for a more faithful application of Chirac's 1995 manifesto.

Overall, these problems highlighted the difficult standing of the right in the mid-1990s. Despite (or because of) recently winning the presidency and also boasting a thumping majority in the National Assembly, the right appeared divided and demoralised and on the defensive. As Jaffré explained, the right was imperilled for, in late 1996 – for the first time since 1990 – French public opinion put more confidence in the left's (37 per cent) rather the right's (31 per cent) capacity- 'to govern the country'.[12]

An especially problematical issue for the right was the question of leadership. First, there was intense rivalry for leadership, as was evident in the manoeuvring and campaigning for the 1995 presidential election. The divisions created here would have repercussions for the next few years, not least as the right looked to retaining the presidency in 2002. Second, once installed, there were serious questions (both within the right and without) about the direction and image of the Chirac-Juppé tandem. Juppé's style of government was seen widely as technocratic, remote and elitist, hardly calculated to redress the so-called 'crisis of representation' in France. Interviewed in early 1996, for instance, UDF vice-president François Léotard called for a political style of leadership from the prime minister, that was more in touch with the people.[13]

According to Léotard, Chirac had succeeded in bringing a 'more human, less monarchic' dimension to the French presidency. Nevertheless, opinion polls indicated that the French voters wanted more hands-on leadership from Chirac, particularly to help resolve some of the damaging socioeconomic conflicts that beset his early presidency. As Jaffré astutely points out, 'The return to a Gaullist [i.e. regal] presidency in a world profoundly different from the 1960s did not match up to people's expectations'.[14] Indeed, this observation confirms the view that the role of a (Gaullist) president since de Gaulle's day covers more than the grand questions of state.[15]

Unquestionably, the most controversial and dramatic leadership decision of the Chirac presidency was the decision to go for an early election in 1997, a year ahead of schedule. Gently buoyed by slightly better opinion ratings and fatigued by internecine sniping on the right, the president announced the dissolution of parliament. The 21 April 1997 decision was rationalised by Chirac as an opportunity to provide 'a new élan', in order to take France 'further along the path of change'. Essentially, he was asking for a new parliamentary majority to complement his presidential mandate and enable the government to continue its course.

Allegedly, a right-wing victory would enable the country to meet the difficult decisions ahead, notably in a European context as France prepared to participate in the first wave of single currency membership.[16] Chirac did not want elections to coincide with signing up for the single currency, as this might expose divisions on Europe within the right. Here is not the place to rehearse the details of the 1997 legislative election.[17] The discussion is confined to examining what were the main consequences and implications for the right.

The result of the election transferred government power back to the left, under the leadership of 1995 presidential candidate, Lionel Jospin (PS) and, inevitably, this stimulated criticism of Chirac's leadership and judgement. Key political figures on the right (including Balladur and Séguin – both seen as potential successors to Juppé) were hostile to the gamble that dissolution represented. Certainly, there were (or had been) other options open to the president, notably a cabinet and prime ministerial reshuffle, a significant policy change or an immediate dissolution in 1995, in the wake of presidential election success – and before 'the going got tough'. The measure was interpreted widely as a tactical and political decision by Chirac, but one that backfired. The four previous dissolutions in the Fifth Republic (1962, 1968, 1981 and 1988) had all resulted in the president's hand being strengthened. By contrast, the 1997 dissolution left the president weakened and the right as a whole devastated – after losing 220 of its 477 seats won in 1993 – and prone to further division.

Indeed, first ballot failure had forced Chirac and Juppé, belatedly, to offer a change of prime minister, but this concession was not enough to avoid left-wing victory on the decisive second ballot. Juppé also, quickly and reluctantly, lost the leadership of the RPR to a resurgent, combative and unstoppable Séguin, who now emerged as a serious threat to Chirac's presidential ambitions in 2002.

When, in March 1998, the right suffered further losses in the regional elections, this again was seen (not least, by Séguin)[18] as another consequence of Chirac's dissolution – a botched dissolution, according to Séguin. Furthermore, there were also rumblings that President Chirac had become semi-detached from his 'troops' and apparently disinterested in the outcome of the regional election.

The outcome of the 1997 legislative election had signalled a new phase of 'cohabitation' (power-sharing) between a president (Chirac) and prime minister (Jospin) of different political families.[19] On the right, too, a de facto 'cohabitation' emerged within Gaullism, as Chirac and Séguin both vied with each other for leverage. Although the first mode of power sharing proceeded relatively harmoniously, with neither side wishing to 'rock the boat' too much, the latter experience (itself conditioned by the former) culminated, in April 1999, with the embittered resignation of Séguin from leadership of the RPR party and the right's Euro-election list (see below). There were various protracted developments that led up to Séguin's dramatic step and it will be instructive to highlight the main elements of conflict and disunity.

First, Chirac was not content to see Séguin take control of his RPR. Chirac's initial moves to maintain the *status quo* or promote loyalist Jean-Louis Debré to Juppé's succession came to nought. Moreover, Séguin spent the first half-year or so of his leadership trying to change the internal dynamics and even the name of the RPR, but with limited success. From the start of Séguin's RPR presidency, Chirac and his supporters began to reactivate or create parallel structures of influence. These included Bernard Pons's Association des Amis de Jacques Chirac and Debré's successful capture of the presidency of the RPR group in the National Assembly. At the RPR public meeting in Paris, on 31 January 1998, Séguin's very mention of Chirac's name prompted a prolonged and pointed ovation, no doubt encouraged by Chirac loyalists.[20]

A second difference between Séguin and Chirac emerged over cohabitation dynamics. As RPR boss, Séguin adopted an aggressive 'leader of the opposition' stance towards Jospin and his government's policies. However, this contrasted with the more consensual and even conflicting (with Séguin) approach of Chirac. The latter strategy paid dividends for the French president as his opinion poll ratings (as well as Jospin's) benefited considerably from 'cohabitation' (and, arguably, from France's 1998 World Cup soccer victory), while coincidentally Séguin's personal popularity scores trailed well behind.[21]

None the less, Séguin clearly expected a more systematic and supportive opposition from Chirac against the PS-led government. Moreover, the former and his supporters were mindful of the electoral timetable in 2002: the parliamentary election was on schedule to precede the presidential contest and would, no doubt, have a bearing on the latter. In these circumstances, *séguinistes* (and others) could argue that it made good political sense not to neglect attacking the opposition and focusing on the legislative election, rather than massaging a candidate's (i.e. Chirac's) presidential ambition. Alternatively, Chirac and his advisers probably do not expect Jospin's already extended honeymoon period to last forever and are conscious of the fact that every parliamentary election over the past two decades has been lost by the incumbents.

Whatever the interpretation on long-term strategy, things came to a head between Chirac and Séguin in April 1999, with the latter's abrupt and acrimonious resignation announcement. Séguin took offence at an article (in *Valeurs actuelles* (17–23 April 1999) by Pons, which – leading up to the June European elections – claimed two, rival, right-wing, Euro-election lists (those of François Bayrou [UDF] and Charles Pasqua/Philippe de Villiers) as part and parcel of Chirac's presidential majority. Both the UDF and de Villiers had supported or fronted rival candidatures in the 1995 presidential election – although both had rallied to Chirac on the second ballot. Nevertheless, Séguin interpreted Pons's article and, more pertinently, Chirac's unwillingness to promptly contradict it, as an open encouragement of disunity on the right.

Additionally, Chirac's all-too-obvious courting and reception of Bayrou (a Balladur supporter in 1995) seemed to add insult to injury, especially since the UDF leader was known to be critical of Séguin's allegedly lukewarm Europeanism, as evidenced during the Maastricht referendum debate. In fact, Bayrou – a strong advocate of deeper European integration – saw Séguin, too, as an obstacle to right-wing unity and, thus, became increasingly persuaded of the virtues of running a separate, centre-right, European-friendly list in June 1999. While this step was hardly unprecedented on the right, the overall, widespread impression of the above developments was of a right divided on personality, strategy and policy (i.e., Europe).

UNION POUR LA DEMOCRATIE FRANCAISE (UDF)

The second major component of the mainstream right is the UDF. Created by Valéry Giscard d'Estaing in 1978, the UDF developed as a loose confederation of small parties. As such, it was 'originally a confederation of those non-Gaullist parties supporting Giscard's presidency' (1974–81).[22] Historically, it has brought together economic ultraliberals, Christian and social democrats, right-wing 'radicals', political clubs and other centre-right elements.

A strong sense of localism and *notabilisation* pervades the party. Indeed, as Elgie suggests, in the introduction to this volume, the organisation brought together various fiefdoms, each quite jealous of their identity and autonomy within the overall structure. While an undisguised (and unfulfilled) aim of the UDF politicians has been to displace the RPR as the leading right-wing party in France, party spokespersons have often ruled out any intention to copy or reproduce the neo-Gaullist movement.[23] Even so, in 1977, Giscard's old Independent Republicans metamorphosed themselves into the more structured Parti Républicain (PR), aspiring to rally the UDF and challenge the recently established RPR.

However, the UDF has, more often than not, been cast in the role of RPR-support team and, significantly, has not even fielded its own, official, presidential candidate since Giscard's 1981 defeat. Seemingly, too, where the RPR has preached (though not always practised) internal party discipline, the UDF has made a virtue out of giving free rein to its component parts. In essence, then, the UDF has celebrated what divides it and this reflex has conditioned the ability of the movement to speak with a concerted and coherent voice.

Here is not the place to dissect the various components of the UDF.[24] But, writing in 1997, Hanley usefully offers the following view of the UDF: 'It is more than the sum of its variegated parts, but arguably not much more; at the same time it is less of a unitary actor than any typical member of the socialist, Christian democrat or even liberal families.'[25] The same author goes on to portray the UDF as 'a party in a phase of arrested development'[26] while Fysh disparagingly refers to it as a 'ramshackle confederation'.[27] If anything can be said to have united the party ideologically, it is support for European integration and the free market, but again with varying degrees of emphasis and interpretation across the different components of the UDF.

There are five specific factors of division worth emphasising in so far as they shed light on the contemporary workings of the UDF and the French right: personal rivalry; arguments over political structures; ideological dispute; attitudes towards the RPR; and also perspectives and practices vis-à-vis the FN. Most of these factors will be dealt with collectively here, rather than individually, in view of their interconnected character – and, as indicated, the next section discusses the FN.

As regards personal rivalry, Giscard has dominated the history of the UDF and his on-off relationship with Chirac has been a central feature of right-wing politics since the mid-1970s. In 1974, Chirac had played the role of king-maker to help Giscard win the French presidency and was rewarded with the prime minister's position. However, as Knapp points out, 'the first Chirac premiership was marked by an increasingly bitter power struggle between the two men',[28] ending with the neo-Gaullist leader's resignation in 1976. Further differences between the two men helped the right to lose the presidency when they both stood in 1981.

According to Cole, 'Once Giscard d'Estaing had lost the presidency, the UDF became little more than an electoral cartel'.[29] In this capacity, the UDF has done reasonably well, attending to the internal arrangements in order to put up a single UDF candidate at elections and negotiating with the RPR to field common candidates or support each other on the second ballot of elections. A single UDF-RPR presidential candidate or an all-embracing right-wing party have been less realisable.

Within the UDF realms, Giscard passed control of the PR to his up-and-coming colleague, François Léotard in 1982. However, later years witnessed increasing rivalry between the two, as Léotard endeavoured to establish his own presidential ambitions. In 1994–95, Giscard was unhappy with the lack of support within the UDF for his renewed ambitions to capture the French presidency. Significantly, the 1995 presidential election found the party very divided and each of these two UDF-PR leaders backing different candidates: Giscard, unusually, was for Chirac and Léotard for Balladur. The distinct lack of empathy between Giscard and Léotard was apparent in March 1996, when eventually Giscard stood down as president of the UDF, in what one journalist called 'the biggest shake-up in the conservative right since the founding of the multi-party Union pour la Démocratie Française'.[30] Although Léotard (strongly backed by Bayrou) won the contest to succeed Giscard, the latter supported the main rival candidate, Alain Madelin.

Madelin's political trajectory since backing Chirac in 1995 (see above) had seen him promptly rewarded with a cabinet seat, only to soon clash with Prime Minister Juppé over the pace of economic liberalisation – a disagreement which led to his dismissal after only several months in office. Thwarted next of the UDF presidency, Madelin 'succeeded' renaming the PR – it became Démocratie Libérale (DL) – and later took it out from the UDF umbrella in May 1998.

Behind these manoeuvres were not only personal rivalries, but also ideological and strategic considerations. The PR (and Madelin especially) had come to be identified with economic ultraliberalism and this did not always sit comfortably with the Christian and social democratic wing of the UDF, represented largely, but not exclusively, by the Centre des Démocrates Sociaux (CDS) (renamed Force Démocrate (FD) in 1994, under Bayrou's leadership, and including the small Parti Social Démocrate). Moreover, the previously dominant PR was increasingly challenged within the UDF by FD and felt uneasy about Bayrou's wish to create a more structured, 'resolutely centrist' UDF (or equivalent), possibly along the lines of the German Christian Democratic Union (CDU). This possibility was subsequently enhanced by Bayrou's election to the presidency of the UDF, in September 1998, and his 're-centering' (*recentrage*) and unifying of the UDF the following November.

Ideologically, DL was closer to the free market liberalism of the RPR and it was no real surprise to see the RPR and DL run a joint list in the 1999 European elections. The resignation of Séguin, a social and somewhat national-populist Gaullist by tradition, may have exposed the divisions on the right, but it also gave a tighter ideological thrust to the RPR-DL 'Euro-ticket' under a Sarkozy-Madelin leadership. At the same time, it was also not illogical to put forward a Bayrou-led UDF list, even if this again showed up divisions on the right. The decision to run a separate UDF Euro-list, together with the resignation of Séguin, dealt a severe blow to the Alliance, from which it may not recover. The Alliance, constructed after the 1998 regional elections, had been the initiative of Séguin and UDF leader, François Léotard, aimed at reconciling the two main right-wing forces. However, from the off, the new structure appeared elitist, even personally, driven and lacked grassroots support.

Moreover, the RPR's decision to run the Euro-list with the DL, under Séguin's non-negotiable position as list-leader, squeezed the UDF and again pushed Bayrou and colleagues towards the logic of a separate list. As Elgie's introduction to this volume suggests, the Alliance is 'nothing more than the sum of its divided and somewhat demoralised parts'.

THE FRONT NATIONAL (FN) AND THE RIGHT

The divisions and problems on the right in the mid-to late-1990s were compounded by the success of a third force, the FN. After spending its first 13 years in the political wilderness, the FN emerged as a durable feature of French politics during 1983–99, winning between 10 and 15 per cent of the vote in recent years. According to Shields, 'The rise of a powerful extreme-right party is arguably the most important political development of the past fourteen years.'[31]

The mainstream right has had persistent difficulties in knowing how to 'play' the FN and strategy has ranged from ostracism to alliances, and from policy-clothes stealing to outright condemnation or ignoring. The FN has impacted upon the right in various ways, winning over right-wing voters, influencing the policy agenda of the right and acting as a power-broker at the regional level. Again, below, the emphasis is on the period 1995–99, and the consequences of FN electoral successes.

As Cole suggests, the 1995 presidential election saw displayed 'shades of René Rémond's three families of the French right (bonapartism, orleanist conservatism and the counter-revolutionary right)'[32] as Chirac, Balladur and Le Pen all faced one another – (with de Villiers, too, representing the last-named strand, plus a dose of orleanism).[33] Le Pen's impressive 15 per cent share of the poll deprived the right of first ballot victory – although, especially given the 'popularisation'[34] of the FN electorate in recent years, it is clear that Le Pen not only took votes from the right.

The success of the presidential election for Le Pen was carried over into the June 1995 local elections, which saw the FN make some important breakthroughs. The towns of Toulon, Orange, Marignane and (in early 1997) Vitrolles were all won by the FN in its south/south-east bastion area. Right-wing division, mismanagement and corruption were certainly strong factors in the FN local government successes, which represented new landmarks in the legitimisation of the party.[35] Corruption, of course, is a practice that has implicated both the right and the left in France. Exploitation of the issue enabled the FN to articulate an anti-establishment, populist discourse against the other parties and elites, thereby trading upon the crisis of representation and public disaffection against corrupt politicians within French society.

The above electoral developments refuelled a debate on the right about the virtues of 'republican discipline', that is, 'should the right join forces with the left in presenting a united front against the FN, even if it meant losing seats to the left?'. Responses to the question varied, depending upon local factors and personalities, and, therefore, a degree of incoherence characterised the right's practice of dealing with the FN. Since the FN's historic local election breakthrough at Dreux in 1983, the right had practised varying degrees of collusion with the extreme right at sub-national level (see below). Certainly, ambiguity was a feature of the right's response to the FN.

In the 1990s, however, the right-wing leadership hardened its approach to the FN. Thus, the 1993–97 right-wing government pursued a strategy of appeasing (likely or actual) extreme right voters – via tough legislation on nationality and immigration (the Pasqua-Debré laws) – while at the same time ostracising the FN. In response, Le Pen adopted (in July 1995) a 'neither left, nor right' position. In practice, this involved punishing right-wing candidates in by-elections, by refusing support on the second ballot – thus assisting a left-wing victory here.

Overall, the FN was continuing to prove troublesome against a right, whose leaders (Chirac, Juppé, Léotard and Séguin, conspicuously) preached non-co-operation with the extreme right party. This state of affairs was all too evident in the 1997 legislative elections, when the FN reached record scores (almost 15 per cent, against a parliamentary election best of 12.7 per cent in 1993) and was able to maintain its presence in 132 second ballot contests. These included 76 'triangulars' (involving left, right and FN candidates) and, with almost two-thirds of these constituencies won by the left, the FN voters certainly made a contribution to the right's defeat.

While, as Ysmal illustrates, the actual impact of the FN (or rather the party's voters) on the final outcome of the 1997 election (albeit a narrow left-wing victory) should not be exaggerated,[36] it was clear that Le Pen's 'nuisance value' to the right was enhanced by the results. On the first ballot, the FN made striking gains among artisans, shopkeepers, traders and *industriels* (up 11 points since 1993), and benefited here from a reaction against the policies of Balladur (1993–95) and Chirac-Juppé (1995–97).

Appreciable progress among blue-collar workers (up 6 points since 1993) also indicated disillusion with the right's lack of success in healing France's 'social fracture'.[37] The two-ballot majority voting system and the political isolation of the FN meant that the party only won one seat (in Toulon – and this was lost in a rerun election for the constituency).

The March 1998 regional elections reproduced the broad result of the 1997 parliamentary elections: gains for the left and losses for the right, but it was the creditable performance of the FN that also stole the headlines. Moreover, because of the proportional voting system in place for these elections, the FN won tangible rewards for achieving yet another record score (15.2 per cent and 275 seats, compared to 13.7 per cent and 137 seats in 1992). Significantly, too, the process and arithmetic of post-election jockeying for regional presidencies serves to give the FN some leverage over its right-wing rivals, and therefore tests the right's official policy of non-co-operation with the extreme right. Following the first regional elections in 1986, and amidst criticisms and recriminations, a handful of right-wing regional presidents had owed their election to FN assistance – and the same pattern was in evidence in 1992.

The rewards to the FN generally came in the form of a share of the spoils and offices. Thus the exercise tends to compromise the right and legitimise the FN. In 1998, the success of the FN led to divisions, expulsions and regional presidency/executive losses on the right, as right-wing national leaderships imposed, to the letter, their declared policy of non-co-operation with the FN. Consequently, in Languedoc-Roussillon (Jacques Blanc), Rhône-Alpes (Charles Millon) and Picardie (Charles Baur), three regional presidents were expelled by Léotard from the UDF for accepting support from the FN.

Elsewhere, several right-wing potential presidents or presidents-elect handed the regional executive office to the left, either to avoid the same fate or to resist collusion.[38] Jean-Pierre Soisson (president of Bourgogne) uprooted his Mouvement des Réformateurs from the UDF, after accepting FN support.

In this context, then, the FN continued to act as the scourge of the right, forcing the latter to make difficult choices or compromises and fomenting division therein. In fact, the result was to create even further right-wing fragmentation as dissidents then proceeded to set up new political structures, notably Millon's launching of the (interestingly-named) La Droite.[39] When, in 1999, Millon was ousted from the regional presidency by a UDF rival adopting a 'republican front' strategy, the episode was again noteworthy for laying bare the divisions on the right.

Tensions on the right were also apparent as Madelin was unwilling to take a hard line towards dissidents. The DL leader was against demonising the FN totally, believing that on some policy aspects (such as security) a dialogue was possible.[40] Jean-Pierre Delalande, chair of an RPR working party on the FN, also argued that demonisation had tended to reinforce the cohesion of the FN, and strengthen bonds with its voters.[41] Balladur, too, even proposed a national commission on the key FN policy issue of 'national preference' (that is, a strictly applied policy of 'France for the French' – not immigrants – in employment matters, state benefits and other spheres). Critics viewed this proposal as counter-productive and likely to legitimise the FN's discourse.[42] In contrast, and as already indicated, the Séguin-Chirac-Léotard approach was rather to vilify the FN, but not to reject its voters. At times, this involved clothes-stealing on key (FN) issues, such as immigration. However, in his 1995 election campaign, Chirac was credited by some observers with not pandering to first ballot FN voters, a strategy that in any case would have alienated the centre ground.[43]

Paradoxically, in view of the FN's disruptive impact on the right, the question of right-wing alliance strategy proved to be the factor that severely split Le Pen's party in 1998–99. The FN's number two, Mégret, was receptive to the idea of striking some kind of electoral arrangement with the mainstream right, to minimise each other's losses against the left. (The 1997 legislative election had seen the collective right unable to turn numerical advantage into seats and victory.) The recent example of the Berlusconi-Fini alliance in Italy was influential upon Mégret, not least since it had helped to legitimise the extreme right National Alliance and even realised seats for it in the government. Moreover, after the 1997 electoral reversal of the French right, a few right-wing voices were openly canvassing the possibility of reaching a limited accommodation with the FN.

Le Pen, though, was hostile to such manoeuvres and anxious to retain his party and personal status as a national populist, opposition force, which benefited from attacking the rival parties, including the RPR-UDF bloc. Mégret and his supporters were increasingly of the opinion that Le Pen's public image was preventing the party from breaking out of the 15 per cent electoral 'ghetto'. Behind the question of strategy was also a bitter internal struggle, which had been building up for several years, to control the party.

Matters came to a head over the FN's European election plans, with Le Pen (initially banned from standing for striking a rival candidate in the 1997 election campaign) favouring his wife, instead of Mégret, to head the party's Euro-list. Friction between Le Pen and *mégretistes* at internal party meetings and the prospect of fielding de Gaulle's grandson (Charles de Gaulle) ahead of Mégret on the Euro-list further strained relations.

The FN split was consummated at special conferences in early 1999, with each side going its own way, indulging in a vicious war of words and vying for control of party resources, members, elected representatives and name.[44] Ironically, the site of the FN's initial breakthrough – European elections (in 1984) – became the arena in which the division was all too apparent, as the two sides prepared to field separate Euro-lists in June 1999. There was a danger too that neither might pass the 5 per cent quota hurdle and the French extreme right could thus lose its presence in the European parliament.

Both the FN and the mainstream right/centre right were threatened by the formation of a Pasqua-de Villiers Euro-list, whose construction again testified to the divided state of the French right. The two maverick politicians hailed originally from the mainstream right – Pasqua, the RPR and de Villiers, the UDF – and had enjoyed ministerial office in recent decades. However, their potentially attractive policy mix of national populism (Pasqua) and Euroscepticism, combined with a discourse that overlapped with the FN's, meant that votes could be won from an internally divided extreme and mainstream right. In 1994, de Villiers' 12.3 per cent had been (with Bernard Tapie's Energie radical success) the shock story of the previous Euro-election.[45]

In electoral free-fall subsequent to that poll, de Villiers – with Pasqua's close association – stood a chance of reviving his political fortunes in the 'second order election' and political opportunity structure afforded by the June 1999 contest. The broad Euro-consensus of the leading right-wing parties left a space to be exploited by the Eurosceptic list – which provocatively and tellingly adopted the historic Gaullist label of the Rassemblement pour la France (RPF).[46]

CONCLUSION

The divisions on the right in recent years have been illustrated by the fact that two main (or mainstream) parties have been jockeying for power, a situation compounded by factionalism within and breakaways from these organisations. The rise of the FN and its divisive and diluting impact upon the right has further fragmented the broad right-wing 'family', although the FN is now at a critical point in its own history. Divisions on the contemporary right predate, of course, the 1995–99 years (the period of focus). However, in contrast to the initial Gaullist dominance of the Fifth Republic – which benefited from left-wing divisions and fears of a strong PCF – the past 20 or so years of the regime have witnessed an increasingly hegemonic left-wing party, the PS. The one-party predominance on the left in effect has served to highlight, perhaps even exaggerate, the divided nature of the pre-millennium right.

Additionally, Jospin's retention of power through a pluralist left-wing coalition (see Szarka, in this volume) – albeit not without problems and also fielding separate Euro-lists – contrasted somewhat with the inability of the right to keep its house together. Pipe-dreams of creating a single powerful right-wing party are precisely that. Paradoxically too (in view of the right's idealisation of the Gaullist presidency), Chirac's capture of France's highest political office served to divide the right in the mid- and late-1990s, whereas Mitterrand used the power base provided by presidential victory (i.e., popular approval plus resort to dissolution of the National Assembly by way of Article 12 of the Constitution) to boost the electoral fortunes of the PS in 1981 and 1988. The fact that Chirac inherited a right-wing parliamentary majority in 1995 was also significant: it was never his majority in the sense that Mitterrand had personally created left-wing majorities on the backs of his 1981 and 1988 presidential election victories. Chirac's 1995–97 majority was therefore fractious, and the nature of the legislative election defeat then left the president greatly weakened and his political judgement and leadership qualities in question.

The 1999 Séguin resignation exposed the division on the right and should be seen as the latest salvo in a leadership struggle focused around Séguin–Chirac rivalry, the legacy of Gaullist values, attitudes to deepening European integration and presentation and priorities of socio-economic policy. Constrained by the office of RPR president, Séguin probably felt that his French *présidentiable* future would prosper better in another role. Association with a poor Euro-election would have been unhelpful too, as it was to Michel Rocard's (PS) ambitions in 1994. Immediate public opinion reaction to the resignation tended to see Séguin's decision as justified and a 'bad thing' for the French president.[47]

Nevertheless, as the Balladur–Chirac duel of 1995 showed, access to a good party apparatus is a useful basis for winning the French presidency. Strategically, Chirac has impeccable connections with the RPR, good working relations with DL leader Madelin and, as Séguin's resignation demonstrated, a *rapport* with UDF leader Bayrou. Overall, these factors – and a FN in crisis – are bonuses for Chirac and potentially strengthen his (expected) bid to construct a winning coalition for the 2002 presidential election. However, the reconstruction of the PS under Jospin, a working plurality on the left and the extended honeymoon period of the PS-led government are indications of where the main threat to Chirac and the right will come from.

NOTES

1. See Joseph Szarka, 'The Winning of the 1995 French Presidential Election in France', *West European Politics* 19/1 (Jan. 1996) pp.151–67.
2. See Byron Criddle, 'The French Referendum on the Maastricht Treaty', *Parliamentary Affairs* 46/2 (1993) pp.228–38.
3. Howard Machin, 'The 1995 Presidential Election Campaign', in Robert Elgie (ed.) *Electing the French President, The 1995 Presidential Election* (London: Macmillan 1996) p.41.
4. David Hanley, 'Change and Continuity in the Mitterrand Years', in Elgie (note 3) p.14.
5. Alain Guyomarch, 'Voting Behaviour', in Elgie (note 3) p.156.
6. Alistair Cole, *French Politics and Society* (Hemel Hempstead: Prentice-Hall 1998) p.98.
7. Cole (note 6) p.39.
8. Nick Parsons, 'Economic despondency and social division: a political review of the year, 1996', *Modern and Contemporary France* 5/2 (1997) p.245.
9. Parsons (note 8) p.248.
10. The opinion polls in this paragraph are drawn from Jérôme Jaffré, 'De 1995 à 1997: l'opinion publique, l'impopularité et le vote', in Pascal Perrineau and Colette Ysmal (eds.) *Le vote surprise: les élections législatives des 25 mai et 1er juin 1997* (Paris: Presses de Sciences Po 1998) pp.27–52.
11. Jaffré (note 10) p.32.
12. Ibid. p.36.
13. *Figaro-Magazine*, 9 March 1995.
14. Jaffré (note 10) p.31.
15. For a useful discussion on the role of the president see Vincent Wright, *The Government and Politics of France* (London: Unwin Hyman 1989).
16. See Paul Hainsworth, 'The Return of the Left: The 1997 French Parliamentary Election', *Parliamentary Affairs* 51/1 (Jan. 1998) pp.71–83.
17. See Perrineau and Ysmal (note 10).
18. See *Le Monde*, 18–19 April 1999.
19. Hainsworth (note 16) pp.79–83. See also, for a fuller study of 'cohabitation', Jean Massot, *Alternance et cohabitation sous la Ve République*, (Paris: La documentation française 1997).
20. See *Le Monde*, 23 and 27 March 1999, and esp. 17 and 18–19 April 1999.
21. For example, see the opinion polls in *L'Express* (19 Feb. 1998) and *Le Point* (7 March 1998).
22. Alistair Cole, 'The Return of the Orleanist Right: The Union for French Democracy', in Cole (ed.) *French Political Parties in Transition* (Aldershot: Dartmouth 1990) p.106.
23. See, for instance, the interview with François Léotard in *Figaro-Magazine* (9 March 1996).
24. See Cole (note 22) pp.106–39; David Hanley, 'Compromise, Party Management and Fair Shares: The Case of the French UDF', *Party Politics* 5/2 (1999) pp.171–89.

25. Hanley (note 24) p.173 (the article was accepted for publication in 1997).
26. Ibid.
27. Peter Fysh, 'Candidates and Parties of the Right', in Elgie (note 3) p.76.
28. Andrew Knapp, 'Un parti comme les autres: Jacques Chirac and the Rally for the Republic', in Cole (note 22) p.143.
29. Cole (note 6) p.159.
30. Paul Webster, *The Guardian*, 23 March 1996.
31. James Shields, 'Le Pen and the Progression of the Far-Right Vote in France', *French Politics and Society* 13/2 (1995) p.37.
32. Cole (note 6) p.141.
33. For a comprehensive discussion of the political location of de Villiers, see P. Mitchell, 'Philippe de Villiers: Politics, Parties, Ideology' (U. of Ulster at Jordanstown, unpub. PhD thesis, 1998).
34. See Pascal Perrineau, *Le symptôme Le Pen: Radiographie des électeurs du Front National* (Paris: Fayard 1997).
35. See, for useful analyses of FN local government success, R. Martin, *Main basse sur Orange* (Paris: Calmann-Lévy 1998); V. Martin, *Toulon la noire* (Toulon: Denoel 1996).
36. Colette Ysmal, 'Le second tour: le prix de l'isolement de la droite modérée', in Perrineau and Ysmal (note 10) pp.297–301.
37. Philippe Bréchon and Bruno Cautrès, 'La cuisante défaite de la droite modérée', in Perrineau and Ysmal (note 10) pp.238–9.
38. For a review of the regional elections, see W.M. Downs, 'The Front National as Kingmaker Again: France's Regional Elections of March 1998', *Regional and Federal Studies* 8/3 (1998) pp.125–33.
39. Millon's own account of relations with the FN is given in Charles Millon, *La paix civile* (Paris: Odile Jacob 1998).
40. *L'Humanité*, 12 May 1998.
41. *Libération*, 21 March 1997. For the FN's view on Delalande – the 'Monsieur anti-FN' of the RPR – see *National Hebdo*, 14 Nov. 1996.
42. See J.-P. Moinet, 'La notabilisation du FN: engrenage et dangers', *Revue Politique et Parlementaire* 955 (1998) pp.23–6.
43. Elgie contrasts Chirac's 1988 and 1995 French presidential campaigns – 'He eschewed any compromise with the FN and consolidated his position with the centrists. Consequently, he was able to reconcile the conflicting needs to be both populist and centrist and succeeded where before he had failed'. Robert Elgie, 'The Institutional Logics of Presidential Elections', in Elgie (note 3), p.70.
44. *Libération*, 23–24 Jan. 1999; *Le Monde*, 30 March 1999.
45. Patrice Buffotot and David Hanley, 'Les élections européennes de juin 1994: élection européenne ou élection nationale?', *Modern and Contemporary France* 1/3 (1995) pp.1–18.
46. The full title of the list is Le Rassemblement pour la France et pour l'Indépendance d'Europe.
47. See the CSA poll in *Le Parisien*, 19 April 1999; and also *Le Monde*, 20 April 1999.

The New Social Movement Phenomenon: Placing France in Comparative Perspective

ANDREW APPLETON

As with many facets of the French polity, the phenomenon of new social movements (NSMs) has previously been described in terms of exceptionalism. NSMs in France, it was argued, have never been as vigorous, as embedded in society, or as weighty in impact as other post-industrial polities. For exceptional reasons, the classic triad of the NSM universe did not appear in France with the same presence as in neighbouring countries. The anti-nuclear movement, the ecology movement, and the women's movement were all subject to the cultural, historical, and institutional particularities of the French system and as such were somehow qualitatively and quantitatively different from similar movements outside France.

In this essay, it will be argued that, contrary to this view of NSMs in France as exceptional, current trends show that on many dimensions France is not so atypical in terms of the organisation and activities of these NSMs. Rather than conceptualising the NSM universe in contemporary France as unique, an attempt is made to place it in a comparative and theoretical context and in doing so, demonstrates that (a) the general concepts and theoretical approaches that have been developed in the field of NSM research are readily applicable to the French case, and (b), perhaps more importantly, the French case is a good one with which empirically to test many of the rival propositions that have emerged in the NSM literature.

The essay will begin by reviewing the main lines in the important debates in the comparative NSM literature that purport to be portable across cases. Next, it will examine the literature on NSMs in France, highlighting the distinction between first and second wave movements. From this base, it will move to an empirical examination of NSMs in contemporary France, developing some explanations for the renewed activity of such movements since the mid-1980s. Finally, it shows that these explanations, indeed the general contours of the NSM phenomenon in France, fit well with the more general and comparative theories of NSMs that have been developed most often to the exclusion of the French case.

APPROACHES TO THE STUDY OF NEW SOCIAL MOVEMENTS (NSMs)

The first analytical task facing the researcher is to distinguish between social movements as a conceptual category and the particular class of those movements that have been afforded the appellation 'new'. In their comparative study of new social movements in Western Europe, drawing upon a large body of literature, Kriesi *et al.* note that there are important qualitative distinctions between traditional and new social movements.[1] For them, the new social movement phenomenon is linked to the weakening of traditional structures in a slow transformation of society. In this perspective, the erosion of traditional class distinction has produced new forms of class differentiation that have in turn given rise to new demands for collective action. To a great degree, they note, these demands are based upon post-material and libertarian values.

Such a perspective is concordant with the observations of other theoretical and empirical treatments of new social movements. Dalton and Keuchler observe that new social movements are not only distinguishable from traditional social movements and/or interest groups on the basis of social cleavages and value structures, but that they have adopted new forms of mobilisation and new modes of organisation. New social movements, therefore, can be adjudged a separate class of participatory institution not only by the forces that have acted as catalysts for their inception, but by the forms that the collective action expressed within this class of movement have taken.[2] Together, these parameters help differentiate NSMs from other forms of participatory institutions and more empirically to locate them in a particular time and space. The post-material and libertarian value structures have arisen in post-industrial societies in the aftermath of the post-war growth period,[3] and the NSM phenomenon occurred coterminous with the emergence of these new value sets.

In France, such a distinction is important for, as Charles Tilly has brilliantly noted, the French have had a long history of popular struggle against authority structures.[4] Eric Hobsbawm noted that large-scale transformations of society such as the onset of modern capitalism backed by state power have thrown up protest movements, often at the periphery, to resist and challenge the authority of central institutions.[5] Yet the link between values and styles enables us to focus upon the movements that emerged in the 1960s in France and which were loosely intertwined with the *autogestionnaire* left. The struggle for the recognition of women's rights, the student movements of 1968, the fledgling ecology movement of the early 1970s all represent qualitatively different forms of collective action than previous social movements or protest actions described by Tilly.

Moving from the definitional to the analytical, it is important to examine competing theoretical explanations for the emergence of NSMs at this particular juncture in the development post-industrial society. To pinpoint the social bases of NSM action, and to observe the different organisational forms that such movements have encompassed does not provide a satisfactory or sufficient explanation of why NSMs are as they are. For example, if we apply the non-decisional analogy to NSMs, we might come to the conclusion that there are an infinitely large number of theoretically possible social movements; thus why do some take actual form and others not?[6] Or, placing new social movements into a cross-national perspective, we might ask; why do certain movements appear in some countries and not others? For example, why was there so little organised opposition in France to nuclear energy when it was a major point of mobilisation in Germany and Sweden in the 1970s?

The social movement literature generally advances three explanations for the genesis of such movements. The first of these stresses the institutional incentives and/or constraints upon social movement action. This approach in widely known as the political opportunity structure perspective, and as the term implies focuses upon political institutions and institutional structures in the search to determine roots of social movement behaviour. The second theoretical strain emphasises the rational incentives for collective action that can be marshalled by nascent organisations. Termed the resource mobilisation approach, such theorists borrow from the organisational literature that highlights the core process in the formation and maintenance of organisations as being the ability to successful mobilise key resources from the social environment. The third of these general explanations relies much more upon social psychological theories to explain the proclivity of new social movement activists to engage in collective forms of behaviour.

Although these three explanations for the origins and formation of social movements coexist, they are not necessarily mutually exclusive. McAdam *et al.*, for example, have argued that a synthesis of these perspectives is both theoretically possible and desirable.[7] By borrowing from organisational theory and social psychology, they continue, the predominant paradigm found in the political science literature, that of the political opportunity structure, can be modified to overcome serious weaknesses and shortcomings. Closely linked to the new institutionalism, the notion of the political opportunity structure as the predominant force in shaping actors strategic preferences was attractive to disciplinary advocates whose work focused in large part upon institutions and structures of power.

The concept of the political opportunity structure is not particularly new; for example, Joseph Schlesinger utilises the notion of the structure of political opportunities in his classic 1966 work on political parties.[8] However, the use of the term in the cross-national study of new social movements was popularised, as noted by Chris Rootes, by Herbert Kitschelt in his study of anti-nuclear movements in four countries, including France.[9] Kitschelt suggested that the environment for social movement action is formed predominantly by the 'openness' or 'closedness' of states to inputs from civil society and the 'strength' or 'weakness' of the potential for state outputs. France, one of his cases, was characterised as having a state that is closed to easy access from civil society but that has a strong capacity to deliver and implement policy once it is made.

Beyond criticisms of some of the simplistic and *post hoc* characterisations of the nature of the state in empirical work such as Kitschelt, critics of the political opportunity structure approach have focused on the lack of conceptual clarity of the opportunity structure itself. It should be noted that the very notion of the political opportunity structure has been approached in two rather different ways. On the one hand, political scientists such as Tarrow and Tilly have focused more upon longitudinal changes within the configuration of power as being at the core of their conception of the opportunity structure.[10] On the other, the work of those such as Kitschelt and Kriesi *et al.* is more cross-national in scope and relies more upon the static comparison of institutional structures. McAdam, a proponent of the approach, outlines no less than four different schemes for measuring the political opportunity structure that he finds in the general literature.[11] None the less, he argues that the concept is still theoretically useful and empirically relevant, despite the need to refine some of the inconsistencies in the way the term has been utilised.

Despite the scepticism of those such as Rootes who see the concept of political opportunity structure as leading to either tautological reasoning or the voiding of meaningful content, the approach has been applied specifically to the French case to investigate the phenomenon of new social movements in the contemporary era. For example, in his recent work on mass protest in France, Fillieule argues that a modification of the static conception of the political opportunity structure derived from cross-national work can be accomplished to benefit the study of social movements in Fifth

Republic France.[12] Closer to the cross-national approach is Duyvendak's analysis of new social movements in contemporary France using a four-dimensional configuration of the political opportunity structure that includes national cleavage structures, formal institutional structures, prevailing strategies, and alliance structures.[13]

On the reverse side of the coin, two recent studies of new social movements and social movements impacts in France have challenged the application and utility of political opportunity structure as a conceptual framework. In her essay in a previous issue of this same journal, Waters suggests that the externally developed notion of political opportunity structure is much less persuasive as a lens through which to view French social movements than the indigenous work of Alain Touraine and others.[14] She suggests that the recent resurgence in new social movement activity in France, which will be discussed below, has resulted from the increasing bifurcation of French society between those who benefit from post-industrialism and those who do not. The result of new social movement activity is a new form of citizenship, she argues, in which the excluded are drawn into the political process in meaningful and determinant ways.

In a different vein, Stetson and Mazur argue that the political opportunity structure approach falls short in predicting the impact of new social movements upon the policy process in the area of equal employment policies and job-training. They contend that the political opportunity structure approach would predict that women's movements should have a greater impact on such policy in the United States than in France; yet in a preliminary study they find that the reverse appears to be true.[15]

Despite these criticisms of the more general approach and the specific application of political opportunity structure theories to the case of France, it would be a mistake to jettison the paradigm entirely. Both Rootes and Filleule agree that the approach can be modified to incorporate a less deterministic and tautological line or argument, although coming to different conclusions. In the analysis of new social movements in France that follows in this essay, it will be argued that, contrary to the theoretical objections of Rootes and the empirical assertions of Waters, new social movements can be understood within the framework of the political opportunity model, albeit in modified form.

NEW SOCIAL MOVEMENTS IN FRANCE: THE TWO WAVES

Most of the relatively scant literature on new social movements in France distinguishes two different periods, or waves, of NSM activity. The first wave is associated with the events and generation of May 1968, and has come to be lodged in the public consciousness as exemplifying the French capacity for spontaneous mobilisation and popular protest. In the immediate aftermath of the student rebellion of that year, new social movement activity flourished in several domains; women's rights, ecology, regionalism, and anti-nuclear protest. The demands espoused by these movements resided predominantly at the macro-societal level and explicitly addressed the 'quality of life' concerns that Inglehart and others have identified as being at the heart of the post-material revolution.[16]

However, unlike neighbouring European countries such as West Germany, the Netherlands, and Switzerland, where NSMs continued to flourish and grow through the 1970s,[17] the same period witnessed a decline in new social movement activity in France. For reasons that will be discussed below, these classic forms of collective mobilisation faded from the scene by the early 1980s (although it must be noted that they were of variable strengths to begin with and faded with greater or lesser intensity).

However the latter half of the 1980s was to witness a resurgence of new social movements that has in many ways gathered momentum during the 1990s and today is at the forefront of the contemporary French political scene. Yet this second wave of NSMs[18] has emerged around somewhat different issues than the first; anti-racism, AIDS and gay rights, and above all 'social solidarity' dominate the agenda. Rather than macro-societal concerns, these movements appear to be predominantly focused on subcultural goals. They have tended to be less prescriptive in orientation than their first-wave counterparts and more defensively oriented. Equally so, according to Waters, they have been much more pervasive in terms of organisation at the local level and less concentrated on building national movements.

Placing France in a cross-national perspective, much of the evidence about the development of the NSM phenomenon stresses the comparative weakness of them when viewed alongside other selected post-industrial societies. If we gauge NSM strength from the character of protest activity, Kriesi *et al.* find that France has a much lower rate of NSM protest activity than three other West European countries over a 15-year period beginning in the 1970s. From newspaper accounts they categorise unconventional protest events in France, West Germany, the Netherlands, and Switzerland from 1975 to 1989; only 36.1 per cent of all such events were associated with NSMs in France as compared to 73.2 per cent in West Germany, 65.4 per cent in the Netherlands, and 61.0 per cent in Switzerland.[19]

Adding Great Britain and Spain to this list, Koopmans portrays France as having just moderate levels of NSM activity along with Britain; West Germany, the Netherlands, and Switzerland are shown as having high levels, while Spain lags behind with very low levels.[20] However, these figures obscure the dynamic changes in social movement organisation that seem to have taken place during this period; thus it is instructive to unpack the data and consider the two waves of French NSM activity in a discrete fashion.

The First Wave: the comprehensive data assembled by Duyvendak shows that the events of May 1968 had a catalytic impact upon the development of new social movements in France. From 1968 through to the end of the 1970s, there was a relatively consistent level of NSM activity from year to year with no great fluctuations. However, from 1980 to 1984, the data show the level of NSM activity dropping to pre-1965 levels.[21] From this information alone, coupled with the general perception that May 1968 in France was really the epitome of the new social movement phenomenon, it is tempting to conclude that NSMs during this first wave in France were rather extended in their scope and impact. Especially when added to the vigour of the *autogestionnaire* left at the end of the 1960s and the collapse of the old Section Française de l'Internationale Ouvrière, May 1968 seems a seminal event for the development of NSMs.

However, a little caution needs to be exercised in this regard. First, the same data reveal that the overall proportion of NSM to traditional social movement activity did not change in the aftermath of 1968. In other words, the large scale revolt against authority that was unleashed by the student protests at the Sorbonne in the early days of May had as much impact upon the activity levels of traditional social movements (such as trade unions) as it did upon new forms of collective action. Whereas NSM activities rose in proportion to those of traditional social movements in countries such as West Germany and the Netherlands and continued to rise through the 1970s, there was no such occurrence in France. Duyvendak attributes this to the persistence of the traditional left, bolstered by a large and relatively orthodox Communist Party. While this argument may be overstated and is possible magnified by the nature of the data, it is certainly true that the recomposition of the Socialist Party under the leadership of François Mitterrand tended to emphasise the traditional values of the socialist left and marginalise the new left in its *autogestionnaire* incarnation.

A second caveat to the interpretation of May 1968 as an event that emanated from a dynamic outburst of NSM activity is provided by Rootes' analysis of the student protest movement.[22] According to his view, the protest wave in France occurred relatively late in comparison to other countries (such as the United States) and not without stimulus from the outside. The degree to which the French student movement was inspired by external forces has been demonstrated elsewhere in accounts of the historical development of student organisations in France.[23] Although Rootes does acknowledge that the outburst of 1968 was contingent upon the prior failure of the left to achieve political power after the legislative elections of 1967, the determinant effect of international forces is hard to ignore.

Thus the characterisation of the wave of new social movement activity set off by the events of 1968 as either comparatively vigorous or unique to the French polity is rather misleading. Duyvendak suggests that the predominant effect of 1968 was to reinforce and emphasise traditional French class cleavages, rather than to forge different and enduring cleavage structures based on the new politics of post-materialism and quality of life concerns. Overall, his conclusion is that the post-1968 period, at least until 1974, represented an institutionalisation of nascent NSM activity into the resurgent left.

The hopes of victory in the 1973 legislative and the 1974 presidential elections effectively tied the aspirations of the NSMs to the communist and socialist parties; it was only in the wake of Giscard's victory in 1974 that new social movements began to assert more autonomy from the burgeoning left coalition. What did occur after 1975 was the increase in new social movement activity that took place without the co-operation of (or co-optation by!) either the communists, the socialists, or the trade unions.[24]

The differentiation of the relationship between new social movements and the organisations of the traditional left in the period of the 1970s is one that carries weight. For example, the decision of the ecology movement to seek an independent electoral avenue in the 1970s spurred on by the relative success of Jobert's candidacy in the presidential election of 1974, or the formation of a women's party, *Choisir*, to contest the 1978 legislative elections, show that these movements were pursuing strategies of independence.

Yet the limits of such an assertion must not be overstated, for both the ecology movement and a large portion of the feminist movement were to tie their fortunes to those of the Socialist Party over the same period. The problem of the analysis of new social movements becomes clear; France has a tradition of parallel movements, that do not allow us to speak accurately of 'The Ecology Movement' or 'The Women's Movement' but of Movements. Furthermore, there is a constant dynamic between movements that are created or sponsored by existing organisations, especially the political parties, and those that arise more spontaneously to resist the forms of co-optation just described.

For example, the women's movements in France pursued very different trajectories through the 1970s that had very different consequences for their relations with the parties of the left that were to come into office in 1981.[25] Furthermore, these movements were complemented by an active women's movement (the *courant* G) within the Socialist Party replete with its own internal battles over questions of action and co-optation. Even beyond that, other political parties either already had or created their own women's auxiliary organisations that further divided the field and range of action. Once the Socialist Party came to power (with their communist allies) in 1981, the majority of women who acceded to positions of power in women's policy agencies were drawn from the ranks of the party (women such as Louise Brocas and Yvette Roudy).[26]

The thesis of co-optation and then distance in the 1970s, thus, has its limits. Again, it is incontestable that some notable forms of social protest were encapsulated in new social movement activity in the late 1970s as the left appeared to become more comfortable with the prospect of wielding power from the heights of the state within the Gaullist institutional framework. The resistance to the creation of a military training ground at Larzac is one of the best known of these autonomous movements and received much attention from Touraine and others as a possible example of a new kind of counter-cultural movement that could spawn new forms of state–society relations. Yet detailed analyses of that movement show that it is ambiguous as to whether the Larzac phenomenon really represented a new social movement in the strict sense or whether it is more easily understood as a curious and fragile alliance of traditional rural interests with regionalist and ecological movements that may have sometimes complementary but sometimes competing claims.[27]

The second wave of the new social movement phenomenon was to occur in France in the mid-1980s, and the echo continues to be felt. Most accounts of the upsurge of social movements in France during this period emphasise the difference between the issues addressed by the first wave of new social movements and their more recent counterparts. Kriesi *et al.* suggest that NSMs may have essentially one of three primary goals, which in part define key differences between them; instrumental, counter-cultural, and subcultural. The first of these NSM goals pertains to the strategic outcomes pursued by such movements, whereas counter-cultural and subcultural goals deal more with the identity of either external society (counter-cultural) or within-group identity (subcultural).[28] This categorisation may be applied to the French case to illustrate the contrast between first and second wave NSMs that emanates from the literature; first wave movements tended to be (although not exclusively) oriented towards instrumental goals while second wave movements have been either counter-cultural or subcultural in nature.

The onset of a new wave of NSM activity was heralded by the emergence of the anti-racist movement in direct reaction to the rise of the Front National to prominence at the national level. Neither the FN nor the racist movement were created in the 1980s,[29] yet the electoral breakthrough of the party in Dreux thrust the immigration debate into the national limelight as never before. The most well-known counter-reaction to the anti-immigrant themes espoused by the FN was SOS-Racisme which succeeded in gathering 500,000 people to Paris in 1985;[30] Duyvendak traces the birth of the national anti-racist movement to the march organised by local immigrant groups in Les Minguettes (Lyon) in 1983 with about 100,000 participants.[31] However, two things clearly happened at this juncture; first, the anti-racist movement began to take on a much more national character and, second, as it did so, SOS-Racisme began to supplant the myriad of other groups until it became the core of the consolidated opposition to the anti-immigrant sentiments expressed by the FN and its sympathisers.

The prominence of SOS-Racisme and some of its leaders, such as Harlem Désir and Julian Dray, serves as a fascinating case of the new social movement phenomenon in France. One of the surprising aspects of the anti-racist movement at the beginning was just how fast local groups mobilised to counter the explosive growth of the FN. At the beginning of the 1980s, one estimate put the number of local immigrant organisations groups at about 4,200;[32] while not all of these groups were primarily formed to combat racism, they formed the backbone of the network of oppositional groups that took on the agenda of the FN in local clashes all over France. Yet just as fast as these groups succeeded in coalescing into an identifiable and distinct national *rassemblement*, so too were they supplanted by the organisational might of SOS-Racisme. Harlem Désir's group (and he himself) began to monopolise media attention and, perhaps more importantly, were recognised by the leadership of the PS – then in power – as the privileged interlocutors for the concerns of young immigrants.

Covertly funded and helped by the Elysée,[33] much to the subsequent detriment of the PS, SOS-Racisme swept other groups such as the MRAP from the political map. While the anti-racist movement did witness the emergence of yet new groups, such as Ras l'Front and SCALP, it is SOS-Racisme that led the national debate in the late 1980s. Such a status conferred on its leaders an instant access to the French political elite and served as the springboard to national office for those such as Julian Dray.

What clearly separated SOS-Racisme from other groups, and explains the palatability of it to Mitterrand and his close advisers, is that it preached the discourse of equality rather than difference, a message that coexisted fairly well with the jacobinism entrenched within the more traditionalist ranks of the PS. The same discourse permitted SOS-Racisme to form alliances with other, non-immigrant groups and protest movements such as the student demonstrations against the loi Devaquet in 1986. None the less, the integrative quality of its message began to shift in the late 1980s under the combined pressure of local discontent and the continued strength of the FN, which strained and finally broke the tight relationship with the PS.

Out of the anti-racist movement emerged a more general concern with the rights of immigrants in general, particularly those without official permission to reside in France (*les sans papiers*). One of the first attempts to deal systematically with the question of illegal immigrants and asylum seekers was the formation of the Réseau Intercommunautaire d'Aide aux Demandeurs d'Asile in 1985, which quickly became the Réseau d'Information et de Solidarité. A co-operative effort on the part of four existing groups with concerns encompassing immigration (FASTI, GISTI, CIMADE, and MRAP), the Réseau concentrated its efforts on obtaining a blanket amnesty for illegal immigrants and a regularisation of their status.[34] As the question of immigration, legal and illegal, fused with that of anti-racism, a broad coalition emerged between both existing groups and newer ones that had sprung to life in the second wave period.

The solidarity movement, as it came to be known, is, thus, a combination of different groups and ideas loosely co-ordinated around the notions of social solidarity and social insertion. Older human rights groups (such as the LDH or Terres des Hommes) and established anti-racist groups (the CIMADE, MRAP) joined forces with newer internationalist organisations, such as Médecins sans Frontières or Amnesty International, with the burgeoning anti-racist movement, and with *ad hoc* groups advocating on behalf of asylum seekers and the *sans papiers* to form a broad front that by the early 1990s was highly visible in daily French life.

The issue of social insertion was wrestled from the hands of the French policy and academic elite and became a rallying point for the concerns of those at the margins of French society. The increasing salience of the twin processes of globalisation and European integration, which both call into question many of the foundations of French republicanism, only served to intensify the debates in these issue areas.

The solidarity movement also came to overlap with an attempted mobilisation around the concerns of the unemployed. In the early 1980s, at least three national organisations were created to advocate on behalf of those without work; the Syndicat des Chômeurs, the Mouvement National des Chômeurs, and the Fédération Nationale des Chômeurs. Fillieule notes that the presence of these movements caused much initial consternation in the traditional trade unions, which regarded the organisation of the unemployed into an autonomous movement as potentially dividing and weakening the working classes.[35]

The movements faltered through the 1980s, primarily as a result of their inability to gain members and to disentangle their collective action from that of the unions. Yet the question of whether the failure was also strategic – that is, whether they had any impact upon the public consciousness of unemployment – is altogether rather different. At the beginning of the 1990s and then most recently in the strike wave of 1995, the overlaps between the solidarity movement and the unemployed were clearly evident, reflecting the degree to which the notion of the bifurcated, or two-speed society, has penetrated the arena of political and social mobilisation.

A third area of mobilisation that has appeared in the second wave era is that of advocacy of issues relating to AIDS; this has come to join with the growth in the political visibility of the gay movement in the 1980s and 1990s. The appearance of the HIV-virus at the beginning of the 1980s in France had an early impact upon the public psyche through the transmission of the virus as a result of blood transfusions. The affair of the contaminated blood, which echoes still today, is now well-known and need not be chronicled here, but the number of contaminations by non-homosexual contact meant that the issue was fairly early-on defined as one of public health and not simply relegated to a subgroup status.

Groups such as Aides, created in 1984, and Arcat-Sida, organised one year later, pushed to maintain public and political focus on dealing with the AIDS crisis. However, the government was less willing to recognise these movement as interlocutors, and this has only taken place in the 1990s. Duyvendak ascribes the lack of interest from government to the absence of a unified gay movement organised around instrumental goals, but this statement must be read more as hypothesis than empirically demonstrated.[36]

The slow response of the public authorities to both the epidemic itself and the groups that had crystallised around the issue led to a radicalisation of the AIDS advocacy movement and the rejuvenation of gay activism. The earlier groups had sought to pursue the attention of the state through non-confrontational means, but this strategy was supplanted by the tactics of newer groups such as Act Up. Confrontation with the state became the norm rather than the exception during the early 1990s, which produced a crisis of self-examination within the gay movement as a whole. Moderates feared that such tactics would lose support for AIDS advocacy and homosexual rights among the French population, in a country not noted for its sympathies towards its homosexual population.[37]

The gay movement itself has had a long history in modern France, although the conditions under which being homosexual was socially and politically 'acceptable' depended upon one's position in the social and intellectual elite. Thus, intellectuals and artists enjoyed a sort of 'immunity from repression'[38] during the 1950s and 1960s which was not particularly prevalent in the general population. However, the flowering of the NSMs in France in the wake of the revolt of 1968 had its impact upon the gay community as well, and several organisations were born at the start of the 1970s. Initially these groups were dominated by Marxist and/or Trotskyist ideas, but the decade ended with the creation of a new peak movement, the CUARH, that tied its fortunes more closely to that of the PS. Thus in 1981 it supported the candidacy of Mitterrand for the presidency.

The PS proved to be the only one of the political parties even slightly sympathetic to the concerns of the gay movement, although it favoured groups that espoused instrumental concerns over those that were more subculturally based. The party also sponsored its own organisation, Homosexualité et Socialisme which was set up in 1983 by party activists seeking to influence the party platform. Yet the links between the CUARH and the PS proved to be the downfall of the former; once the PS moved into government in 1981, it moved with a speed that astonished many in the gay community to reform many of the provisions of the civil and penal codes relating to homosexuality. This occurred without any form of institutionalisation of the relationship between party and movement in the framework of state institutions; in other words, the socialist government did not afford the same kind of institutional shelter through subsidy and other mechanisms than it did to parts of the women's movement, for example. This left the CUARH as an organisation without a purpose, and it withered away fairly quickly.

The mid-1980s witnessed the shift of the gay movement, as noted above, to more subcultural concerns and more radical action. The movement was hastened by the attempt of the Chirac government in 1986–87 to ban *Gai Pied*, a magazine that had begun more as a media forum for the advocacy of political issues and yet which had become increasingly oriented towards non-political articles dealing with sexual and cultural concerns. Although

Gai Pied was rescued from the axe of government, it was in large part due to the intervention of non-gay organisations (such as the LDH and SOS-Racisme).[39] Coupled with the AIDS crisis, the gay movement was galvanised into action at the end of the 1980s; yet this action has been hampered by the lack of a unified and co-ordinated national organisation than can speak for the gay community as a whole.

Thus, the second wave of the new social movement era in France is quite clearly different in character than the new social movements of the 1970s. The goals of the movements have tended to gravitate more towards the counter-cultural or the subcultural; where instrumental concerns have been clearly articulated, by groups such as SOS-Racisme or the CUARH, those concerns have been channelled through the political party avenue and have circumscribed the autonomy of the movements themselves. The looser, more localised, subcultural movements of the second wave have ebbed and flowed, yet there are broad areas of overlap that have inserted them in the public eye in a manner that might initially seem inconsistent with the notion of counter-cultural or subcultural groups.

With many sociologists and social commentators promoting the view that France has inculcated a two-speed society, in which globalisation, technology and mobility favour one privileged half of the population, while the other half suffers the harm of these processes, it is tempting to view the second wave of new social movement activity in France as a reflection of this phenomenon. The alliances that have seemed to be almost natural outgrowths of the movements, that have forged the broad label of the solidarity movement with all its subsidiary manifestations, appear to show that something about these movements varies so much from the first wave that perhaps an alternative theoretical framework needs to be employed to explain them.

THE NEW FRENCH SOCIAL MOVEMENTS: EXCEPTED OR EXPECTED?

At the beginning of this essay, the question was posed as to whether existing theories of social movements elaborated in the cross-national comparative laboratory of post-industrial society can adequately explain the dynamics of NSM activity in France. Put another way, do these theories lead us to except France from the predictions of these theories, or do they push us to expect the kinds of outcomes that can be observed in the French case? Much of the comparative literature that has been cited sees France as exceptional not so much in terms of the ability to apply the broad theories of new social movements, but in terms of outcomes. The level of NSM activity in France has not been as marked as in neighbouring countries (although it compares relatively evenly with the UK), and the outburst of new social movement activity in the late 1960s and early 1970s was not as sustained in France as elsewhere. Little has been written since, however, comparing the second wave of NSM activity, particularly into the 1990s, against other countries.

In this absence, a counter-view has been forwarded that suggests that this second wave of NSM activity in France is so markedly distinct from the first that it calls into question the applicability of the aforementioned theories. This view asserts that there is a uniquely French component to the phenomenon; indeed, pushed to the furthest it even questions whether contemporary social movements in France are really new social movements at all in the way that they have been defined in the literature.[40] Rather than applying the lens of comparative social movement theory, this approach stresses the relevance of the paradigm fashioned in France by Touraine and others.

What makes these movements so different from the previous wave is three factors; their independence from major political parties, the new forms of action (such as the mobilisation of cultural symbols to further their goals), and the short-term and *ad hoc* nature of their organisation (often locally based with no clearly defined leadership). These movements are not striving for instrumental outcomes, nor for national level access to the system; they are more expressive in character, stemming as they do from the parts of society that have been left behind by the technological revolution and the globalisation of the political economy. Suffused with a strong dose of normative and affective reasoning, these movements are seen as the harbingers of a new participatory culture among the marginalised elements in society. The broad coalitions that have formed and reformed around the solidarity movements appear to those such as Touraine suspiciously like a new basis for mass mobilisation against prevailing structures of dominance and power.

Persuasive though this approach may be at first sight, it contains some important weaknesses. The first problematic area is in the empirical data themselves. Two criticisms may be raised on strictly observational grounds. The first of these concerns the characterisation of previous NSM activity as being overtly linked to the organisation of political parties within the French political system. The new citizenship perspective asserts that the first wave of new social movements had little autonomy from political parties, whereas the second wave is almost totally separate from the reach of party influence.

The contention here is that this fundamentally mischaracterises the first wave of new social movements. It is true, as narrated above, that some parts of the feminist movement, the ecologist movement, or the anti-nuclear movement sought accommodation and entry into the party orbit. But this was not the whole story; as we have noted, these movements were plural in nature, and even where some organisational elements of the movements did develop alliances with political parties, that relationship was frequently fraught with tension. Equally so, the second wave of new social movements has seen important organisations that have done much the same; SOS-Racisme, CUARH, etc. It is more accurate to portray the organisation of new social movement activity as being caught, whether in the first or second wave, between instrumental and non-instrumental goals.

The second objection to the new citizenship view at an empirical level concerns the lack of emphasis it places upon the continuation of the 'old' new social movements from the first wave period. Despite the institutionalisation and claimed demobilisation of these movements in the years following the victory of the left in 1981, they have continued to manifest their presence in important ways. It is true that the character of the movements underwent serious evolution in the 1980s, and that there was a fairly incontestable drop-off in activity in the early part of the decade.

An examination of the women's movement is quite revealing. Rather than disappearing, or at least fading, the decentralisation of state activities and the creation of specialised policy machineries for women at both the regional and local level has opened up access to the policy-making system in interesting ways. The concerns of the women's organisations of the 1990s are rather different to those of the 1970s; broad themes of equality and emancipation have been replaced by complex policy agendas involving issues such as prostitution, domestic violence, and sexual harassment. These organisations may have a rather closer relationship with the state than previous incarnations and exist at the local level rather than staging national forms of political action, but our research suggests that they retain the essential characteristics of NSMs as previously defined.[41]

At the theoretical level, it is hard to see what predictive qualities can be gleaned from the adoption of the new citizenship approach. It is perhaps compelling in some respects as a characterisation of the contours of NSM activity in contemporary France; but it does not help predict trends on the basis of observed relationships between different elements of the political system. It is argued here that the political opportunity structure framework, while in need of some refinements in its operationalisation, stills performs in a superior manner on this level.

How does the political opportunity structure approach explain the two wave phenomenon experienced by France? Simply put, the answer resides in the logic of partisan control of the state apparatus. The unprecedented victory of the left had the effect of completely recasting relationships between state and civil society, between government and social movements. Groups which had staked their instrumental claims on that victory in many cases found quick satisfaction after the victory of the left; other non-instrumental groups found themselves equally as speedily disenchanted.

The left did pass important new social legislation in many areas; yet the style of policy-making was distinctly Gaullian for the most part. Instrumental groups faded as their concerns were addressed, only to reemerge as these policy areas were threatened by the return of a right-wing government in 1986. In this respect SOS-Racisme is an excellent example; Mitterrand used the movement as a vehicle of opposition to the right, both in the immediate run-up to and the period following the left's victory.

The biggest weakness of the political opportunity structure approach, as clearly articulated by Rootes and acknowledged by many of its proponents, is the continuing lack of precision in the operationalisation of the concept. Particularly weak is the lack of sophistication in the conception of the state itself. For example, the portrayal of the French state as 'closed' reverts to some of the more stereotypical views of it and ignores the important literature in both English and French on the real impacts of deconcentration and decentralisation. Indeed, the burgeoning new citizenship at the local level is greatly shaped by these processes. The decentralisation of the French state has opened up important new arenas of action, with significant resources and tangible opportunities.[42] Decentralisation also brings, it should be noted, variance in policy outputs and implementation at the local level, thus once again stimulating and facilitating local action.

The second weakness of the operationalisation of the political opportunity structure is that it does not adequately incorporate exogenous processes. Defensive movements – those that seek to protect established social and political rights – have to a large degree (and not just in France) been stimulated by forces outside the state. Globalisation and integration have become watchwords, yet they capture important truths about the changing capacities of states and the changing relationships between states and civil societies.[43] Transnational forces have forged a new conception of the political, and in doing so have engendered new incentives and constraints on NSM action. None the less, the underlying value structures that were at the core of the new social movement phenomenon in the early 1970s are still with us in the 1990s.[44]

Put in such perspective, France does not look quite so exceptional from other European polities. To be sure, there is a uniqueness about the French political opportunity structure that makes it tempting to conclude that it cannot be easily compared. Yet all cases in a comparison are by definition unique; the importance of the theoretical framework articulated in this essay is that it allows us to model and predict social movement outcomes in France using the same set of explanatory variables and the same set of hypothesised relationships as in other countries.

The more interesting questions for the future perhaps reside in the direction of new social movement activities in an era of integrative convergence, where the range of state action (or inaction) is severely constrained by exogenous factors.

NOTES

1. Hans Peter Kriesi, Ruud Koopmans, Jan Willem Duyvendak, and Marco Giugni, *New Social Movements in Western Europe: A Comparative Analysis* (Minneapolis: U. of Minnesota Press 1995).
2. Russell Dalton and Manfred Keuchler (eds.) *Challenging the Political Order. New Social and Political Movements in Western Democracies* (NY: OUP 1990).
3. Obviously there is a major body of literature on the existence of such value structures. See in particular Ronald Inglehart, *Culture Shift in Advanced Industrial Society* (Princeton UP 1992), and idem, *The Silent Revolution: Changing Values and Political Styles Among Western Publics* (ibid. 1977).
4. Charles Tilly, *The Contentious French: Four Centuries of Popular Struggle* (Cambridge, MA: Harvard UP 1986).
5. Eric Hobsbawm, *Primitive Rebels: Studies in Archaic Forms of Social Movement in the 19th and 20th Centuries* (NY: Praeger 1963).
6. The question is posed by Peter Eisinger in his classic article, 'The conditions of protest behavior in American cities', *American Political Science Review* 67/1 (March 1973) pp.11–28.
7. Doug McAdam, John McCarthy, and Mayer Zald, 'Opportunities, mobilizing structures, and framing processes: towards a synthetic comparative perspective on social movements', in idem (eds.) *Comparative Perspectives on Social Movements: Political Opportunities, Mobilizing Structures, and Cultural Framings* (Cambridge: CUP 1996).
8. Joseph Schlesinger, *Ambition and Politics: Political Careers in the United States* (Chicago: Rand McNally 1966).
9. See Chris Rootes, 'Political opportunity structures: promise, problems, prospects', *La Lettre de la Maison Française* 10 (1998–99) pp.75–97; Herbert Kitschelt, 'Political opportunity structures and political protest: anti-nuclear movements in four democracies', *British Journal of Political Science* 16/1 (1986) pp.57–85.
10. See, e.g., Sidney Tarrow, *Power in Movement: Social Movements and Contentious Politics* (Cambridge: CUP 1994); Tilly (note 4).
11. Doug McAdam, 'Conceptual origins, problems, future directions', in idem *et al.* (note 7).
12. Olivier Filleule, *Stratégies de la rue: les manifestations en France* (Paris: Presses de Sciences Po 1997); Olivier Fillieule, 'L'analyse des mouvements sociaux: pour une problématique unifiée', in idem (ed.) *Sociologie de la protestation: les formes de l'action collective dans la France contemporaine* (Paris: L'Harmattan 1993) pp.29–66.
13. Jan Willem Duyvendak, *The Power of Politics: New Social Movements in France* (Boulder, CO: Westview 1995).
14. Sarah Waters, 'New social movement politics in France: the rise of civic forms of mobilization', *West European Politics* 21/3 (July 1998) pp.170–86.
15. Dorothy Stetson and Amy Mazur, 'Toward a Comparative Theory of Women's Movements

and the State: State Feminism and Job-Training Policy Debates in France and the United States', unpub. MS.

16. See, for confirmation, Ruud Koopmans, 'New social movements and changes in political participation in Western Europe', *West European Politics* 19/1 (Jan. 1996) pp.28–50.

17. Kriesi *et al.* (note 1).

18. Duyvendak (note 13) sees a second wave of social movement activity from 1975 to 1980; however, his own data do not necessarily demonstrate that NSM activity levels from 1975 to 1980 should be termed a 'wave' in comparison with 1968–74. Thus I adopt the view that there have been two broad waves of NSM activity from 1968 to the late 1990s, echoing other characterisations (such as Waters, note 14).

19. Wilson has criticised the data collection technique as introducing potential bias in the study. Reviewing Duyvendak's book, he suggests that the choice of the Monday edition of *Le Monde* for the content analysis is flawed, as the Paris edition appears at a different time than the newspapers selected from other countries. See Frank Wilson, review of Duyvendak's *Power of Politics* (note 13) in *American Political Science Review* 91/2 (June 1997) pp.479–80.

20. Koopmans (note 16).

21. Duyvendak (note 13) p.115.

22. Chris Rootes, 'Student activism in France: 1968 and after', in Philip Cerny (ed.) *Social Movements and Protest in France* (London: Pinter 1982) pp.17–46.

23. A. Belden Fields, *Student Organizations in France: A Study of the Union Nationale des Étudiants de France* (NY: Basic Books 1970).

24. See Duyvendak (note 13) p.126.

25. See Claire Duchen, *Feminism in France from May 1968 to Mitterrand* (London: RKP 1986).

26. Amy Mazur, *Gender Bias and the State: Symbolic Reform at Work in Fifth Republic France* (Pittsburgh UP 1995).

27. An excellent treatment is to be found in Alexander Alland, *Crisis and Commitment: The Life History of a French Social Movement* (Yverdon, Switzerland: Gordon and Breach 1994).

28. Kriesi *et al.* (note 1).

29. See Duyvendak (note 13), and Nona Mayer and Pascal Perrineau (eds.) *Le Front National à découvert* (Paris: Presses de la FNSP 1989).

30. Waters (note 14).

31. Duyvendak (note 13) pp.158–9.

32. Cathérine Whitol de Wenden, *Les immigrés et la politique* (Paris: Presses de la FNSP 1988).

33. Anthony Daley, 'François Mitterrand, the left, and political mobilization in France', in idem (ed.) *The Mitterrand Era: Policy Alternatives and Political Mobilization in France* (London: Macmillan 1996) pp.1–32.

34. Johanna Siméant, 'Le mouvement des déboutés du droit d'asile 1990–92', in Fillieule, *Sociologie* (note 12) pp.181–210.

35. Olivier Fillieule, 'Conscience politique, persuasion, et mobilisation des engagements: l'exemple du syndicat des chômeurs', in idem, *Sociologie* (note 12) pp.123–56.

36. See Duyvendak (note 13) p.193.

37. The then Prime Minister Edith Cresson's 1991 remarks about the character of British manhood was only one flagrant manifestation in recent years of these general attitudes.

38. See Duyvendak (note 13) p.187.

39. See ibid. (note 13) p.194.

40. This view is articulated in English by Waters (note 14).

41. The author is currently engaged in the preparation of an inventory of local women's groups under the auspices of the French government. The study will include a detailed observational account of the interactions between such groups and state and party actors in three regions.

42. See Emanuel Négrier's essay in this volume.

43. This proposition is copiously described in Jerry Mander and Edward Goldsmith (eds.) *The Case Against the Global Economy and For a Turn Toward the Local* (San Francisco, CA: Sierra Club Books 1996).

44. See Inglehart (note 3).

Amendments to the French Constitution: One Surprise After Another

GUY CARCASSONNE

If the 1958 Constitution still has some way to go before it breaks the French record for longevity (though this is probably only a matter of time), it has already set one for the number of amendments made.[1] Of course, the regimes which preceded it more often than not underwent the most radical, if also the least profound, of changes as a result of their early and sometimes rapid demise. It can be deduced from this that a large number of amendments is first of all a sign of health, both of body and mind.

It is a sign of a healthy mind because it would not be thought worth altering a rotten structure. The care which the Constitution has received indicates a real commitment to it, strong enough for people to take the trouble to develop it, which they would not do unless it were expected to last.

It is also a sign of a healthy body which finds within it the strength necessary to evolve in what is on the whole a rather calm and not always insignificant way. This is not to say that in the past, particularly under the Third Republic, there were no perceptive individuals, no inspired doctrine or wise propositions. Pronouncing on institutions whose weaknesses everyone perceived and many condemned, reform might have been expected to result all the more easily given that Article 8 of the Constitutional Law of 25 February 1875 apparently placed no insurmountable obstacle in its way. However, after 1884, the Third Republic could not find enough motivation to avert or at least try to avert the final collapse. As for the one amendment made to the Constitution under the Fourth Republic, it seemed more like a case of resignation, adapting the law to the fact, instead of a reaction, which would have forced the fact to fall back in line with the law.

By comparison, therefore, the amendments made under the Fifth Republic must first and foremost be seen for what they are: a tangible sign that, by inclination, by choice or at worst, but probably less commonly, out of self-interest, the actors have accepted that from now on the Constitution belongs to everyone, that it seems destined for certain longevity which has dispelled the fantasy of a constitutional revolution.

Undoubtedly, in 1958 very few would have been prepared to bet on such an outcome. There were so many doubts hanging over this new Republic that while even the most optimistic might have hoped to see it take root, they would certainly not have ventured to guarantee it.

In fact, the Fifth Republic avoided very early on – as can be easily gauged with hindsight – a curse which might have proved fatal: as the product of an imposing will and sometimes difficult compromises fuelling the mystique of new institutions which had yet to establish themselves, it could have become an immutable text which no-one could or would dare to touch for fear of upsetting its delicate balance or reopening old wounds. Thus, sooner or later, it would have become fossilised by its very rigidity.

This only too real danger was averted very early on. Although it was marginal and ultimately had no effect, the first amendment, that of 4 June 1960, assumes in retrospect a special prominence. Adopted just 20 months after the promulgation of the Constitution, it was sufficient to demonstrate that the text could be modified and was not condemned, out of fear or reverence, never to change.

The 13 constitutional laws adopted to date have confirmed this rather relaxed approach to the Constitution. Indeed, so little is it set in stone that its volume has varied considerably. The 92 initial articles increased to 96 in June 1992, then 99 in July 1993 before reaching 100 in November 1993, falling to 85 in August 1995, rising again to 86 in February 1996 and standing today at 88 following the reinsertion of the new Articles 76 and 77.

Of the 88 articles currently in force, only 54, less than two-thirds, have rigorously retained the exact wording of the original, while 23 have been modified to a greater or lesser extent and 11 have been added.

Of course, these quantitative elements conceal major qualitative differences: the addition to Article 61 of just six words had a much greater impact than the 1995 amendment which affected 29 articles (modifying 12, adding one and abolishing 16). This is not to say that these figures are of no significance since they intrinsically rule out the fossilisation of a text which it has never become taboo to change, something which did not go without saying at the start.

Having established this, the use which the Fifth Republic has made of constitutional amendment is consistent with what it has demonstrated in other fields: its potential for paradox and surprise. Ironically, the amendments which were expected have not been made, the amendments which were made were unexpected, in their principle or in their effect; those of which great things were expected have changed nothing substantially; those whose importance was played down have proved to be fundamental; no major procedure has ever worked while one which was initially considered minor has been effective; strong majorities have failed in their intentions while amendments have been made during periods of 'cohabitation'; new opportunities have been opened up by those whose firm intention was never to use them, while others have grabbed at opportunities introduced against their will, and so on.

The exposition which follows will be devoted to all of this, in an attempt to set it in order so as to reveal that, rather strangely, timidity of content does not actually result at all from genuine problems of form.

GENUINE PROBLEMS OF FORM ...

These are familiar to everyone. Even before the final adoption of an amendment, the need for a proposal from the Prime Minister, an initiative from the President, an identical vote in each of the two assemblies, presupposes a union of wills which may be difficult to achieve. So for this convergence to come about, a reform has to be seen as essential.

In fact, it is nothing of the sort and when all is said and done the right moment proves to be much more elusive than the right procedure.

The Right Moment

Logically, one would expect the period after a national election to be the best time for amendments: having committed themselves to reforms, coalitions or candidates are eager to carry them out as soon as (and if) victory gives them the opportunity to do so. Conversely, yet still logically, if there is a period which seems *a priori* unsuited to constitutional amendment, it is that period of hostility commonly known as 'cohabitation'.

As is so often the case, what appears on the face of it to be sound common sense is found to be flawed. Politics stands logic on its head.

De Gaulle, Pompidou and Mitterrand (I and II periods in office) either gave very few constitutional commitments before their election or did not keep them afterwards. The coalitions which were successful in the legislative elections never had the ludicrous idea of putting institutional matters at the heart of their manifestos, and when they did mention them at all, it was generally with caution. For this reason, national elections have rarely been a prelude to significant changes.

However this is only a statement of fact. There are doubtless several reasons for it. Among them, and to varying degrees, could be cited a probably low level of interest on the part of the French, a strong feeling that there are more urgent priorities, a wish to save up an opportunity for a time when it could be put to better use. To this list could be added a sincere conviction of the pointlessness, even the harmfulness, of amending a text which is judged on the whole to be satisfactory.

Nevertheless, three elections have been directly followed by changes: the election of Valéry Giscard d'Estaing in 1974, of Jacques Chirac in 1995 and the changeover of ruling parties in 1997: that is, two presidential elections and one legislative election.

Yet these precedents should not be credited with greater significance than they possess. In the 1974 campaign, the future president emphasised changes which have not been made (the introduction of at least a measure of proportional representation in the legislative elections, progress towards a presidential system of government, the strengthening of parliament). Whereas those which were effected, and then only after several drastic cuts, took up just a small part of what he had to say. In 1995, every possible opportunity was taken to stress that the amendment's most tangible contribution – the introduction of the single session – was primarily a response to the demands of the President of the National Assembly, whereas the widening of the scope of the referendum, which was actually wanted and announced, without too much of a fanfare, by the future head of state, has had no effect to this day. As for the amendment adopted in 1998,[2] it had not been envisaged during the spring 1996 campaign.

So on close examination, the apparent exceptions do not invalidate the rule: until now, national election campaigns have not produced commitments which would be kept after a victory. Even when the French are called on to give their opinion, no-one has seen fit to seek their backing for the introduction of institutional reforms and with one important exception those which have been made were made without reference to them.

While the subject of institutional change generally comes up during election campaigns, it is more a question of general ideas being floated rather than firmly fixed in formal commitments. If the presidential election sometimes departs from this pattern, it amounts to the same thing, as in 1995 when Lionel Jospin gave what was probably a sincere commitment to introduce a five-year presidential term but did so during an election which by his own admission he had very little chance of winning. On the eve of the elections which he quite rightly expected to win, on the other hand, he found it expedient not to return to this subject which might have been unpopular.

Thus, during those periods which seemed the most favourable the Constitution has not been amended, or not in the way one would have expected. It has, on the other hand, been amended during those periods which seemed the least appropriate.

Let us pass over the amendment of July 1993.[3] Not that it was insignificant but because it was carried out during 'cohabitation' and not brought about by it. In the proposal previously introduced by François Mitterrand on the recommendation of Pierre Bérégovoy, Edouard Balladur and his government nibbled at what they thought was good, only accepted their inheritance strictly without liability. Ultimately, that government thought it more convenient to exploit the opportunities for constitutional 'self-service' than to appeal to the head of state whom they were thus able to do without.

Stranger still is the amendment of November 1993.[4] This was only possible with the consent of the President. His feeling, which was highly debatable, was that he could not refuse. Two lessons follow from this. The first, which is strictly historical, is that for a lightweight head of state, even inertia may be beyond his strength. The second and more repeatable lesson is that a given political situation can force a president to do, and not just passively accept, something which he might not be inclined to do of his own accord.

It would be presumptuous at the time of writing to prejudge the prospects for amendments which are in progress or have been announced.[5] It is, on the other hand, easy to establish that plans exist, that they have been deliberated in the Council of Ministers, reviewed in parliament and above all that they have all received beforehand the two eminent signatures which one might have thought incompatible here.

Far from it, as has been shown. The dedicated followers of de Gaulle will despair over this muddying of responsibilities. Others will rejoice at seeing it thus confirmed that the Constitution really is a matter for everyone, since the right moment to reform it proves to be when powers are more or less shared out among everyone.

So, with few amendments directly following elections, several amendments begun or completed during 'cohabitation', there are two outcomes which no-one would seriously have bet on.

As for the other amendments, they were primarily a matter of circumstances: so the right moment to reform is whenever amendments can be made easily without the timing being dictated by the interests or even the wishes of the author, who notes rather than chooses it.

The Right Procedure

It is difficult to be sure exactly what the right procedure is, but it is imperative to know what the wrong one is: a procedure which has never been followed before. And to add to the already long list of paradoxes of the Fifth Republic, it is obviously a question of which of the competing procedures finds favour with its text and found favour with its sponsors.

Article 89 provides for a rule – approval by referendum – and it appears only by foresight, almost reluctantly, that it provided for an exception – recourse to Congress. Eleven amendments later (if we restrict ourselves to those carried out in accordance with the article), the rule remains half asleep and the exception is wide awake. This can be interpreted in two ways.

The first appeals to the founding fathers: Michel Debré himself explained to the first joint session of Congress in 1963, that it was welcome to make technical alterations but that a referendum was the only legal mechanism for making fundamental choices. The conclusion which can be drawn from this is not without relevance: none of the amendments adopted at Versailles was really essential. The choice of procedure therefore qualifies the content of the amendment.

The second interpretation stresses the unsuitability of this procedure: bearing in mind the precautions taken to guarantee the existence of a minimum of consensus, a referendum would doubtless contribute nothing that is not already guaranteed by the exceptional procedure. Either the issue is not really very contentious and popular consultation is superfluous or it is contentious and those who would be in a position to call a referendum are wary of doing so if the outcome cannot be assured. It is either unnecessary or dangerous. This is certainly regrettable. After all, there is nothing to prevent the people from being asked to decide; indeed the opposite is true. And whoever were to canvass their opinion in this way could quite easily avoid linking his own fate to the outcome of the vote. Given a clear issue, if it is of some significance – for example, the five-year presidential term – it is even possible to imagine a president revealing his preference for a no vote while recognising the right of the French to decide for themselves, and inviting them to do so.

The fact remains, however, that the theoretically standard procedure set out in Article 89 is probably doomed to remain a victim of the dual competition between Congress on the one hand and the referendum procedure set out in Article 11 on the other.

There is, nevertheless, one scenario in which the procedure might be revived: if there were real hostility, for example during 'cohabitation', between the head of state and the other actors. There would then be nothing to prevent members of parliament from taking the initiative, or the government from putting it on the agenda, or the chambers from debating and adopting it. In this totally new situation, either the head of state would have to resign himself to a referendum being called, or if he refused or delayed excessively, he would certainly be made aware that, after all. Nothing in the Constitution says, or suggests, that this is necessarily a presidential power: a determined prime minister or government, assured of the support of the assemblies and confident of the popular sentiment, might consider themselves entitled to take it upon themselves to call a referendum. This would be in accordance with Article 89, which (unlike Article 11 which as we know is so different) does not explicitly require the intervention of the head of state. Of course, such a scenario is not very likely, but a particularly strained 'cohabitation' might lend it a plausibility which it lacks today.

To return to more well-trodden paths, the standard procedure suffers, of course, from a fault in its design and flaws in its implementation. The design fault stems from the fact that an identical vote in both houses is prerequisite. It is one thing not to be able to make ill thought-out amendments, but for one assembly, or rather its governing party, to have an insuperable veto is quite another, and this is made worse in the case of the Senate by its political imbalance. Of the two major coalitions which confront each other democratically, only one can, whatever happens, determine the fate of an amendment. That is, whether to carry it out, let it mature or reject it, and the other has to admit defeat without even, in theory, being able to get round this by appealing to the French people.

The proposals on the subject put forward by the committee chaired by Georges Vedel are sufficiently well-balanced to win unreserved approval here despite the fear that they will never see the light of day due to the effects of the very thing which they were intended to remedy.

The flaws in implementation stem from the incompetence or timidity of governments. if Article 45 is cancelled out by Article 89, this does not destroy all the weapons at the executive's disposal. Of course, it loses the advantage provided in Article 49, paragraph 3, since the second paragraph of Article 89 requires the text to be 'passed' which it would not be if the Assembly were only asked to pronounce on a possible motion of censure. Yet the government retains, informally, the possibility of appealing to a joint committee and, formally, that of forcing a vote.

A meeting between the influential members of the two assemblies and of all their groupings would probably make the search for an agreement easier. And do so in a more effective and less dubious fashion than was the case when only the senior members of the parties in power at the time of the 1995 amendment met.[6] Of course, this kind of informal committee, if it existed, could not produce any of the effects provided for in the last two paragraphs of Article 45. It might, however, be very fruitful in cases where a compromise was being genuinely sought.

In other cases, Article 44, paragraph 3, might offer a considerable resource. No-one can question its validity and many would find it useful. Each assembly can in fact reject an amendment. But each can also pretend to accept it in principle while imposing conditions which it knows to be insurmountable, thus ensuring that sooner or later the plan will be shelved. The *vote bloqué* (forced vote) was devised precisely to confront members with their responsibilities: either to take or leave a text whose author feels that he has compromised as much as he can.

When applied to the amending procedure, this weapon would discourage hypocrisy, or force it out into the open, and would make it possible to avoid an amendment being overtaxed to the exclusive benefit of anyone who wants his consent to be paid for with some new power or unwarranted privilege. It is normal for assemblies not to reach agreement of their own accord and natural that they set themselves objectives which may be different. Nevertheless there comes a time when the final whistle has to be blown to force one or the other to rule on a text which can be amended no further.

It is odd that governments have resorted to the *vote bloqué* where minor issues are concerned but have forgotten about it in more important matters and have to date never used it as a means of closing any loophole which might have been exploited duplicitously.

Any amendment requires such a favourable astral and political conjunction that it is a miracle so many have been made. The coincidence of the right moment and the right procedure forms a tight mesh through which only relatively modest changes have so far been able to pass. It is unlikely, however that it is the former which explains the latter.

... DO NOT EXPLAIN THE TIMIDNESS OF CONTENT

To amend is not to reform. Admittedly, no change is gratuitous. Each one affecting, to a greater or lesser extent, directly or indirectly, sooner or later, the positive law has changed the way it works and is applied.

However, an important distinction has to be made between those amendments which were a cause and those which were an effect. In the first case, it has been a question of modifying more or less successfully the arrangement of powers in a clear direction. In the second case, where simple questions of competence and hierarchy of rules are concerned, it has on the contrary been a question of ensuring that the Constitution is not an obstacle to what has been decided outside and independently of it.

It is probably not incorrect to use the word reform only in the first case whereas in the second it would be more appropriate to speak of adaptation. Viewed in this light, the Constitution seems to have been adapted more often than genuinely reformed.

Adaptation

Nine amendments fall into this category.

The first, that of 4 June 1960,[7] carried out in accordance with the special procedure set out in Article 85, had as its stated aim an attempt to make the law correspond to the fact, to make the constitutional tools more flexible so that they could respond to the suddenly accelerated pace of decolonisation.

The amendment of 30 December 1963,[8] whose ambitions were so modest that it was hardly worth the price of the ticket to Versailles, introduced a welcome simplification but one which no-one would think of claiming to have been a profound innovation.

In the amendment of 18 June 1976,[9] the Assembly, helpfully if not completely, corrected an oversight which might have proved extremely unfortunate. This is duly noted and to be commended. Yet its intention was not to change anything whatsoever in the constitutional order of things. It was on the contrary to maintain its course in case one of the scenarios for which it provided should occur.

If it is true that Article 88-4 restores to some extent the powers of the authorities with regard to Europe, it is no less true that this was certainly not the primary objective of the amendment of 25 June 1992 as a whole. If there is a case where it is justifiable to speak of adaptation, then this is it. Having once acknowledged incompatibility in April, parliament got down to remedying it in May, achieved this in June. And it was in September that the French people gave it their tacit if grudging approval. It was definitely the Constitution which complied with Maastricht. Its amendment was an effect and by no means a cause. And the same was true after the Treaty of Amsterdam which was taken account of in the amendment of 25 January 1999

Is the new Article 53-1, inserted in the amendment of 25 November 1993, to be interpreted as a reform? Certainly not in the mind of its initiator who has always pretended to see it as a strengthening of the traditional right of asylum. Nor in the mind of those who passed it, in whose eyes it was only stating the glaringly obvious which, according to them, the Constitutional Council had blindly disregarded. Let us acknowledge then that if this provision has contributed anything, it is less in terms of its content that the proof which it offers that an amendment can obliterate a judge's decision. Was this not once again confirmation of what everyone knew, even if until then it had only been a hypothetical scenario?

What is there to say next about the new Articles 76 and 77? Apart from underlining that they are certainly very innovative in that they give a rough ride to several tried and tested principles and set up totally new procedures. The scope of these innovations is very limited and very remote geographically and perhaps historically. They only affect one local authority which in future will in fact be the only one to be mentioned by name in the supreme law.

Finally, the two most recent amendments of spring 1999 fall into this same category.

The one which introduces the principle of equal access for men and women to political office is obviously a genuinely important reform. But its insertion into the Constitution is purely reactive. It is only intended to remove for good the legal obstacle which conflicted with an earlier law that had already been adopted to that effect in 1982.

As for the other amendment adopted at the same time, it aims to make possible the ratification of the treaty setting up the international penal court and so follows, in another sphere, exactly the same logic of adaptation as that which has already operated for the Treaties of Maastricht and Amsterdam.

In all of these cases, the Constitution has, like a well-behaved child, submitted to all sorts of adaptations, varying in their scale, scope, sphere, causes and consequences, but none of which claimed, strictly speaking, to represent constitutional reformism at work. The latter has manifested itself on other occasions and rarely with the anticipated effects.

Reform

Success is never the order of the day. Either the reform falls through and failure is complete, or it succeeds and its consequences do not live up to expectations, even though others which had not been appreciated may be fulfilled. In short, genuine failures have alternated with false successes.

Let us begin with an inventory of those failures which have been authenticated as such. That of 27 April 1969[10] simultaneously sounded the death knell for Gaullism and regionalisation. Of course, Gaullism has survived its vicissitudes but by increasingly distancing itself from the initial model. As for regionalisation, 12 years later a form of decentralisation based on very different principles, which seemed designed to inhibit the growth of the regions rather than promote it, was preferred. In the process, the Senate recovered its strength, which is good, as well as its capacity to oppose reforms affecting it which is not so good.

Five five-year terms later, we are still waiting for the five-year presidental term voted for in 1973. This was in no way perceived as a failure for Georges Pompidou, who was rather given credit for trying, but it was certainly one for the French people who, whatever their response might be, have never managed to get asked the question.

Although he was the author of two amendments, Valéry Giscard d'Estaing had to resign himself to abandoning two more. However, the one which would have allowed former ministers to get back their parliamentary seats would have been welcome. The incompatibility rule, introduced when it was necessary to enhance the prestige of the executive, fulfilled its function. At a time when it is the image of the legislature, which needs restoring, it would be wise to allow those whose experience and renown, or even their recalcitrance, might enrich it to return without having to resort to subterfuge. This was already true in 1974. It is even more so in 1999. As for the other failure, which was contemporaneous with the first, it passed relatively unnoticed. From experience, however, one can gauge the importance which the Constitutional Council's power of self-referral might have assumed, while being wary of saying that this would have been a good thing. It cannot be denied that it would have been important if the parliamentarians had not refused to establish it as was proposed to them.

The same could be said of what was attempted in 1990 with regard to the exception of unconstitutionality. The latent hostility of the Senate was enough to block this, all the more so since its official initiator, the President of the Republic, was far less motivated than its actual initiator, the President of the Constitutional Council.

It might be surprising not to find on this list of failures that of 1984. This is not accidental, since it was a success. In proposing a modification to Article 11 which would make possible a referendum on state aid for private education, François Mitterrand was obviously not seeking to carry out an amendment but simply to get out of the political trap in which he had ensnared himself, and this he did. The amending procedure can be used to divert attention as well.

Let us now come to the false successes. They are not synonymous with failure, but refer sometimes to lack of success and sometimes to inadvertent success.

To give credit where credit is due, the sudden, passionate amendment of 6 November 1962,[11] which was the most spectacular and important of all, did not in the end fulfil all the expectations that de Gaulle had placed in it. Through this amendment, he wanted a strong president, and he got one, but he also wanted a head of state who would be above cleavages and parties. Not only did his reform fail in this respect but it had the opposite effect, being a major factor in the revival of the parties. He wanted a sharing out of responsibilities between president and prime minister, and he got it. Yet he certainly never imagined that the latter would be able to decide virtually everything while the former would be put out to pasture, which he would not altogether savour. Thus, depending on whether one's criteria is the attachment which the French showed towards the law they were given in 1962 or the effects which its initiator expected it to have, this key reform is either a triumph or a semi-failure.

The amendment of 27 July 1993 would have to be termed a semi-success. It brought genuine innovation and improvement to the career development of judges. This appreciation is only tempered by its incomplete nature, since the subject will have to be looked at again in the light of a plan which is under review.

As for the Court of Justice of the Republic, it revealed in its first trial, the indictment of a former prime minister and two former ministers in the case of the contaminated blood, that its setting up had been the wrong answer to the right question and it will no doubt be necessary to review the system which was adopted in haste and under pressure in 1993.

Conversely, there is no point in waiting to see the effects or lack of them of the amendment of 4 August 1995. Let us pass over the referendum. Its scope was considerably widened but as might have been expected, it has remained unused and is likely to remain so for some time to come. Believing that the root of the problem lay in its definition when obviously the main obstacle was rather the monopoly of initiative of a president who has little to gain and much to lose in this kind of consultation, was an idle fancy. If it was not a deliberate move to reform in order to be seen to reform, with the quite firm intention of never changing anything and leaving it to someone else, as reckless in their handling of Article 11 as the court was with Article 12, to prevent the referendum from becoming obsolete.

As for the single session, this was certainly not a prolific success for the person who had imposed it and was only able to enjoy it for one year. But beyond the case of the President of the Assembly of the day, it does not yet seem that this genuine reform has borne all its fruit. It is too early to speak here of failure. If by some miracle the *cumul des mandats* were to decrease, then parliamentarians would rediscover, as some have already begun to do, the attractive and substantial powers which they possess and the lengthening of the session would offer the necessary space in which to exercise them.

Perhaps the most exemplary of the amendments is the one adopted on 22 February 1996. The elected representatives had already demanded for some time a right to look at the national social budget. In 1986, they had even taken an initiative along these lines which the Constitutional Court had judged to be untimely Their perseverance was finally rewarded ten years later. Rewarded? Perhaps.

Out of a claimed concern for rigour, the introduction of the laws on social security financing was accompanied by a strict mechanism. The procedure is subject to tight deadlines since, justifiably, no-one wanted parliament to resurrect for the social budget the 'provisional twelfths'[12] from which the general budget had suffered prior to 1958. But the logical counterpart to this which was called for had to be a rigorous system of protection against all those who might want to jump on the bandwagon. A carelessly drawn-up organic law, an excessively lenient constitutional judge, and the foreseeable happened. From its introduction, the law on social security financing became a sort of DDOS[13] (*Diverses Dispositions d'Ordre Social*), a cargo plane designed to take on board virtually all the junk which the ministers concerned take it into their heads to cram it with.

Where it was naïvely thought that parliament was being given a new and essential power, the government has in fact been provided with an unwarranted additional opportunity, that of getting measures which have no unity, clarity, often no urgency or necessity other than the purely bureaucratic, rapidly adopted. Hell is not only paved with good intentions.

In this sequence of genuine failures and successes which were either deceptive or at least qualified, ultimately only one amendment is out of place, that of 29 October 1974.[14] Its proposer, Valéry Giscard d'Estaing, unquestionably saw its potential. He was aware, because three years of proven experience had already demonstrated this, that it undermined the supremacy of the executive and could, in the case of a censure, politically damage the image of the government, which ultimately had more to lose from it than parliament itself. It deserves all the more credit for having been pursued with such clear-sightedness.

Everyone is familiar with what happened next and the effects of the amendment and it would not be an exaggeration to consider this reform to have been almost as important as that of 1962. It has ultimately had consequences which are more in line with the expectations of its author.

This is not quite to say that this amendment alone produced no surprises. It is merely that (and once in a while this does no harm) those who were most surprised were not the initiators but the beneficiaries.

Ignoring the term '*réformette*', which is as well-known as it is inane, it is more interesting to note that it was the opposition of the day which, despite itself, forged the legitimacy of the Council, something which it totally denied.

If the left advocated setting up a Supreme Court, it was less from any attachment to the control of constitutionality, which is as foreign to its instincts as to its traditions, than in order to condemn by contrast the arrangement for French constitutional judges. The year 1971[15] had not obliterated 1962[16] and the Pavillon Montpensier (the Council's home) continued to be seen as handing out services rather than sentences.

Yet since in politics any new power is worth having, the socialists seized both it and the Council. Each session brought them its share of censures, which were seen as blows struck against the enemy. They were almost making fun of this president who had been so naive as to hand them a weapon and the means of using it against him. They hardly gave the Council any credit for their satisfaction, which they attributed rather to the merits of their own shrewdness, and there were very few of them who saw a little further ahead.

So it was a cruel disappointment when, having become the majority party, it was the socialists' turn to incur the displeasure of the constitutional censure. All past cases have come up again, on the instructions of the very people who had tried to throw them out. There was fierce condemnation, which was fortunately shortlived. Although belatedly, everyone rapidly understood that having boasted for a whole presidency about the successes won before the Council, they no longer had any right to condemn it for the successes being offered to others. Unwittingly, they themselves had closed the circle in which they had trapped themselves and which they would discover to be ultimately virtuous only once calm had been restored.

Beyond these cases, the fact remains that amendment is possible. Yet apart from the amendments of 1962 and 1974, it certainly cannot be maintained that they had any real impact.

This would be unsurprising if it was because there was no need for amendments, or no proposals, or because their supporters could not get them adopted, or even because of the reservations which the French allegedly had about them. However, this was not the case. Whether it was a question of the five-year presidency, the referendum on minority initiatives, the exception of unconstitutionality, to take major constitutional changes, or the number and powers of parliamentary committees or basic principles relating to the status of the opposition to take less spectacular constitutional changes, but ones which would nevertheless be very significant, nothing stood in the way of the changes affecting them. There would be no insurmountable obstacle to them. None of these ideas was the property of one tendency, something which would have been enough to ensure that the other opposed it. And the precedent of 1973 is certainly not sufficient for procedural requirements to be seen as inviolable under any circumstances.

In fact, it seems that the relative timidity of the initiatives which succeeded has to be put down to a combination of fear and egotism. Not one of them, in almost 25 years, has significantly altered the balance or imbalance of powers. The rules of the game have only changed at its margins. The French themselves have never directly benefited.

Two consequences follow from this. The first is a reappraisal of the state of health of the mind alluded to at the beginning. It is real but delicate, rather sensitive to the climate. The second is that the French might end up growing weary of changes which they would be forced to remain outside of, amendments which they could see neither the importance nor the point of, while those which they might want would be continually rejected. Then, the future of the Fifth Republic would be threatened, arbitrarily, not by a lack of reforms but by their unsuitability.

Thus, to reflect for a moment on past amendments is to recognise that they were full of surprises, rich in paradoxes. These surprises and paradoxes force us to view future amendments warily. This certainly does not mean abandoning them but on the contrary approaching them with rigour and ambition. And all of this should only serve to inspire tenacity in their champions and humility in all constitutionalists.

NOTES

1. This is an updated version of the article which first appeared in *Revue du Droit Public* 5/6 (1998) pp.1485–97. This version was translated from the French by Sally Marthaler.
2. An amendment reintroducing Articles 76 and 77 in a new form devoted to the future of New Caledonia.
3. An amendment which strengthened the independence of judicial authority by providing for the election of members of the Higher Council of Magistrates.
4. Following a decision of the Constitutional Council which, out of respect for the right of asylum, had revoked some of the clauses of a law on immigration, the Constitution was amended to allow these clauses to be readopted.
5. A new amendment relating to judicial authority was adopted in identical terms by both assemblies but the President of the Republic has not yet convened a Congress (a meeting of the two chambers) which must ratify it definitively. Moreover, an amendment extending to Polynesia a statute similar to the one already given to New Caledonia is to be examined shortly.

6. At the time of the 1995 amendment, decisions later imposed on the two assemblies were taken at a dinner attended by the majority leaders.
7. This amendment concerned the Communauté française, which no longer exists.
8. This amendment specified the dates for the opening of ordinary parliamentary sessions.
9. This amendment established the mechanisms to be applied if the course of the presidential election were disrupted by the withdrawal of one of the candidates.
10. Following the failure of the referendum which he had called, de Gaulle resigned from the presidency of the Republic in 1969.
11. This was the amendment introducing the election of the President of the Republic by direct universal suffrage.
12. The 'provisional twelfths' (*les douzièmes provisoires*) were monthly budgets which parliament passed every month since it had been impossible to pass the annual budget within the allotted time.
13. *Diverses Dispositions d'Ordre Social* are bills in which all sorts of measures are lumped together.
14. This revision gave 60 deputies or 60 senators, and thus in effect the opposition, the possibility of referring a law to the Constitutional Council whereas before this capacity had been reserved solely for the President of the Republic, the Prime Minister and the Presidents of the Assembly.
15. The date of the first decision in which the Constitutional Council abolished in its entirety a law based on the Preamble to the Constitution.
16. The date on which the Constitutional Council declared itself incompetent to assess the validity of recourse to the referendum called by de Gaulle.

The Fifth Republic: From the *Droit de l'État* to the *État de droit*?

VINCENT WRIGHT

Political scientists have once again become more interested in institutions, and even, at last, in the law. It is now generally accepted that individual and group preferences are embedded in and shaped by institutions, an historically-forged amalgam of bodies, rules, procedures, norms, customs, rites, which generates its own conventions, path dependencies and notions of appropriateness. Law plays a vital role in institutions: it is woven into the fabric of public and private action, it is a medium of conflict avoidance and resolution, and it is rooted in a set of pervasive political theories and ideological assumptions. Law is both the articulated expression of collective preferences mediated through the filter of the legal profession, as well as the map of procedures for aggregating and channelling preferences, for rendering them operational and enforceable. Any understanding of a political system requires a recognition of the output and the input dimensions of law. Perhaps one of the major reasons for the renewed interest in law for political scientists lies in the alleged increased juridification of institutions, politics and public policy – a phenomenon common to all West European countries but felt particularly in countries such as France.

An attempt is made here to outline the various strands of this juridification, and to explain the process in terms of a set of discrete yet often interlinked factors connected with the profound changes taking place in France, leading to a reshaping of the relationships within the sacred trinity of state-society-market. It is both a top-down and a bottom-up phenomenon. Increasing juridification is taking place, driven by multiple factors. It has provoked a debate in France about the emergence of an *État de Droit* – a state bound by and respectful towards the rule of law and due process. However, there remain important limits to the processes of juridification and the *État de Droit* in France is more incipient than fully realised. It is essential, first, to describe the judicial inheritance of the Fifth Republic.

THE FRENCH JUDICIAL TRADITION: *ÉTATISATION DU DROIT*

By 1958, the French judicial system had acquired several features which were powerfully anchored, even if they were neither consistent nor entirely coherent. The system had been forged, both deliberately and unwittingly, by a set of doctrines which blended selective readings of Montesquieu and Rousseau with the ideas of a host of lesser known but influential legal thinkers and practitioners. The system came to absorb features acquired from the *ancien régime*, the Jacobin Revolution, the two imperial regimes (but more especially the first) as well as of the post-1870 Republic – features which were distinct yet interconnected and which jostled with one another in uncomfortable fashion. These features may be summarised as follows:

• *The formal equality of individuals before the law* – a fundamental principle established in 1789, and never formally called into question thereafter, even though traumatic political events could lead to the creation of tribunals with exceptional powers. These tribunals (which were sometimes military or mixed judicial and military in character) invariably behaved with repressive zeal, violating even the most elementary rights of defence.

• *The ubiquity of law*. France was quickly to be contaminated by *Verlichtung* – 'legal pollution' – as an increasing number of sectors came to be regulated and bureaucratised by legal stipulations.

• *Law which was established and policed by the 'imperial state'*.[1] This *Étatisation du droit*, which was one of the major legacies of the Revolution and of Napoleon Bonaparte and was pursued by all successive regimes, was rooted in a deep mistrust of autonomous self-regulating institutions. Regulation and control should emanate exclusively from the state which was invested with superior rights and which legitimised its actions in terms of 'the general interest'.

• *An abiding disrespect for the current constitution* which, despite all the rhetoric, was viewed as a mere rule in the wider game of politics – a means of regulating conflict rather than the foundation of political order.

• *Law which was instrumental*. It has been argued by Cohen-Tanugi that in the US law was a mechanism for managing a diverse and pluralistic society, and applied equally to individuals, groups and public authorities.[2] It could not be the expression of the general will since the existence of such a will was denied (if it was ever considered ...). France, on the other hand, was not only legalistically liberal, ensuring equality before the law – law which arbitrated between the interests in contention. Law was also seen as a mobiliser and legitimiser of the sociopolitical system. It was not neutral, but embodied 'technocratic normative justice': it was instrumental and output-oriented, intimately involved in social guidance and social engineering, and served as a tool for ensuring social integration (based on a legally-constructed concept of citizenship), political centralisation and economic *dirigisme*. In short, law was a top-down system of homogenisation.

• *An enduring hostility towards jurisprudence (the expression of judicial creation and the adjudication of individual conflicts) as a source of law, and towards judicial review* which was both ideologically and politically inspired. The 1804 Civil Code (Article 5) expressly forbids judges from making decisions of a general character. Legal sovereignty lay with the legitimate representative authority (parliament or executive depending on the regime), itself the embodiment of the popular will (through election or referendum). Law, as the expression of the general will or the popular will, is, by definition, not perfectible and not contestable – a point re-emphasised in an important decision of the Council of State. Implacable hostility to judicial review was also inspired by deep suspicion of the politics of the judiciary. Lawyers and magistrates had played an important role in undermining the *ancien régime*, and the revolutionaries of 1789 (many of whom came from the legal profession) were determined to demolish their wrecking potential. Bonaparte and all subsequent rulers agreed on this point.

The problem was compounded by regime instability in France between 1789 and 1958: two empires, two monarchies and four republics, each the object of anti-regime assaults. The rulers of each regime were instinctively suspicious of the judiciary they inherited. Hence, there were massive purges of the magistrature at the beginning of each regime and lingering mistrust of those who escaped the purges. This mistrust of the judiciary was given early and enduring expression in the celebrated proclamation of August 1790, which insisted on the separation of judicial and administrative powers – the next feature of the French judicial tradition.

• *Law which was dual in character.* Ideological factors (the state as the expression of the general will, separation of powers, and legal sovereignty vested in political authority) combined with political suspicion of judges underlined the need for a separate administrative jurisdiction. Judges of the ordinary courts should not, in any way, be able to upset the operation of administrative bodies. Nor could they call those bodies to account by virtue of their functions. Indeed, after 1790 any interference by the ordinary courts in the administration was officially a criminal offence.

The state created its own internal system of justice to try alleged illegalities, and at the head of this system lies the Council of State. Theoretically, in this scenario the state is the alleged offender, judge and jury. For freedom-loving French liberals and British constitutionalists such as Dicey, administrative law was a perversion: the British tradition of common law guaranteed equality before the law and 'the equal subjection of all classes to the ordinary law of the land administered by the ordinary law courts'. In truth, Dicey was profoundly to misread the nature of administrative law which, even by his time, had begun to generate a set of rights against the abuses committed by state officials.

• *The subordination and politicisation of the judiciary.* In the practice of separation of powers, the judiciary was not even considered to be a 'power' similar in status to that of the executive and the legislature. Rather it was portrayed as an 'authority' – a term which clearly indicated its lower ranking. And this subordination was given practical expression: the hierarchical supremacy of the Justice Ministry over part of the judiciary; the requirement that prosecuting magistrates become electoral agents for the regime and keep a close and punitive eye on the 'enemies' of the regime; the involvement of the judiciary in special tribunals established to try political 'crimes' (which included, in 1851, defending the Constitution); the persistent interference in political appointments; the constant pressuring of prosecuting magistrates into shelving politically embarrassing *affaires*.

• *Judicial self-restraint* both of a collective and individual nature. Judicial creativity or activism was frowned upon by a profession which was socialised into a role of discretion, and which was docile in accepting the doctrines of state supremacy and political sovereignty.

Legal pollution, law which was state-based and highly instrumental, disregard for the constitution, absence of judicial review, civil-administrative legal duality, a mistrusted, subordinate and politicised judiciary, and judicial restraint – such were the dominant characteristics of the French judicial tradition, and each was rooted in and connected by a set of ideological and political assumptions. Of course, there is a danger of investing the system with a simplicity and rationality which it lacked in practice. Thus, the separation of powers was constantly violated, and the formal locus of political authority was not always the real locus (parliamentary sovereignty was undermined by the executive's increasing recourse to statutory instruments (*décrets-lois*).

The borderline between civil and administrative law often proved difficult to trace, and led to disputes between ordinary and administrative judges – hence the creation of the *Tribunal des Conflits* in May 1872 to settle such disputes. More significantly, the role of judges as policy makers was more important than official texts and doctrines suggested. As early as 1800 the Council of State was given important powers in the public works sector and slowly transformed itself into a reasonably impartial, if politically sensitive administrative court, with protection against dismissal for its members, and committed to the protection of citizens against the abuses and illegalities of state officials.

The celebrated *arrêt Blanco* opened 'the golden age' of administrative law, which was to last until 1920. During this period, there was a progressive narrowing of the area within which the Council was prepared to treat executive acts as non-justifiable. The two bases of administrative law – the *recours pour excès de pouvoir* and the *régime de la responsabilité administrative* – were established, refined and extended, providing the citizen-plaintiff with the right to seek the annulment of an act or decision, and the Council of State with a capacity to create, through a set of coherent and flexible principles of tortuous liability, an important jurisprudence.

The Council of State was largely responsible for almost all the law concerning the public administration and its officials: it defined the rules, regulations, procedures and responsibilities of the administration, and provided the basic ideas of what constituted *service public*, a public agent and the public domain (these concepts have become critical in the current privatisation debates). And, the Council went much further. Long before 1958, it had begun to define a set of constitutional principles that could be cited in cases of litigation. These 'fundamental general principles of law' included conveniently elastic concepts such as 'equality before the law', 'freedom of conscience', 'non-retroactivity', 'individual freedom' which provided the Council with a certain interpretative latitude.

While the jurisprudential role of the Council of State was important, its direct impact should not be exaggerated. It always insisted that 'the general principles of law' were implicit in, or accorded with the spirit of legislation. It specifically stated that it could not test the constitutionality of the law, which was the expression of the general will. There is no doubt that at the beginning of the Fifth Republic the constitutional and political tradition of the country remained permeated by an *Étatisation du droit* rather than an *État de Droit*.

Furthermore, the early years of the Fifth Republic were far from promising for those who favoured the latter. Even the Constitutional text was far from reassuring: the Council of State, the supreme administrative court was not mentioned as a judge (and its consultative role was strengthened); the Constitutional Council was to be composed exclusively of political appointees, and its role was defined less as a judge than as a policeman of the executive/legislative spheres of competence; the independence of the judiciary was to be protected by the President of the Republic, while the *Conseil Supérieur de la Magistrature* was given only an advisory function over appointments.

Constitutional practice was even more alarming, as the President of the Republic constantly abused and misused the letter and spirit of the Constitution. Moreover, during the early years of the regime there were several disturbing incidents involving the judiciary: there were some flagrantly political appointments to key posts: there were public rows between the government and the Council of State (notably, over the Council's leaked unfavourable response to the 1962 referendum which it considered to be unconstitutional; over the sacking of Jacomet, a member of the Council, who, in his capacity as an official in Algeria; had openly sided with the rebels against government policy, and, most spectacularly, over the Canal affair which involved the Council, in emergency session, saving the life of Canal who had been condemned for treasonable activities in Algeria by a special military court).

Several highly dubious *affaires* were hushed up as the result of pressure on the judiciary: the Ben Barka affair (involving the assassination of the leader of the Moroccan opposition with the connivance of the French Intelligence Service); the mysterious murder of the Prince de Broglie, a politician of high social credentials but low social contacts; the no less mysterious suicide of Boulin, Labour Minister and prominent Gaullist; the *Canard Enchaîné* affair (yet another) that revealed that the police had been bugging the newspaper which named the policemen involved to a government which refused to take the required legal measures against them.

THE JUDICIALISATION OF PUBLIC POLICY: UNBUNDLING THE PACKAGE

Against this background there has been an increasing judicialisation of public policy during the Fifth Republic. Based on the work of institutions such as the European Court of Justice (ECJ), the European Court of Human Rights (ECHR), the Constitutional Council, the Council of State, the Court of Cassation, the Court of Accounts, the Court of Justice of the Republic, investigating magistrates, the *Médiateur* and regulatory agencies, this judicialisation has taken several forms which have been triggered by a somewhat different mix of factors.

• *The quantitative leap in litigation in all branches of law*: constitutional, administrative, civil and criminal. This phenomenon is by no means restricted to France, where administrative courts are having great difficulty in coping with the workload. The same story is repeated in the civil courts: in the Paris Appeal Court, for instance, during 1980–89, criminal litigation rose by 31 per cent and civil litigation by 36 per cent, and the rate of increase was said to be accelerating.

• *The establishment of the parameters of public policy by the process of judicial review* – the legal mechanism by which a decision of a public authority may be challenged in the courts on the grounds that it is unconstitutional. The Council of State has, in its judicial capacity, continued its tradition of developing its jurisprudence in the light of general principles of law, which are framed by the wider context of republican legality. It has made several important decisions which have established the supremacy of European Union (EU) law, have defined fundamental human rights (e.g., the right of aliens to bring their families to France or the conditions surrounding expulsion), and the rights of public officials (e.g., the rights of pregnant women) and of their clients (e.g., hospital patients). Of great legal importance were two decisions of the Constitutional Council – in 1980 and 1987 – which recognised as having a constitutional status the litigation status of the Council of State – although, in practice, it had already acquired this status. The role of the Constitutional Council as parameter setter has given rise to both intellectual and political controversy. There is no dispute, however, about its importance as a public policy maker, by entrenching the principles, practices and legitimacy of judicial review.

The emergence and consolidation of judicial review by the Constitutional Council from the mid-1970s as a major feature of the regime have been due to the combined efforts of politicians and members of the Council itself. In 1974, newly-elected President, Giscard d'Estaing, sensitive to the need to provide a limited counterweight to the executive dominance of the regime (the right had won every parliamentary and presidential election since 1958), pushed through a constitutional amendment which opened access to the Constitutional Council to any 60 deputies or senators. Denounced initially as a '*réformette*', reference to the Council was to become a major avenue for all parliamentary oppositions intent on fighting a particular law.

In the 14 years between 1959 and 1974 the Constitutional Council was called to give only nine decisions on the constitutionality of a law. During the Giscard d'Estaing presidency, from 1974 to 1981, this figure rose to 47 (45 at the request of members of parliament). From 1981 to 1986, when the socialists dominated the executive there were 66 rulings; during the 1986–88 *cohabitation* period, there were no fewer than 26 references to the Constitutional Council; the renewed period of socialist dominance from 1988 to 1993 saw 46 rulings on constitutionality; and in the first four months alone of the Balladur government in 1993, the left petitioned the Council on nine occasions. Today, all major controversial laws and all annual budgets end up in the Council.

If deputies and senators made increasing use of the Council it was because the latter was proving itself as much a constraint as a facilitator of Executive action, reshaping itself and its political environment in the process. Members of parliament discovered that judicial review was not necessarily a zero-sum game: indeed, it empowered opposition members and revitalised parliament as a whole. Annulments of government laws in part or whole became more frequent, from a quarter during 1974–81 to about half since then.

By a series of audacious decisions, beginning in July 1971, the Council has widened and deepened the scope of its action, building on precedents and principles. In its celebrated decision of 16 July 1971 which struck down an Act designed to restrict freedom of association by subjecting the registration and the acquisition of legal personality to the prior approval of a prefect, the Council, by six votes to three, ruled that, by virtue of the Preamble of the Constitution, the right to form an association could not be subject to the prior permission of an authority either judicial or administrative. Invoking 'fundamental principles recognised by the laws of the Republic' embedded in principles defined in the Declaration of the Rights of Man of 1789 and the Preamble of the 1946 Constitution, the Council has succeeded in articulating a set of general political, economic and social principles implicit in the above sources which are not always consistent.[3]

It should be noted that the Council of State had already paved the way in this direction in a decision of 1936 which invoked 'principles enjoying constitutional status' (*principes à valeur constitutionnelle*) and the

Constitutional Council was, therefore, building on an established legal tradition. Also, when confronted with imprecise legislation which might give rise to abuse by the Executive, the Council has elaborated a doctrine of acceptance subject to certain conditions, and outlines those conditions for interpretation and implementation. This would enable the law to be considered as constitutional. So, the role of the Council is not merely negative, it has acquired an advisory role. Furthermore, it is now customary for the government, in amending those parts of a law struck down by the Council simply to copy the precise terms relating to the conditions contained in the judgement. The Council has also extended its control to the constitutionality of Acts amended by new legislation.

The Council has continued to monitor the executive/legislative boundary (but in a more impartial way) as well as exercise its electoral functions. It has also, by its jurisprudence, provided the framework for other branches of law – administrative, electoral (including conditions on redrawing constituency boundaries), penal, fiscal, budgetary.

Perhaps most visibly, the Council has become a key actor in protecting public freedoms. It has restricted police powers notably over car searches (1977), the detention of suspects (1980 and 1986) and has protected various freedoms: the freedom of association (1971); the inviolability of domicile against the tax authorities (1983); the freedom of education (1977); the independence of university professors (1984); the right to strike (1979); the independence of magistrates (1978); the freedom of press and communications (1986). It has made key decisions on asylum and immigration issues which have strengthened the rights of immigrants and ensured that magistrates be involved in any expulsion proceedings.

Some of its rulings have raised an immediate political outcry: its ruling on abortion in January 1975; its generosity to the expropriated shareholders of the enterprises and banks nationalised by the socialists in January 1982; its hostility, in 1984, to the conditions surrounding the socialists' attempt to dismantle the media empire of Hersant, a right-wing press baron; its rejection, in 1986, of important provisions of a series of laws inspired by Charles Pasqua, the Interior Minister; its annulling, in January 1984, of several key provisions of the Savary Act on Higher Education, which had provoked mass protests by outraged Catholics and which was eventually withdrawn by President Mitterrand; its renewed attack, in 1993, on the illiberalism of Pasqua, back in the Interior Ministry, and whose legislation intended to tighten up on immigration rules. (The decision of the Council triggered a public row between the government and the President of the Constitutional Council and led to a government-promoted amendment of the constitution.)

The Council has also been involved in ruling on the constitutionality of important treaties – the 1976 Treaty on direct election to the European Parliament, the 1985 Convention on protecting fundamental rights and freedoms, and, most famously the Maastricht Treaty. In the latter case, the Constitutional Council (decision of 9 April 1992) objected to the single currency, common visas and the right of citizens of other member states to vote in French local elections. As a result, constitutional amendments were required, were proposed to Parliament (which amended the bill further), were passed by a joint sitting of the two chambers at Versailles, and were submitted to the people in a referendum and won by only a whisker.

• *The expansion of the intervention of the courts or of judges at the expense of politicians and administrators* involves either the courts rendering policy issues justiciable (subject to the law) or by the transfer to judges of decision-making power in new policy areas hitherto regulated by the government, the legislature or the public administration. Thus, the late 1980s and early 1990s saw the juridification of competition law under the impact of the EU (highly publicised affairs dealing with supermarkets, book price-fixing and civil aviation liberalisation), and the active role of the Competition Council (in 1996 it fined 36 companies for price-fixing and other anti-competitive price-fixing practices in public sector projects) many of whose decisions have led to legal appeals. Even the ECHR – normally considered a weak body – has helped to bring administrative decisions into the judicial domain, and France has been condemned by the Court on several occasions – over irregular detention, excessive slowness of procedures before an administrative court, telephone tapping, customs controls, and discrimination against transsexuals.

• *The criminalisation of activities which previously fell outside the scope of the law.* This process has several distinct strands. For example, there has been an intensification of repression in areas such as juvenile delinquency and immigration policy, and financial market malpractices have been criminalised. Another example is the increasing process of rendering political and administrative officials personally responsible for their acts and subject to criminal proceedings in the event of negligence. No longer can they hide behind the principles of anonymity and political responsibility. Since the mid-1980s, France has witnessed the dismantling of immunities. At the end of 1996 six prefects or sub-prefects were under judicial investigation for negligence (in one case, for something which had occurred 30 years previously). Thus, when one part of a football stadium collapsed and an ill-regulated camping site was swept away by a freak flood, with disastrous consequences for the campers, the prefects in question were investigated and faced with prison sentences. Similarly, the Director-General of the Health Ministry who was implicated in the use of contaminated blood was tried and sent to prison.

The Court of Justice of the Republic, established by the Constitutional Reform of 27 July 1993, was quickly charged with three affairs: the highly emotional affair of contaminated blood (which involved three ministers, including the Prime Minister); a sordid financial fraud allegedly perpetrated by the ex-Junior Minister for Handicapped People; the ministerial implications of the Noir-Botton affair (a complicated matter involving national and local politics, family feuds and financial impropriety).

• *The increasing role of judges, outside the judicial arena, as public policy makers.* The British tradition of asking judges to chair *ad hoc* commissions has spread to France. Marceau Long, the vice-president of the Council of State, was a ubiquitous policy maker, presiding several important commissions, including one established on the vexed question of citizenship. Members of the Council of State are invariably recruited as members or chairpersons of the independent administrative authorities which have grown in number and influence in recent years. From 1986 to 1992, the post of *Médiateur* was held by Paul Legatte, a member of the Council of State.

Another – and important – arena of policy activity by administrative judges is at executive and parliamentary level. Members of the Council of State and, to a much lesser extent, of the Court of Accounts, have penetrated the higher echelons of political decision making: the presidency (Pompidou from the Council of State, Chirac from the Court of Accounts), the premiership (the Council of State has provided, for example, Debré, Pompidou, Fabius and Balladur), the Council of Ministers, the Senate and the National Assembly have all been penetrated by the state *grands corps* in general, and by the Council of State in particular.

Members of the Council of State and of the Court of Accounts also figure prominently in the private offices (*cabinets ministériels*) of all executive actors, dominate the General Secretariat of the Government (responsible for the administrative co-ordination of government business), are present in key posts in Brussels, and, by the process of *pantouflage*, have taken over major posts in public and private industrial and banking groups. Finally, members of the Council of State play an important role in chairing the various disciplinary bodies of the professional self-regulating bodies.

• *The juridification of questions previously dealt with by exceptional non-judicial bodies*: thus, in 1981, the Mitterrand presidency abolished the Court of State Security (*Cour de Sûreté de l'État*) which had been established in the aftermath of the Algerian War, and in 1982, it dismantled some military tribunals.

• *The spread of judicial-making methods outside the judicial province proper* (referred to in French as *juridictionnalisation*). There are many examples of this process: increasing the rights of the defence; insistence on the presence of a judicial authority in cases such as the expulsion of foreigners; greater transparency. The Constitutional Council has forced the independent administrative authorities to juridify their procedures, and their decisions are subject to appeal either to the Council of State or the Court of Cassation.

• *The increasing role of judges as policy advisers.* Since 1958 the Council of State has had to be consulted for all government bills, proposed ordinances and all decrees which modify any pre-1958 law in an area now covered by decree. Since 1992, the Council of State has had to be consulted on all EU acts having a legislative character. This compulsory consultation represents a heavy burden for the Council: in 1992, for example, it examined some 946 bills or decrees. The advice of the Council is not officially binding on the government, although it is invariably followed: unfavourable *avis* which are ignored are sometimes leaked to the press and can be exploited by hostile pressure groups, or by opposition members of parliament who can refer the issue to the Constitutional Council. Moreover, measures regarded unfavourably at the consultative stage may eventually return to the Council of State, acting in its judicial capacity.

The Council of State may also be consulted by a government which is in need of advice. The government has done so on some 30 occasions each year. It requested the advice of the Council on matters such as the price structure of the TGV (the high-speed train), the personal status of workers of France Télécom which was scheduled for partial privatisation, and the rights of asylum-seekers. Perhaps the best-known *avis* of the Council arose in November 1989, over the highly emotional *foulard* affair (the right of young Muslim girls to wear the veil at school): the government – embarrassed by the whole issue – was happy to agree to the muddy compromise suggested by the Council.

Finally, the Council may carry out general studies at the request of the Prime Minister or of its own Vice-President (generally two or three a year).

They have covered a wide range of administrative and judicial questions (including an important report on the impact of EU law), but also complex issues such as information technology, urban planning or the ethical problems arising out of medical and biological progress. Several of these reports have served to shape future legislation.

• *The growing independence and autonomy of the judiciary*. The legislators of the Constitutional Council have reaffirmed the independence of judges, and extended the status of judges to members of the Court of Accounts, and to members of the various administrative courts and tribunals. The Constitutional Council has made it clear that neither the legislature nor the executive can censure the decisions of the courts, nor try to replace them in the exercise of their *compétences*. Successive presidents of the Republic have expressed their respect for the independence of the judiciary, and President Chirac even announced in 1997 the creation of an independent commission to re-examine the link between the *parquet* and the Justice Ministry, with a view to weakening or abolishing the umbilical cord. The Commission will also examine the presidential idea of making proposals for judicial appointments by the *Conseil Supérieur de la Magistrature* binding upon the government.

• *The increasing propensity fully to implement the law* by activist judges and by a judicial system under pressure from some politicians, the media and pressure groups. First, legal decisions (such as recently promulgated EU directives and national laws and decrees) are more assiduously transmuted into action. One of the sections of the Council of State has the task of tracking implementation performance, and the results are published in the annual report of the Council.

Second, legal redress is not only increasingly sought but is increasingly effective in punishing wrong-doers. In the past, the corrupt practices of politicians or businessmen were often covered up. Since the mid-1980s legal action has been taken against prominent politicians such as the mayors of Lyon, Grenoble, Cannes, Nice and Angoulême. By 1997, Prime Minister Juppé had been publicly rapped over the knuckles over a housing scandal in Paris, and the legal system was investigating Jean Tiberi, President Chirac's successor as Mayor of Paris. No less significantly, by the mid-1990s, a host of important French businessmen were in court for alleged personal or corporate corruption.

• *The increasing internalisation of judicial constraints by public officials*. French civil servants have always had to beware of ignoring the legal consequences of their acts: a condemnation by the Council of State or the Court of Accounts was always an unwelcome episode. However, officials could – and regularly did – ignore judicial constraints, either inventing ingenious means to circumvent them or recognising that legal authorities were often lenient, and penalties invariably followed several years after the offence. In any case, it was an anonymous state which was held responsible for making amends.

However, one of the recent trends in French legal practice is to hold politicians personally responsible for their acts: thus, prefects and mayors now face severe sentences (including prison) for neglect deemed to be criminal in impact. This personalisation of responsibility has had a sobering effect on public officialdom. No less important, is the impact of judicial review in rendering governments sensitive to the need to anticipate the reaction to any law of the Constitutional Council.

JURIDIFICATION: TOWARDS AN EXPLANATION

In trying to explain the growing juridification of French public policy in terms of quantity, it is relatively easy to identify the major factors – many of which may be found in other European countries, and some of which are peculiarly French. Yet, we must make a fundamental distinction between factors which are increasing the scope of law, and those which involve and enhance the role of the judiciary in that law. Furthermore, even if we focus only on the latter any satisfactory explanation must, in the first place, be sensitive to sectors: the juridification of competition policy has been the result of factors which bear little relationship to those for juvenile delinquents.

Moreover, the analyst must attempt to distinguish between the different types of juridification: the growing autonomy of the judiciary was driven by factors which differ sharply from those which provoked other forms such as the extension of soft-law generated by regulatory agencies.

Finally, a distinction must be made between the various types of law – constitutional, administrative, civil and criminal – since the increasing role of each was inspired by a different set of motives and different agents.

Judicial expansion is easily explicable. State regulation is probably on the increase despite – and possibly because of – privatisation, liberalisation and deregulation. Thus, deregulating the labour market requires a sustained legislative and legal effort. Moreover, as noted above, a changing political agenda – law and order, immigration, gender issues, consumerism and environmentalism – have forced the state to enter into new legislative territory.[4] The current omnipresence of law must also be seen as a response to the breakdown of traditional modes of social regulation – deference and trust – as well as the decreasing hold of regulatory institutions such as the family and the church. In short, the juridification of society is a reflection of its increasing weakness.

Explaining the increasing recourse to judges and judicial processes in that overall increase in legal activity is more difficult, since it involves several factors, each of which is complex. They may be listed as follows:

• *Europeanisation*: the full impact of European law is difficult to assess although, clearly, it has gradually penetrated domestic law. It is generally drafted in less specific terms than French law, thus providing judges a measure of interpretative freedom. Moreover, European law has socialised judges into the idea that parliamentary statutes can be overridden by a higher judicial authority, and the ECJ has provided pro-EU constituencies with new avenues of pressure by giving them a direct stake in the promulgation and implementation of EU law. Thus, individuals, firms or groups can now invoke European law in the national courts.

• *Ideological*: the slow breakdown of an ideological paradigm based on collective goods, the public interest and citizenship, and its replacement by one which emphasises private goods, individual rights and consumerism. Rights-based political cultures involve more questioning of authority and increased demands for legal arbitration. Individualism is coupled with anti-statism, and the latter is translated into a desire to withdraw the state from certain economic activities and from direct control of others: privatisation and arms-length regulation have replaced the traditional modes of state *dirigisme*. However, economic regulation has invariably meant a juridification of decision making.

• *Economic*, which has several dimensions. The dismantling of traditional *dirigisme* through privatisation and liberalisation and the creation of new modes of legally-based regulation: hence, telecommunications in France, in keeping with the situation in an increasing number of other European countries, is to be regulated not by the traditional methods of ministerial control but by a regulatory agency. Paradoxically, the withdrawal of the state in financial, industrial and labour markets has generated a massive need for indirect regulation of a quasi-legal sort.

Another economic factor which has been advanced as a cause of juridification is the stubbornly high long-term unemployment rate, seen as one of the major roots of social problems family breakdown and rising crime rates (all of which provoke legislative action of a remedial and criminalising character), and a source of political friction fed by xenophobia.

Immigration is seen as the cause of unemployment, and it is being slowly brought into the judicial domain with a view to regulation and the criminalisation of offenders. Hence, an economic problem becomes a social and political problem which is then transformed into a legal problem.

• *Cultural*: the increasing recognition that the traditional model of citizen integration through the homogenising pressures of education and parliamentary legislation may have to give way to a recognition of the growing diversity and multi-culturalism of French society. This situation is creating potentially explosive tensions in the one, indivisible and secular Republic: for instance, should young Muslim women be allowed to wear the veil – a symbol to them, of their cultural and religious identity, but which is, to others, an expression of their subjugation? Such a question is increasingly typical of a multi-cultural society: it provokes the clash of two concepts of liberty, involves a particular group and is particularly fraught. It becomes, therefore, expedient for an embarrassed government to transfer the problem to the courts.

• *Technological*: the pace of technological change in some areas has raised urgent practical and ethical issues that regulators have neither the will nor the time to process: copyright; the flow of pornography across national frontiers; the multiple problems raised by medical advances, biotechnology; artificial insemination.

• *Managerial*: the managerial ambitions of the more market-oriented modern state have several implications for juridification. Thus, the need to relieve the overloaded state of policy responsibilities has led to what has been described as the process of autonomisation – transferring state authority (of a politico-bureaucratic nature) to self-regulating agencies which control their own destiny, and which function by more informal, and bargained quasi-legal ('soft-law') processes.

A second feature of the new public management paradigm is 'customer empowerment' – the desire to create a public-choice style exchange between producers and consumers, an exchange in which consumer choice rather than bureaucratically-brokered or producer-driven production becomes the norm. The shift from the pursuit of collective political goals for citizens to the definition of rights for individuals or clients harbours an immense emerging potential for litigation.

A third aspect of new managerialism is the creation of administrative agencies with operational autonomy which are tied to the central state by contracts of a quasi-legal character. Contractual relations are also increasingly important in the emerging 'enabling state' – a state which is no longer directly responsible for service delivery, but which entrusts such delivery to other (often private) agents. The importance of contractual relations is particularly evident at local level (where most public services are delivered): increasingly, major local authorities in France are locked into contracts with the two major privately-owned public utility groups.

• *Political*: the deliberate attempt of the legislator to enhance the role and autonomy of the judiciary. This may be seen in several ways; in conferring upon judges decisions relating to the propriety of elections and party financing in legislating for increased legal aid; in President Giscard d'Estaing's opening up of the access to the Constitutional Council to 60 deputies and senators to redress the constitutional settlement of 1958; in the strengthened consultative role of the Council of State; in the government's judicialisation of procedures at local level and in the spheres of planning, environment and immigration; in President Chirac's creation of a commission to examine, among other things, means of loosening (and possibly abolishing) the hierarchical chain that binds part of the judiciary to the Justice Ministry.

Perhaps one of the most significant areas of juridification willed by the legislator concerns local government. The socialist government, as part of its decentralisation reforms of 1982, transformed the nature of local authority supervision, transferring responsibility from prefects (who exercised *a priori* political control) to magistrates, who were henceforth called upon, at the request of the prefect, to organise *a posteriori* legal control. Furthermore, the 1982 reforms and other reforms of the 1980s have had the effect of rendering public officials personally responsible for their acts – even for those carried out many years previously.

• *Democratic*: 'civil society is on the move' and is demanding greater consultation, participation and transparency. These pressures are both territorial and sectoral in character. The territorial pressure has been translated into growing demands for decentralisation and for greater independence *vis-à-vis* state authorities at local level by a loosening or even abolition of prefectoral supervision and control. This was achieved by the 1981 reforms introduced by the Mauroy government. However, as noted above, prefectoral *tutelle* of legal propriety has simply been handed over to local legal authorities.

At the sectoral level, many pressure groups, deprived of satisfaction at the political level, are using the courts as an alternative arena for expressing their grievances and seeking redress. In the case of the Council of State, pursuing a case is both cheap and remarkably simple. Some groups are seeking to establish rights, through public interest litigation or test case strategies. Others are intent on pursuing specific wrong-doing: in the corruption cases involving the mayors of Cannes, Angoulême and Grenoble, well-organised and determined citizen groups pressured the authorities into judicial activity. This has spread to other cities, and is becoming more effective because groups have acquired legal expertise, and are able to exploit the doctrine of 'legitimate expectations' (groups have the right to be consulted) and the erosion of the rule which insists that access to a court should be restricted to a party having a direct interest.

Finally, public opinion, as tested by successive opinion polls, is firmly behind the major judicial institutions and approves the activity of judges in pursuing miscreants, particularly party politicians.

• *A more attentive media*: the *Canard Enchaîné*, that ancient champion of publicising the legal laxity of politicians, industrialists and public officials, has now been joined by other newspapers (notably *Le Monde* and *Libération*) in the encouragement of investigative journalism. With liberalisation, the habit is spreading to radio and television.

• *The growing collective demand for autonomy and independence by the judges*. Recent reports of the *Conseil Supérieur de la Magistrature* have been openly critical about the appointments policy of the government. During the 1997 election campaign over 100 senior magistrates of all political persuasions signed a petition to the President of the Republic in favour of greater autonomy.

• *Internal organisational*: new legal or quasi-legal institutions (the ECJ, the Constitutional Council, independent administrative agencies, regulatory bodies) are, at least in part, driven by a dynamic of expansion, and, together with existing judicial bodies, wish both to broaden and to deepen their jurisdictional control. Judicial expansionism can result from both symbiotic relationships and competition between courts. Thus, it has been argued that the ECJ 'empowered' national courts by providing them with a new capacity for judicial review, and that competition between lower and higher and between the civil and administrative supreme courts helped to entrench the power and legitimacy of the ECJ.[5] Often the role of an individual (such as Guy

Braibant, an immensely influential member of the Council of State, Badinter, a particularly dynamic president of the Constitutional Council who left 'a potent jurisprudential legacy', and Adolph Touffait, a fervent pro-European member of the Court of Cassation) or of a small group or clan can be critical.

• *The activity of individual judges*, particularly the investigating magistrates who have often shown great courage in the pursuit of wrong-doing, by resisting political pressures, by-passing their own hierarchy and appealing directly to public opinion. The role of the *petits juges* has sometimes been crucial and is best illustrated by the case of Eric de Montgolfier, a public prosecuting magistrate of Valenciennes, who successfully brought ex-minister Bernard Tapie to justice in a celebrated football bribery case. Indeed, it may be argued that the wave of corruption that has swept through political and business circles has been a prime factor in triggering and legitimising demands for judicial activity, activism and autonomy, and has resulted in the increased juridification of the financial and industrial sectors, both public and private, as well as of the financing of political parties (notably by the laws of 11 March 1988 and 15 January 1990).

From the mid-1980s, political corruption became one of the favourite themes of the French press and of the extreme right. This is scarcely surprising, given the scale and the notoriety of the people involved. Corruption is sometimes personal, sometimes on behalf of a political party. The list of incriminated politicians include Bernard Tapie, a flamboyant businessman and *mitterrandiste* deputy whose corrupt practices led him to a prison sentence. The list also includes Henri Emmanuelli (Treasurer of the Socialist Party and ex-President of the National Assembly); Michel Noir (the Mayor of Lyons and former RPR Trade Minister); Gérard Longuet (the Industry Minister who was forced to resign in 1994; and then leader of the Republican Party), Michel Gillibert (ex-Minister for Handicapped People), Jean-Michel Boucheron (Mayor of Angoulême and ex-socialist minister, who fled to Argentina); Jacques Médecin (Mayor of Nice, and former minister who had to be extradited from Uruguay to face allegations of tax fraud and misappropriation of town funds); and Jean Bousquet (ex-Mayor of Nîmes who was sent to prison in December 1996 for channelling part of the municipal budget into the maintenance of his private chateau).

And to this impressive list can be added the names of the mayors of Grenoble (Alain Carignon, who was also a leading light in the RPR), of Toulon (Maurice Arreckx, who was also the president of the departmental council of the Var), and of Cannes (Michel Mouillot, implicated in a case involving planning permission for the town's casino).

Even the Communist Party has not been spared: in 1996, Georges Marchais and Robert Hue (past and present general secretaries of the party) were placed under formal investigation as part of the inquiry into the relations between a consultancy firm, the Sicopar (a subsidiary of Gifco which was close to the party) and the *Compagnie Générale des Eaux*, the major public utility group which, between 1984 and 1994, had siphoned some 15 million francs into the coffers of Sicopar. The most politically-damaging corruption affairs of the 1980s (the *Carrefour du Développement*, and Urba) involved the ruling Socialist Party.

However, by the mid-1990s, the spotlight had turned on the right, and more especially on the RPR in the Paris region: allegations have involved salaries for non-existent work (Xavière Tiberi, wife of the Mayor of Paris, was said to have been paid 200,000 francs for a 36-page report), kickbacks by businessmen in exchange for public-sector works contracts and the misuse of public money for personal consumption. By 1996, even the Paris Town Hall, President Chirac's power base, had attracted the attention of investigating magistrates. Prime Minister Juppé, previously head of the city's finances, and Jean Tiberi, Chirac's successor as Mayor of Paris, were both found to be using municipal housing stock to favour their families. Tiberi was also accused of the embezzlement of funds from the city's welfare housing budget. Funds, obtained through various corrupt means, were allegedly handed over to Louis-Yvonne Casetta, fund-raiser for the RPR, who was appropriately nicknamed 'la Cassette' (the cash box). Salaries for fictional work, illegal party funding – either directly or through politically sympathetic consultancy firms – inflated personal expense accounts and the public financing of private goods – such were the allegations that were to be levelled at scores of politicians in Paris and its region.

The revelation of widespread corruption among politicians naturally led to investigations into corrupt business practices. The scale of corruption aroused demands for retribution. From the late 1980s an anti-corruption clampdown was orchestrated by the judiciary, and a growing list of captains of industry were placed under formal investigation: by early 1997, the bosses of almost a quarter of the leading French companies were being formally investigated for one infringement or another. The public were treated to a parade of the business misdemeanours of the head of Elf-Aquitaine, accused of using the company's credit card to buy some 500,000 francs worth of personal items for himself and his wife and spending nearly 4 million francs on his private residence; Martin Bouygues, head of the country's biggest construction group, and Patrick Le Lay, head of TF1 (the commercial television station owned by Bouygues), whose use of corporate funds allegedly included the use of false invoices and the funnelling of money, through Swiss bank accounts, to Pierre Botton, son-in-law of Michel Noir, the ex-Mayor of Lyons; the chairmen of Matra-Hachette (Jean-Luc Lagardère who was a personal friend of President Chirac), of Saint-Gobain, and of Alcatel-Alsthom (Pierre Suard who was charged with using company funds to pay for £400,000 of building work in his Paris mansion and his country estate) – pillars of the industrial establishment.

Fears that the investigative zeal of magistrates might be getting out of hand may have been responsible for the extraordinary decision of the Court of Cassation, on 6 February 1997, which overturned a previous ruling of 1992, and restricted the area in which firms could be taken to court. The Court ruled that bribes did not constitute a misuse of corporate funds if the company received something in return. Not unnaturally, the decision of the Court was denounced as being politically motivated. The causes of corruption are multiple. Yet whatever the cause, there is no doubt that it gave rise to public demands for judicial retribution, since there was a widespread suspicion that political or administrative mechanisms were either inadequate or paralysed by the politicians who closed ranks to protect themselves: since each party had a file on the others, none was likely to break ranks.

Juridification must, therefore, be explained by numerous factors, discrete yet interconnected, running in parallel yet uncoupled, some direct, purposive, top-down, others indirect, unwitting and bottom-up. It must be seen both as a reflection of changing state-market society relations and of attempts to reshape the functions of the state as well as an independent phenomenon, having both wider European and specifically French characteristics. It is a multi-pronged process, combining imposition (the role of the ECJ), political will, spill-over (from new public management and new modes of regulation), internal dynamics of an individual and collective nature and street-level pressure.

CONCLUSION: FROM THE *ÉTAT IMPÉRIAL* TO THE *ÉTAT DE DROIT*?

One of the major developments of French politics has been the increasing juridification of public policy. The political role of judges has enjoyed enhanced visibility, since courts have been drawn into highly contentious and politicised issues, ranging from the trials of René Bousquet, Jean Leguay and Maurice Papon, ex-prefects accused of collaborating with the

Germans during the Vichy regime, and of Paul Touvier (a zealous collaborator of the Gestapo at Lyon during the Second World War), to the high profile anti-corruption crusades of certain judges. Judges have been also called upon to make highly politicised decisions in the fields of race relations, asylum policy, controversial environmental projects, police powers, medical problems of an ethical nature, nationalisation, privatisation. Policy areas such as competition policy which were hitherto 'judge-free zones' have been brought within the jurisdiction of the courts or of regulatory bodies exercising quasi-judicial powers. There is more law, and the courts are playing a greater role in creating, interpreting and enforcing it. Decision-making procedures are becoming more juridified, and judges are becoming bolder in asserting their autonomy and independence.

As elsewhere in Europe, the impact of juridification on policy making is clear.[6] It has five essential effects: *a cancelling effect* – the striking down of specific decisions by private or public actors; *a corrective effect* – obliging administrations to review or reverse the policy or procedure underlying the decision which has been annulled; *a restrictive effect* – hampering future policy development, by issuing guidelines explicitly or implicitly – in deciding a particular case; *an inhibitive effect* – compelling public authorities, when taking decisions or developing new policies, to self-restraint in apprehension of judicial challenge (thus, the Chirac government's open confession that certain public service monopolies would escape privatisation because of the probable reaction of the Constitutional Council); *a pedagogical and general steering effect* by articulating the moral and ideological parameters of public and private action: bounding the preferences of actors, and shaping the arenas for the expression of those preferences by enunciating a set of general principles embedded in ethical conventions, bills of rights and the Constitution.

Actors, processes and outcomes are, therefore, affected by the various processes of juridification. The pillars of the Jacobin temple, of the 'imperial state' have been shaken by these processes. And in five essential ways: the acceptance of the supremacy of European law; the general support for 'government by constitution' and of the judicial review of political action which runs counter to the concepts of popular executive or parliamentary sovereignty; the growing role of courts as policy makers; the spread of diverse sources of 'soft law'; the criminalisation of public officials for negligence. But has the strengthening of the *État légal* involved the creation of an *État de Droit*, of a state in which all the actors, including the political elite, respect and uphold the accepted normative order, the hierarchy of laws and the independence and autonomy of the judiciary?

There are several factors which suggest a prudent reply to the question. In the first place, there are rules which restrict the power of the courts. Thus, the Council of State has few effective ways of enforcing its decisions, and, despite some tightening up, administrative wrong-doers can be notoriously slow in taking remedial action. Moreover, the Council can annul an abuse but act only *ex post facto* – a limitation which, combined with delay, may cause real hardship (the case with many asylum seekers or with protesters against politically-motivated expulsions).

It should be recalled, too, that the advice of the Council of State is not binding on the government (which can and has ignored it), that the Council has no right to examine any amendments to bills on which it has already given its advice, and that it does not scrutinise any private members bills. In the case of the Constitutional Council, it should be emphasised that it tends to look only at those parts of the law which have been specifically contested, that its procedures are less than transparent, and that it exercises a preventative veto power. It has no *post facto* reparative function: a law once promulgated cannot be challenged before the Council, despite its reservations.

The Council has to react to a law before promulgation rather than to the defects of a law which may emerge only in its implementation. Badinter, when President of the Constitutional Council in 1989, proposed a relaxation of the rigid rule prohibiting *a posteriori* control, and won the backing of the prime minister and President Mitterrand. However, the Senate blocked the proposal.

It should also be pointed out that a determined government, with a suitably big majority in parliament, can get round an unfavourable Council judgment by pushing through a constitutional amendment. This has occurred on only one occasion, when, on 29 November 1993, a ruling of the Council (on an immigration law) was overturned by a constitutional amendment). Finally, the Constitutional Council will not give a ruling in the case of legislation passed by way of referendum, and since the constitutional amendment of 31 July 1995, the president can, at least in theory, obviate the Council's constraints by submitting major matters, other than constitutional and institutional, to the voters by way of referendum.

The second factor which limits the power of the courts lies in the practices of some politicians and administrators. Thus, the consultative role of the Council of State is weakened by the government's tendency to submit bills only very late in the parliamentary cycle, thus giving the Council very little time to scrutinise them. The vice-president of the body has frequently complained of this situation, and particularly when a highly complex bill is concerned. Another practice which limits the role of the judges may be seen at local level: the so-called *tutelle des juges* has been singularly limited by the activities of the prefects who continue to prefer pre-litigation negotiation to judicial referral. In only very rare circumstances will a prefect refer an abuse to the local administrative courts: generally, fewer than 0.5 per cent of the acts of local authorities end up in court, and many cases are abandoned before the court reaches a decision.

The continued politicisation of justice constitutes a third restriction of the autonomous power of the judiciary. All members of the Constitutional Council are political appointments: and the political balance within the Council has shifted with the vicissitudes of electoral politics (see Table 1), although the Council's appointment and the electoral cycle are out of tilt, with the result that a left-wing government may be confronted with a right-wing Council, and vice versa.

TABLE 1
POLITICAL COMPOSITION OF THE CONSTITUTIONAL COUNCIL, 1981–99

Date	Left	Right		Date	Left	Right
1981	0	9		1989	5	4
1983	2	7		1992	6	3
1986	4	5		1993	6	3
1987	3	6		1995	5	4
1988	3	6		1999	4	5

Several prominent politicians have been chosen (although since January 1995 it is no longer possible to be a member of the Council and an elected official), and a political sympathiser of the ruling majority party coalition is always placed at the head of the body: Léon Noël (Gaullist deputy) in 1959; Gaston Palewski (Gaullist deputy and minister) in 1965; Roger Frey (Gaullist deputy and senator) in 1974; Daniel Mayer (President of the League for the Rights of Man and a life-time socialist sympathiser) in 1983; Robert Badinter (socialist Minister of Justice from 1981 to 1986) in 1986; Roland Dumas (Mitterrand's Foreign Minister) in 1995.

Formally, the President of the Republic remains the guarantor of the independence of the judiciary and presides over the *Conseil Supérieur de la Magistrature*. Formally, too, an important part of the magistrature remains hierarchically attached to the Minister of Justice (who is also Vice-President of the *Conseil Supérieur de la Magistrature*) and prosecuting judges can be moved at will by the Minister. Finally, with respect to the Council of State, the government has the right to appoint all the presidents of the working sections, one third of the *conseillers d'État* and one quarter of the lower-ranked *maîtres des requêtes*. Moreover, ministers can participate in the discussions of the general assembly of the Council of State and may vote on matters within their competence. And, the government can even change the attributions of the Council, although this may be more difficult in the future.

Recent governments have used their formal powers to try to bury or slow down politically embarrassing cases, by bringing pressure on recalcitrant judges – the list of such cases is depressingly long, and involves both socialist and right-wing administrations. Or, governments attempt to place political sympathisers into key judicial posts: the Elysée and Matignon keep a close eye on all important judicial appointments – and not only to the Constitutional Council and the Council of State (between 1972 and 1996 over half the outside appointments to the Council were ex-politicians), but also to the civil courts – particularly in Paris. Several early appointments to the Council of State made by Mitterrand provoked a mixture of incredulity and hilarity, while some of Chirac's nominations in Paris have been met with scandalised consternation: in the untranslatable pun of one critic, '*l'État de Droit tourne au droit de l'État*'.

The problem of a politicised justice is compounded by the activities of many judges. Too many members of the Council of State pursue political careers, openly flout their partisan convictions, or reveal them by taking up posts in the private offices of ministers. On quitting their political or quasi-political function they invariably take up their posts again in the Council. Thus, a change in the political complexion of the government will alter the political balance of the Council. The politicisation of the civil judiciary takes a different form: many magistrates belong to a professional trades union – the *Syndicat de la Magistrature* (left), the *Union syndicale des Magistrats* (moderate right-wing) and the *Association professionnelle des Magistrats* (more muscular right). It is not difficult, therefore, when appointing to key judicial posts, for governments to identify political friends.

The restrictions on the powers of the judiciary, the practices of some officials intent on circumventing (if not breaking) the law, and the continuing politicisation of justice are all manifestations of a much profounder phenomenon, and which calls into question claims about the emergence in France of an *État de Droit*. This phenomenon is the lingering cultural aversion to the rule of law which affects many groups – from ordinary citizens who evade and avoid taxation and who attempt politically to negotiate themselves out of threatened legal proceedings to militant groups which openly flaunt their illegal tactics (and are rarely brought to court for having done so) and to certain state officials who do not disguise their contempt for the 'legal pedantry' of the courts.

The press may denounce illegalities but shows its disrespect for the law by naming 'guilty' people long before they are tried, thus violating the principle of the presumption of innocence. Even some magistrates, by their demagogic attitudes and practice of leaking confidential documents about *sub judice* cases to the media, are guilty of violating the rule of law.

But the most guilty are to be found among the politicians who bay in protest against unfavourable court decisions (the left-wing's hostile reaction to the Constitutional Council's striking down of clauses of the Nationalisation Law of 1981, and the right's outrage at the Council's ruling on the 1993 immigration laws bordered on the hysterical). In the 1970s several parliamentary attempts were made to curb the power of the courts, and especially that of the ECJ and the Constitutional Council, and as late as 1986, the Chirac government's Justice Minister even proposed the creation of a Charter of Rights to be codified by Parliament to stem the Council's 'vast discretionary power'.

Politicians constantly interfere in appointments and in the processes of justice, and close ranks when justifiable legal action is proposed (the case of the *Carrefour du Développement* scandal), and who hinder legal investigations by invoking *secret défense*, for the supposed sake of national security. Politicians have even been known to refuse police collaboration for judges pursuing their investigation.

Far too many French politicians have an attitude towards the law which is at best one of indifference and at worst one of contempt. The telephone tapping affair, which surfaced in 1993, revealed some of the workings of the Mitterrand presidency, having set up an anti-terrorist cell between 1982 and 1986 which spent many more hours keeping the president's private life from prying eyes and ears than in tracing terrorists. The unit illegally tapped the telephones of some 200 people, including judges, politicians, lawyers and journalists. The *Affaire Péchiney* of 1988–89 revealed the links between people close to President Mitterrand and insider dealing, while the 1985 *Rainbow Warrior* Affair – in which Greenpeace's vessel, which was tracking French nuclear testing activity in the Pacific, was sunk illegally by two French agents in another country's waters – caused much more stir abroad than in French political circles. Perhaps more serious is the tolerance shown towards the activities of the *Renseignements généraux* (the police special branch) which is effectively exempt from normal judicial restraints such as obtaining warrants and which has compiled secret files on prominent politicians, businessmen, journalists, trade union officials and even other police units.

Of course, no democracy can be entirely ruled by judges, since there are both practical and philosophical problems – even if judges were wholly independent and value-free (which is rarely the case). Problems are numerous, and include, first, the capacity of the courts which have reached the point of 'asphyxiation' (President Chirac's admission). A serious criminal case now takes on average 39 months to go through the courts, and some cases may take up to five years. The rate of preventative detention in France is one of the largest in Europe: of the 55,000 inmates of French jails, nearly 40 per cent are on remand awaiting trial and the average time spent on remand is eight months.

Second, courts often impose unrealistic standards, involving heavy financial costs on the state, and provoking both avoidance and evasion.

Third, implementation of court decisions is often difficult to monitor.

The fourth practical problem lies in the intermittent and sometimes erratic regulation exercised by the courts: it is essentially reactive and has been likened to 'guerrilla warfare'.

Fifth, judicial processes are generally time-consuming for officials and upset their normal timetables, thus preventing long-term planning.

The sixth practical objection to a 'government by judges' relates to the nature of judicial policy making, since it involves individual decisions whose wider ramifications for other sectors or for the public interest are often ignored or misunderstood. Often, too, an individual legal decision may have the effect of unpicking a complex political bargain that had required time-consuming trade-offs.

Problem number seven: judicial policy making introduces an element of further unpredictability into public policy making, because different types of court may be (and have been) in disagreement, and the same court may be inconsistent (the Constitutional Council, the Council of State and the Court of Cassation have all changed their rulings on important topics over time).

The eighth problem concerns the legitimacy of the courts: the greater the scope of their competence the greater is the danger of their being dragged into political controversies which may undermine the legitimacy of the entire judicial system. This problem is aggravated by the biases of the legal system which, however cheap and simple, favour the rich, educated and informed.

Linked to this is the ninth problem: the greater the sphere of legal control the greater are the incentives for avoidance and evasion (which is already a sport much practised by certain professions and public officials). Finally, there is the crucial problem of accountability in a democratic polity. How can citizens hold independent and irremovable judges accountable?

All democratic polities are locked into the management of a set of trade-offs between market forces, social regulation and mobilisation, efficient processes of government, and judicial review. The construction of an *État de Droit* recognises this requirement. It implies a disaggregation of the various elements of the juridification process, recognising that there is a balance to be struck between them, and identifying those healthy elements that need strengthening. It takes as a basic premise that litigation has an essential role in public policy, but can never serve as its sole basis.

One does not have to subscribe to a conception of the general will or entertain inflated expectations of parliamentary sovereignty to argue that adversarial relations over particular problems may lead to incoherence and to losing sight of the wider public interest. There is no substitute for general laws producing authoritative allocation of goods, and based on electoral assent and political accountability.

NOTES

1. Jeremy Jennings, 'From 'Imperial State' to 'l'État de Droit': Benjamin Constant, Blandine Kriegel and the reform of the French Constitution', *Political Studies* 44 (1996) pp.488–504.
2. Laurent Cohen-Tanugi, *Le Droit sans l'État*, 3rd ed. (Paris, PUF 1992).
3. Alec Stone, *The Birth of Judicial Politics in France: The Constitutional Council in Comparative Perspective* (Oxford UP 1992); and ibid., 'Where Judicial Politics are Legislative Politics: The French Constitutional Council', *West European Politics* 15/3 (July 1992) pp.29–49.
4. Antoine Garapon and Denis Salas, *La République penalisée* (Paris, Hachette 1996).
5. Mary Volcansek, *Judicial Politics in Europe: An Impact Analysis* (NY: Peter Lang 1986); Karen J. Alter, 'The European Court's Political Power', *West European Politics* 19/3 (July 1996) pp.458–87.
6. Simon James, 'The Political and Administrative Consequences of Judicial Review', *Public Administration* 74 (1996) pp.614–37.

The Changing Role of French Local Government

EMMANUEL NÉGRIER

Analysing French local government entails an examination of both the system itself, and in particular its transformation following the decentralisation reforms of the early 1980s, as well as the new concepts and analytical tools which have been developed to understand the basic aspects of the system. In fact, in France the concept of 'local government' has long been criticised by both politicians and academics. On the one hand, it was said to be inimical to the *Jacobin* tradition which was mistrustful of local authorities. On the other, until the period of decentralisation at least, it would have exaggerated the position of local authorities, given the strength of the central state. Prior to this period, the autonomy of the local area, which was one of the basic elements of the concept of *local government*, was too limited either to allow a real role for sub-central actors or to generate truly local policies.[1]

However, even prior to this period, the idea that the central state was able simply to control local authorites was questioned.[2] Parallel to the formal system of centralisation, it was argued that there was a system of negotiation between the state and locally-elected figures (*notables*). All told, French political scientists preferred the notion of a *local politico-administrative system* to the concept of 'local government'.[3] This term highlighted the sociological aspects of the relationship between the centre and periphery, as well as the notion that rules, their implementation and the policies which affected the sub-central level were subject to a ongoing process of negotiation. Here, elected politicians (who in theory were weak) and bureaucrats (or representatives of the state at the local level, who in theory were strong) rather than operating in separate domains were, in fact, bound together by a system of strategic interdependence. The state, through its agents and in particular the prefect, occupied a central place in the social and political domain and had the key instruments of political action at its disposal. However, it had to negotiate the 'territorial feasibility' of its policies with elected representatives who, although lacking legal and economic resources, were still key to the state's policies being accepted and who were also in a position to amend those policies.

This local politico-administrative system was based on a simple political exchange: it guaranteed the state the capacity to maintain and extend the social and political consensus; it permitted elected representatives to obtain a greater share of resources from the state as well as both the legitimacy and respect of the local population. In this system, a good elected representative was one who could provide citizens with easy access to the administration and an excellent representative was one who managed to enlarge and diversify the avenues of local access to the administration. The system allowed elected representatives to have an influence and it also allowed internal problems of communication between state administrative services to be resolved. Indeed, administrators frequently contacted elected officials so as to circumvent internal blockages within the state. This combination of both a hierarchy of problems and the informal resolution of bureaucratic blockages was named 'cross-regulation'.[4]

Several changes were brought about by the decentralisation reforms of the early 1980s. These changes concerned both the substance of local government and the concepts which were used to study it. The reforms helped to create new centres of power by transferring resources in at least six areas to democratically elected local authorities: local authorities now have powers in the areas of urban planning, education, housing, social policies, health and research. The aim of the reforms was simultaneously to ensure a more effective management of public problems by bringing decision making closer to the point of implementation, and to democratise the management process. In terms of the former, powers were shifted *en bloc* with a view to preventing the reconstitution of hierarchical dependencies between different level authorities (communes, departments, regions).

Communes benefited from transfers in the fields of town planning, housing, education and social assistance.

Departmental, or general, councils were responsible for transport, secondary school and social action.

Regional councils were given the responsibility for high schools, vocational training and regional planning. The state, which previously had *a priori* review power over the decisions of the territorial authorities (*la tutelle*), now only enjoys *a posteriori* legal control.

However, this distribution of powers also produced some unexpected results. Most notably, it mobilised local authorities in areas other than those explicitly outlined by the law. In terms of democratisation, the effects of the decentralisation reforms were rather uneven, since the effects of some of the reforms (the extension of direct and universal suffrage at the regional level and the introduction of proportional representation in local and regional elections) were mitigated by a very limited level of participation in sub-central politics.

Over and above the limits of the decentralisation reforms and contradictions they generated, the study of local government was reconceptualised. The French notion of 'cross regulation' was unable to account for the new realities of local power and new theories of public action emerged which were reminiscent of the concepts used to study local government in other European countries.

Against this background, this essay will consider both the transformation of French local government and the ways in which it is studied. It will focus, first, on the emergence of a plurality of levels of local government and, then, on the political dimension of territorial public action. Some concluding remarks will be made concerning the concepts now used to study French local government.

LEVELS OF FRENCH LOCAL GOVERNMENT

There are three levels of French local government, defined as all infra-national institutions (state decentralised administration and territorial authorities). There are 36,763 communes, 100 departments (including 4 overseas departments) and 26 regions (including 21 in mainland France, plus Corsica and four overseas regions). The decentralisation reforms did not change the highly fragmented system of communes. There are still 4,082 communes with fewer than 100 inhabitants, compared with 36 communes with more than 100,000 inhabitants and only 5 with more than 300,000 inhabitants.

There are also great contrasts at the regional level too. Even if we exclude the Ile-de-France region around Paris, the Rhône-Alpes region, which comprises eight departments, contains more than 5,000,000 inhabitants and the Provence-Alpes-Côte d'Azur region, comprising six departments, has more than 4,000,000 inhabitants. However, the Limousin region (three departments) contains only 722,000 people, while the Auvergne (four departments) totals 1,321,000 people. This demographic heterogeneity is important both in terms of the social context within which local authorities operate and the attempts which have been made to rationalise the organisation of territorial public action (see below).

The main features of the new system of local government are the emergence of local authorities as centres of power and the pluralisation of the levels of government. These developments are a function of the increasing budgetary importance of local authorities, the extension of their legal powers and their new-found political resources. They are also related to the changing relationship between the different levels of sub-central government, of which the implementation of the European structural funds provides a good example.

New Dynamics in Old Clothes

The decentralisation reforms were implemented without changing the pre-existing structure of local authorities. The three levels of elected local government continue to coexist and represent one of the densest networks of elected representatives and administrators in the world. In principle the powers of the various levels are clearly defined. In practice, though, they overlap. For example, in the field of education communes are responsibile for primary schools, departments for secondary schools and regions for high schools. And yet, these powers cannot can be exercised independently, which results in ongoing problems of policy co-ordination.

In the same way, social welfare, which was largely entrusted to general councils, and which is managed by the state and the departments *in tandem*, cannot ignore the fact that communes were, and remain, one of the key actors in this area and, moreover, that they are the ones most directly affected by social problems.

As a result of this situation, the *de jure* distribution of power is often amended by the *de facto* pressures which the different levels of local government face. In short, there is a difference between institutional powers and the dynamics of the political process at the sub-central level.[5] For example, although in terms of formal responsibilities regions were most directly concerned with the issue of economic development, all three levels of local government have competed with each other to invent their own policies and policy instruments.[6] Policy co-ordination between the various levels is, therefore, absent. On the contrary, there is competition and policy overlap.[7]

The same is true in the domain of cultural policy.[8] Here, the powers of local authorities are not clearly set out in law. Consequently, communes, departments and regions have again competed with each other for state subsidies. So, the dynamics of the decentralisation reforms were not confined by legal boundaries, but, quite the opposite, resulted in competition in policy areas which were only in part framed by the law. Indeed, this situation applies not just to the areas mentioned above, but also to environmental policy,[9] telecommunications policy[10] and public health.[11]

In this way, even if it was founded on a pre-existing territorial network, the extension of the powers of local authorities considerably amended the landscape of local government. These changes can be further illustrated in three ways.

The Quantitative Rise of the Local Government

The first change concerns the considerable increase in local authority expenditure (see Table 1), the percentage of this expenditure which is spent on investment (see Table 2) and the growth in the number of the local authority employees (see Table 3).

As indicated in Table 1, the increase in the level of public expenditure at the local level remains very strong. Indeed, the rate of rise is stronger at this level than at the level of the state generally. It might also be noted that regions have the highest rate of growth, which corresponds to the fact that the first set of regional elections only took place in 1986 and, thus, that regional councils only emerged as fully fledged political actors after this time. In this context, it should also be noted that regions still account for only 10 per cent of the overall level of expenditure at the local level, compared with the 30 per cent for departments and 60 per cent for communes.

TABLE 1
THE EVOLUTION OF PUBLIC EXPENDITURE, 1986–96 (IN BILLION FRANCS)

	1988	1990	1993	1996
State	1,153.6	1,281.9	1,502.8	1,642.0
Communes	317.9	353.2	412.7	441.7
Departments	153.6	173.6	207.3	228.2
Regions	34.8	47.6	62.6	73.8

Source: The author, based on Ministère de l'Intérieur, Direction Générale des Collectivités Locales, *Les collectivités locales en chiffres* (Paris: La Documentation Française 1998).

These general financial data must be complemented by another indicator: the respective share of expenditure spent on administration, on the one hand, and investment, on the other. Table 2 clearly illustrates the extent to which the different levels of government are able to act autonomously and to develop their own initiatives – the greater the share of investment expenditure in the total, the greater the capacity of local government to act in these ways.

From these figures it is also clear that, although regions are the weakest level of local government, they are, nevertheless, the most autonomous.

They are scarcely constrained by so-called 'obligatory' expenditure. Indeed, in contrast to both departments, to which the transfer of powers from the state was very great but more in terms of specified responsibilities, and communes, which are confronted by rather rigid and fixed expenditure constraints (in particular the cost of municipal employees), regions have very few predetermined budgetary responsibilities. That said, the most recent tendency is towards an increase in administrative expenditure at the regional level, through the transfer of powers relating to vocational training.

TABLE 2
SHARE OF INVESTMENT/ADMINISTRATION EXPENDITURE, 1996
(IN BILLION FRANCS)

	State	Regions	Depart-ments	Communes
Total	1,642.0	73.8	228.2	441.7
Administration	1,455.5	30.1	148.6	306.1
Investment	186.5	43.7	79.6	135.7
Investment (% of total)	11.35	59.21	34.88	30.72

Source: as Table 1.

The increasing importance of local government can also be measured by the number of local authority employees. Table 3 shows that the number of local authority employees expressed as a percentage of the total number of public-sector employees has increased considerably. At the same time, local authorities have given contracts to a large number of professional people which has strengthened their appraisal and management capacity. Even if representatives of the most senior category of public employees (Category A) are more present in the state public service than in local authorities (43 per cent compared with 8.6 per cent), the difference between the respective sizes of the public service at the two levels has been considerably reduced.

TABLE 3
STATE AND LOCAL EMPLOYEES, 1969–96 (TOTAL IN THOUSANDS AND
AS A PERCENTAGE OF THE TOTAL)

	1969	1976	1983	1989	1994	1995	1996
State	2,067	2,560	2,813	2,844	2,200	2,202	2,214
Local	618	859	1,103	1,211	1,407	1,428	1,447
Local (% of total)	20.4	21.7	23.6	24.9	31.7	32.0	32.1

Source: as Table 1.

Centre and Periphery: Towards New Strategic Interdependencies

The second change concerns the nature of centre-periphery relations. Previously, the local politico-administrative system was centred on the state. Access to the state was the sign that elected representatives were important. The policy process usually entailed negotiation between state and locally elected representatives resulting in state-defined laws being amended to suit sub-central realities. This model was radically transformed and for two reasons.

The first reason concerns the pluralisation of local systems of public action and the emergence of institutions with strong executive powers at each level of local government. Paradoxically, decentralisation, which was supposed to end the centralist uniformity of *Jacobin* France, actually led to a presidentialisation of local politics along the lines of the political system of the Fifth Republic itself. This reform has opened up the local political game on account of the rise of regional, municipal and departmental technostructures.

In this new system, the state no longer has the same capacity to regulate local policies as before. Even if prefects now play an increased role in co-ordinating the territorial services of the state (at the departmental and regional level), the extent to which they, and they alone, represent the state, namely the general interest, at the local level has been reduced as has their ability to appraise the problems of public action. Thus, their regulatory capacity, both socially and politically, has diminished, while the capacity of local authorities has increased accordingly.[12]

This opening up of the local political game affects not only the number of actors involved, but also the nature of the problems that local authorities, local interests and the state have to address. The period prior to the decentralisation reforms was one of growth during which time the physical infrastructure of the local area was greatly developed. This development was largely dependent upon vertically organised professions (such as the Ponts-et-Chaussées *corps*, for example, in the case of road-building), which, in turn, was dependent upon a centralised system of administration. By contrast, the decentralisation reforms coincided with a period of economic crisis and structural unemployment.[13] As such, the same type of policy expertise is no longer appropriate and there is a greater degree of uncertainty in the decision-making process.

In short, it is not just the problems themselves which have been called into question but the definition of those problems. This is what Patrice Duran and Jean-Claude Thoenig call the 'lack of problem structuration'.[14]

Policy problems become increasingly transversal (the 'politique de la ville', for example), and the identification of solutions rests on an increasingly complex process of negotiation in which several categories of actors (state experts, local councillors, territorial administrators, private interests and so forth) can legitimately claim an interest.

Thus, most of the policies which are now implemented are more procedural – meaning that policy aims are very general and that policy content is defined by a collective decision-making process which takes place at the local level[15] – rather than substantial – meaning policies whose definition and aims are *a priori* specified.

In this new configuration of actors and problems, the role of the central state as the institution (single or dominant) which defines the general interest is no longer sustainable. The state's resources (legal, regulatory, and so on) are no longer sufficient to provide it with the capacity to influence the decision-making processes, nor can the state decide which of the many local actors are legitimate and must, therefore, be dealt with. It is, thus, through the interactions of a multiplicity of actors that the definition and the implementation of the general interest at the local level is worked out and *a posteriori*.

A Co-operative and Contractual Government?

The multipolar reality of French local government can also be seen in two relatively recent phenomena: contractualisation and intercommunal co-operation.

Contractualisation is a direct consequence of the process of decentralisation, even if in fact the practice dates back to the 1970s. These public contracts, which do not have the same legal force as private ones, are the expression of a need to maintain local government actors within identifiable limits. From the state's point of view, they consist of the attempt to prevent the problems of fragmentation that might occur if local authorities were allowed to act freely. There are various types of contract, including the State-Region Planning Contracts, the *Contrats de Ville*, the Cultural Development Conventions[16] and the European Union Structural Funds. These are good indicators of the new power relationships between centre and periphery because, over and above the legal fiction that the parties to the contract have equal status, it is possible to analyse the effect of the different issues at stake and the dominant position of certain actors. Research in this area has gone in two principal directions.

The first highlights the continuing influence of the state during the negotiation of these contracts. As a result of the sheer number of contracts, the purpose of the negotiations and the end result of the process, some people argue that the nature of contractualisation has enabled the state to maintain a dominant role in system, while at the same time allowing it to hide behind a formal process of consensus building. Evidence for this argument has been found in the area of cultural policy, which officially remains only partially decentralised but which local authorities have regarded as a strategic category of public intervention.[17] This argument is also present in field work about State-Region Planning Contracts: the state can determine up to about 60 per cent of what it wishes to impose on its partners, thus confirming the unequal power relationship while benefiting actors at the central level.[18]

By contrast, the second highlights the opening up of new spaces of negotiation and the differences between the contexts in which negotiations take place. In short, policies vary from one area to another. This is the key finding in field work about both the decentralisation of contemporary art[19] and the implementation of the European Structural Funds at the regional level.[20] The development of specific regimes as a function, in particular, of the political influence of local representatives has been criticised because it calls into question the abstract but, nevertheless, politically sensitive principle of equality of access to public resources: the negotiation of the general interest on a local and contractual basis results in the legitimisation of specific interests, even those expressed by public bodies.[21]

Among the new forms of contracts, the development of intercommunal co-operation holds a particular place. In France, of course, the large number of communes is a historical characteristic which has resisted all attempts at reform. However, decentralisation and the development of local government has raised the issue again. On the one hand, despite the principle of decentralisation (the rejection of any form of hierarchical supervision of one local level over another), small communes quickly became dependent on policies followed by the general councils. This dependence can be explained by both material reasons (their strategic incapacity) and political reasons (localised networks caused by the *cumul des mandats*, or multiple office holding, see below). This new form of supervision led local authorities to measure the consequences of their traditional desire for autonomy against the benefits of intercommunal co-operation.

In addition to the growth of the number of traditional regroupings (single or multi-vocational districts), the 1992 Territorial Administration of the Republic Act defined two new forms of co-operation – communities of communes and communities of cities. These have two main characteristics: the pooling of equipment and services within contractually defined fields;

and the setting-up of a single tax system for local businesses. It should be noted that these two new forms of intercommunality do not threaten the existence of the communes themselves. Instead, their political and administrative identity is preserved (contrary to the attempts in the 1970s to reduce the number of communes by fusing them together). From 1992 to 1997 more than 1,000 intercommunal structures emerged, bringing together more than 10,000 municipalities and 13 million inhabitants.

In addition, the 1994 *Aménagement et Développement du Territoire* law created the concept of *pays* (localities). These are small territorial areas which share a common identity but which do not (at least in theory) coincide with existing administrative limits. These *pays* reflect the desire to establish 'an intercommunality of projects',[22] rather than following a simple developmental logic. This new formula has been a considerable success. For certain social actors the *pays* are a way of capitalising on the resources obtained by territorial mobilisation or by participation in certain local development projects (such as the Leader programmes of the European Union, for example). For the institutional actors (the general councils and the regional councils) they provide the opportunity to constitute new territorial relays for their policies, or to consolidate old ones.

As a result, this form of co-operation, which at the time of writing is the subject of a new bill, is both desired by the various institutions, but also a source of competition. It might also be noted that the local *pays* are often located in districts which predate the administrative organisation of modern-day France, and often correspond to territories under the Ancien Régime, as if to symbolise the end of *Jacobin* France.

In all of these ways, French local government in the 1990s has reversed one of the long-standing tendencies of sub-central policy making: state-centred public action.[23] The emergence of new centres of power has helped to destabilise the role of the state at the local level and has transformed both the foundations of its legitimacy and the resources at its disposal. However, the new distribution of powers has not led to a stable model of co-ordination, but, on the contrary, to varied forms of competition and institutional redundancy in a system which is both complex and not yet stabilised.

THE POLITICAL DIMENSION OF LOCAL PUBLIC ACTION

Does the reinforcement of the French local government go hand in hand with a new and stronger political dimension for local executives? In the years immediately following the decentralisation reforms most commentators, either hoping, or fearing, such a trend, assumed that this was the case.[24] The fact that elected councils (and no longer agents of the state) were entrusted with the responsibility for important areas of local action suggested that important variations might be found as a function of the political complexion of the council in question.

However, if the above question is pertinent, the answer is much more complex than it first appeared. The political work of local councillors is constrained by several structural requirements which mitigate the 'politicisation' of local apparatuses. At the same time, the study of local government highlights a dialectical process of 'territorial differentiation' and 'political standardisation'. Finally, the democratisation of public action, which was one of the major aims of the decentralisation policy, is undoubtedly one of the most underrealised dimensions of this process.

Three Dimensions of Local Political Work

The political work of locally elected officials is constrained in three main ways.[25]

The first concerns the purely elective dimension. Local politicians participate in a daily process of political competition which is independent of the type of collectivity and the size of the institution. They have to be very active at the local level. This activity can be seen in the constitution of local and regional electoral lists where local groups, like any public and private interest, demonstrate their mobilisation abilities. Indeed, the study of the composition of town councils tells us a lot about the way in which heads of local executives manage the heterogeneous and sometimes divergent interests with which they are faced. From this angle, the elected official is first and foremost a representative, whose aim is to embody a community of potentially allied (or opposing) groups.

The second dimension results from the local representative's participation in a territorial system of action, where he or she has to take into account and act upon the set of many and varied strategic interdependencies with which he or she is faced. In this context, the elected representative must demonstrate his or her own capacity to mobilise resources and influence a network of multi-level governmental actors (local, regional, national, European). Here, the credibility of the official is less a function of his or her position as a representative and more a function of his or her capacity to control the uncertainties caused by the complex nature of the system.

The third dimension is directly related to the implementation of public policies. The negotiation of public initiatives and the participation in (regional or national) arenas of debate about the guidelines of policies is now more and more important: the margin of negotiation has increased in line with the 'proceduralisation' of public action; the increasing territorialisation of certain policies (transport, education, research, health, social action) has meant that the elected representative is obliged to operate in areas where policy expertise is one of the conditions of policy-making legitimacy. This is why local governments have strengthened their administrations, in particular through either contract workers, who operate, therefore, outside the traditional grid system of public employment, or the transfer of qualified civil servants to local administrations. They have also contracted out public services to private enterprises, which, over and above any general tendency towards privatisation, reflects the new constraints (standardisation, safety and responsibility) to which local services are subject.[26]

These points suggest that we should play down the importance of the politicisation of the French local government. If the political dimension would seem to be one of the ways in which a coherent territorial system might be established, it must still be noted that it is neither the only way (note, for example, economic or legal logics) nor the one which is the most easy to identify. This assessment is valid whatever meaning one gives to the concept of 'politicisation': the local construction of collective projects or the legitimation of party politics.

Standardisation and Differentiation in Local Government

If the party political affiliation of local executives is not a good analytical tool for evaluating the differences between local governments, it is, nevertheless, possible to identify both qualitative and quantitative variations in the local management of collective problems. These variations occur against the background of territorial standardisation and new logics of differentiation.

The tendency towards standardisation is threefold and examples can be identified at each level of local government:

At the municipal level, the principal trend towards policy standardisation is a function of the relative homogenisation of the problems of public action and the related supply of collective goods, namely, the quality of the physical infrastructure, environmental, cultural and educational resources. In the last years few years there has been the development of service-provider companies (Générale des Eaux-Vivendi; Lyonnaise des Eaux-Dumez; Bouygues) which in the past specialised in one area (the distribution of water, building and public works), but which now operate in an increasingly large number of domains. There is, thus, a tendency towards standardisation in the supply of public policies (and the related representation of citizens' needs).

At the departmental level, the tendency towards standardisation occurs as a function of the main policy sectors which are managed by the general councils: social aid, transport and regional planning. These are fields in which the pressure of demand and the ongoing nature of the expenditure commitments impose a tendency towards policy convergence.

At the regional level, this convergence is related to the weight of state co-financing of regional projects (education, training and economic planning). The fact that European regional funding is now implemented through the State-Region Planning Contracts tends to strengthen the role of the state in the standardisation of regional policies.

Of course, each level remains autonomous in certain areas. Indeed, the dynamism of local and regional authorities can be explained by the desire to loosen the strait-jacket of standardisation. This is true in the field of culture affairs, communication and international exchanges, that is, areas where there are few regulations and where decentralisation left local decision makers free to take the initiative themselves. These fields created the opportunity for local areas to make a distinctive contribution and also fostered political competition between them,[27] even if they are still subject to modern forms of standardisation, such as the contractualisation of cultural policies.[28] Moreover, this tendency is highlighted (in the field of local cultural policies) in the counter-example provided by the case of the cities run by the Front National. The way in which the party manages cultural questions at this level demonstrates a triple process of repoliticisation, nationalisation of the issues at stake and deprofession-alisation of public policies: three tendencies which are quite opposed to those followed by the majority of the local governments (depoliticisation, localisation and professionalisation).[29]

The new forms of territorial differentiation undoubtedly depend on variables other than the political identity of the authority in question. Several theses have been put forward to account for this differentiation. The first, which remains rather underdeveloped in France, tries to explain these differences by the composition of the networks of public action themselves, which are said to be more or less inclusive, dense and centralised and which as a result lead to a greater or lesser degree of efficiency.[30] This approach has been the subject of considerable criticism.[31] Indeed, the use of network analysis does not seem to have gone beyond the metaphorical stage.[32] It has been relatively little used in the analysis of local government, even through this approach may be enriched by taking into account the content of the network interactions.[33]

The second thesis, which is closer to the concept of urban governance[34] or political capacity,[35] tries to explain these differences by analysing the way in which each local government integrates, or fails to integrate, local interests, so providing it, or not, with a unified front to the outside world. According to this line of thought, the quality of the interactions at the local level explains the differences in local government efficiency. In turn, these differences in efficiency are translated into substantively different policy outcomes. In particular, this approach can be used to explain the considerable variation in the use of structural funds by French regions,[36] the divergent ways in which certain sectoral policies have been implemented and the extent to which these strategic interactions have been politicised.

The problem with this approach is that it has great difficulty in integrating historical and cultural variables into the analysis, which, for certain authors, are the real cause of the differences between local areas. For example, some writers try to explain the considerable differences in the levels of intercommunal co-operation in terms of the role of local political culture. According to this line of thought, western France is 'more culturally' amenable to this form of co-operation, while the political culture of southern France means that local authorities are more concerned to preserve their own autonomy which is more likely to lead to inter-institutional conflict.[37]

Consistent with this line of reasoning, the third thesis emphasises the historical reproduction of local behaviour. However, the problems of this contemporary form of cultural determinism are well known and can be found, for example, in the criticisms which have been levelled against Putnam's thesis of 'social capital' in *Making Democracy Work*.[38] The trend towards change, which is clearly visible across France as a whole, contradicts the alleged effect of 'hard' cultural variables. It might be possible, though, to establish a compromise approach which includes both a synchronic aspect, which by itself would remove any historical factors from the equation, and a diachronic aspect, which in turn would place too much emphasis on such factors. If it can be agreed that new forms of local interdependence are not necessarily all innovative and that they associate actors who have consistently been engaged in a process of co-operation and conflicts across time, then it becomes possible to speak about territorialised political exchanges.[39]

This approach takes into account both the historical context in which behavioural interactions take place (the reproduction of 'political configurations of exchange') and the transformation of the framework within which these exchanges occur. Moreover, this dialectic of change and the reproduction of local configurations of exchange indicates at the same time the effects of reducing the levels of effective participation in public action and, thus, raises questions about the nature of local democracy.

The Transformation of Local Democracy

One of the aims of those behind the decentralisation reforms was to deepen French democracy. Local government, whose powers had been confiscated by a centralised elite and which was scarcely representative of the local population as a whole, would be regenerated by the establishment of a truly representative democracy. Fifteen years on, however, there is more talk about the development of 'municipal monarchies' than about 'local republics'.[40] Indeed, the goal of local democracy is usually regarded as the greatest failure of the decentralisation reforms. There are certain ways in which local political life has been democratised, but in practice the extent of local democracy remains limited.

It is useful to consider three aspects of French local democracy: the localisation of decisions; the extension of representative government; and the limitation of multiple office-holding, or the *cumul des mandats*.

The localisation of the decision-making process is a positive element of the decentralisation reforms. The changes described above have all helped local societies to regain control of issues which affect their own community. The concept of local issues, which in the past was very severely restricted by administrative case law, has now been extended both by the decentralisation of local authority powers and by the dynamic of territorialised political exchanges. At the same time, though, the localisation of the decision-making process goes has gone hand-in-hand with what remains a relatively closed circle of public action. This can be seen in two ways.

First, it has already been noted that the relationship between associations and municipalities very much favours the latter. Through their control of financial and political resources, municipalities have a real structural capacity to impose their choices on civil society which is unable to act as a real countervailing power.[41] The associations which do manage to acquire a certain influence are often those which choose to align themselves with the municipal majority. Certainly, some associations do manage to maintain their autonomy by exploiting the competition between the different levels of public decision-making processes. In this case, the power exerted by the local association should be interpreted as an alignment of higher territorial degree.

Second, the weak legitimacy of locally organised private interests[42] continues, despite (official) rhetoric, to limit the nature and the effectiveness of public-private partnerships. Local democracy, understood as the extension of participation in public decision-making processes, thus remains largely theoretical. The multiplication of popular consultation procedures, however formal or informal these may be, does not mean that a (new) type of deliberative government has really been established.[43]

The extension of local representative government is the second aspect of local democracy. It can be identified in two ways: a wider range of assembly elections and the 'proportionalisation' of political life. In terms of the former, the deepening of the democratic system is clear: the French now have the opportunity to elect city councillors, general councillors and regional councillors, in addition to presidential, parliamentary and European representatives. In terms of the latter, the introduction of proportional representation for local and regional elections has institutionalised opposition forces in local councils. In this respect, it has also helped to institutionalise the Front National. That said, the extension of local representative government has not had a uniform effect and its results have led to at least three political paradoxes.

First, discrepancies in the demographic context of local elections remain. This is particularly so in the case of departmental elections, where the basic constituency is the canton but where rural areas are overrepresented. The consequence is that the most powerful level of local government is also the one which rests on the most contestable form of local democracy.

Second, democracy at the new levels of local government, such as the region, is not advanced by the functioning of the political system itself. After three elections (1986, 1992 and 1998), regional councils still remain secondary political units. Here, election to local office is still used to reward party loyalists and client groups rather than as a way of popularly selecting representatives on the basis of their political credentials.[44] The high turn-over of regional councillors from one election to the next, when compared, for example, with the equivalent figures for the Spanish Autonomous Communities, is another indication of the weak regionalisation of the French political system.[45]

Finally, the presence of an institutionalised opposition within municipal and regional councils has not had the effect of intensifying public debate at the local level. On the contrary, municipal governments have tended to deprive opposition forces of access to strategic information by resorting to increasingly larger numbers of personal advisers (*cabinets*). As a result, there is a growing gap between the 'sphere of action' (the higher levels of the administration and the chief executive) and the 'sphere of representation' (elected councils). The presidentialisation of the former has gone hand in hand with a weakening of the latter. Indeed, local opposition forces have played their part in bringing about this situation because they merely intend to continue it when they win office themselves and so do not challenge it when they are out of office. It is striking to note, for example, that opposition politicians have not been instrumental in unearthing any of the scandals that have shaken local authorities over the past few years. Instead, these scandals have come to light either by the personal action of a determined local citizen, or by the investigations of a judge.

The decision to limit the number of elected offices that a person can hold (*cumul des mandats*) is a good example of the desire to put an end to this particular manifestation of French exceptionalism. However, the difficulties of implementing this reform also illustrate the deep attachment to this type of political practice. Contrary to popular belief, the *cumul des mandats* does not date back very far. Indeed, this practice has only become widespread during the Fifth Republic.[46] Moreover, it has merely been strengthened by the decentralisation reforms which increased the intensity and importance of local political work.

This paradox can be explained by the functions which the *cumul des mandats* performs:[47] (a) the chances of re-election increase in line with the number of positions held – the greater the number of offices, the greater the chances of reelection; (b) it rationalises the nature of the otherwise extremely complicated local decision-making process – *cumulards* personalise the political process and 'concretise' the issues at stake; (c) it increases the number of strategic interdependencies in the system (between the elected representative and both the administration and private interests).

At the same time, the *cumul des mandats* is also one of the main obstacles to the creation of a truly pluralistic local democracy and for three reasons: (a) it encourages certain types of local representatives. For example, across the country as a whole 20 per cent of mayors are farmers, whereas farmers account for only 4.6 per cent of the electorate. In a similar vein, in urban areas mayors are disproportionately drawn from the professional classes, middle and senior-ranking executives and employers.[48] The same point also accounts for the underrepresentation of the women (10 per cent of regional councillors, 5 per cent of general councillors, 21 per cent of municipal councillors and only 7.5 per cent of mayors).

Indeed, this phenomenon is all the more important in that there is a very large number of elected representatives in France (544,000, or, put another way, ten times more than in the UK); (b) it leads to inequalities in the influence of local interests. The degree of influence varies according to the presence or absence of a *cumulard*, since the access to resources is at least partly determined by the number of offices that a person holds; (c) it depoliticises the exercise of power and leads to both parliamentary absenteeism (participation in commissions, debates and so on) in that *cumulards* often continue their local work in order to reinforce their political careers as well as to a reduction in the power of political parties which are faced with deeply entrenched local *notables*.

All told, even if the *cumul des mandats*, which was first limited by law in 1985,[49] is once again the subject of legislative reform,[50] the capacity of the political system to circumvent the effects of any such reform is very strong. The fact that the 1985 law (ironically) increased the representation of women at the local level (elected officials who were restricted from holding office were frequently replaced by their wives!) is a good illustration of the difficulties involved in reforming this particular social and political phenomenon.

CONCLUSION

There are important elements of stability in the French system of local government. These can be found in the political system itself, in the nature of the ruling local elite and in the professionalisation, depoliticisation and localisation of the decision-making process. In turn, these elements of stability have led to consistent problems of co-ordination (or the integration of the various levels of decision making), democratisation, representation (male-female parity, socio-professional origins), participation in the political process, problems of public-private partnerships, policy evaluation and so on.

The new analytical tools with which local government is studied have identified the problems of the more established concepts in this area (the local politico-administrative system or 'cross-regulation'), while at the same time time they have also created the opportunity for more cross-national comparisons to be made. It must, however, be recognised that these new concepts engender their own types of problems. For example, network analysis does not go beyond the metaphorical and leads to a methodological dead end; governance analysis of the more prescriptive kind is not supported by the necessary empirical evidence; the notions of 'contractualisation' or 'negotiation' may describe certain processes, but they are difficult to transform into more general concepts.

What is more, even in the now more pluralistic field of French local government studies, it must be noted that certain potentially promising lines of inquiry have yet to be followed up. These include anthropological accounts[51] and historical analyses.[52] Last, the historical weakness of private interests at the local level has been matched only by the absence of academic work on this topic. Over and above the practical application of studies in this area (concerning good governance and best practices), the deepening of analytical approaches in this domain will be one of the key elements in the renewal of interest in French local government studies.

NOTES

1. François Rangeon, 'Le gouvernement local', in CURAPP, *La gouvernabilité* (Paris: Presses Universitaires de France 1996) pp.166–74; Vivien Schmidt, *Democratizing France. The Political and Administrative History of Decentralization* (NY: CUP 1990).
2. Jean-Pierre Worms, 'Le préfet et ses notables', *Revue Française de Sociologie* 8/3 (1966) pp.255–60; Alistair Cole and Peter John, 'Networks or networking? The importance of power, position and values in local economic policy networks in Britain and France', paper presented to the American Political Science Association conference, Washington DC, 28–31 Aug. 1997.
3. Pierre Grémion, *Le pouvoir périphérique. Bureaucrates et notables dans le système politico-administratif français* (Paris: Seuil 1976).
4. François Dupuy and Jean-Claude Thoenig, *Sociologie de l'administration française* (Paris: Armand Colin 1983).
5. Patrice Duran, 'Le partenariat dans la gestion des fonds structurels: la situation française', *Pôle Sud* 8 (1998) pp.114–40.
6. Patrick Le Galès, *Politique urbaine et développement local* (Paris: L'Harmattan 1993).
7. Pouvoirs locaux, *Poursuivre la décentralisation. Réflexions sur le bilan et les perspectives de la décentralisation* (Paris: Pouvoirs locaux 1994).
8. Guy Saez, 'Villes et culture: un gouvernement par la coopération', *Pouvoirs* 73 (1995) pp.109–25.
9. Pierre Lascoumes, *L'éco-pouvoir. Environnement et politiques* (Paris: La Découverte 1994).
10. Emmanuel Négrier, 'The professionalisation of urban cultural policies: the case of festivals', *Government and Policy* 14 (1996) pp.515–29.
11. Olivier Borraz, with Patricia Loncle-Moriceau and Christel Arrouet, *Les politiques locales de lutte contre le SIDA. Une analyse dans trois départements français* (Paris: L'Harmattan 1998).
12. Éric Kerrouche, 'L'apprentissage du rôle de sous-préfet', *Politix* 38 (1997) pp.88–110.
13. By the 1990s France was well equipped overall in terms of infrastructure, even if some inequalities remain in the provision of roads, schools, public health and so on at the local level.
14. Patrice Duran and Jean-Claude Thoenig, 'L'État et la gestion publique territoriale', *Revue Française de Science Politique* 46/4 (1996) pp.580–623.
15. Pierre Lascoumes and Jean-Pierre Le Bourhis, 'Le bien commun comme construit territorial. Identité d'action et procédures', *Politix* 42 (1998) pp.37–66.
16. Pierre Moulinier, *Politique culturelle et décentralisation* (Paris: Editions du Centre National de la Fonction Publique Territoriale 1995).
17. Vincent Dubois and Philippe Poirrier (eds.) *Politiques locales et enjeux culturels. Les clochers d'une querelle XIXème-XXème siècle* (Paris: Documentation Française 1998); Emmanuel Négrier, 'French Cultural decentralization and International Expansion', *International Journal of Urban and Regional Research* 21/1 (1997) pp.63–74.
18. See Michèle Cascales, 'Le contrat de Plan Etat-Région est-il un outil de programmation pluri-annuelle?', *Revue Politique et Parlementaire* 995 (1998) pp.93–102. This question of

power relationship between the state and the regions has a specific meaning now, since the negotiation of the new contracts is occurring in the context where the Front National is present in the majority of three regional councils (Bourgogne, Languedoc-Roussillon and Picardie).

19. Pierre-Alain Four, 'La compétence contre la décentralisation? Création des Fonds Régionaux d'Art Contemporain', *Politix* 24 (1993) pp.95–114.
20. Marc Smyrl, *From regional policy to European networks: interregional divergence in the implementation of the EC Structural Funds in France*, European Univ. Inst. Working Paper, Florence; Emmanuel Négrier and Bernard Jouve (eds.) *Que gouvernent les Régions d'Europe?* (Paris: L'Harmattan 1998); Bernard Jouve and Emmanuel Négrier, 'Multi-Level Governance 'French Style'? The Contribution of the European Structural Funds to Redefining Intergovernmental Relations in France', *European Planning Studies* 6/5 (1998) pp.555–72; Patrice Duran, 'Le partenariat dans la gestion des fonds structurels: la situation française', *Pôle Sud* 8 (1998) pp.114–40; Andy Smith, 'Putting the Governance back into Multi-level Governance. Examples from French Translations of the Structural Funds', paper presented to the European Consortium for Political Research, Oslo (1996).
21. CEPEL, *La négociation des politiques contractuelles* (Paris: L'Harmattan 1996).
22. Alain Faure, 'L'intercommunalité de projet, un modèle d'action publique innovant?', *Observatoire sur l'Intercommunalité de Projet en Rhône-Alpes* (Rapport 50, CERAT-IEP de Grenoble 1998).
23. Olivier Borraz, 'Pour une sociologie des dynamiques de l'action publique locale', in Richard Balme, Alain Faure and Albert Mabileau (eds.) *Politiques locales et transformations de l'action publique en Europe* (CERAT: Grenoble 1998) pp.85–101.
24. Yves Mény, *La corruption de la République* (Paris: Fayard 1992); Jacques Rondin, *Le sacre des notables. La France en décentralisation* (ibid. 1985).
25. Alain Faure, 'Les apprentissages du métier d'élu local. La tribu, le système et les arènes', *Pôle Sud* 7 (1997) pp.72–80.
26. Dominique Lorrain, 'Après la décentralisation, l'action publique flexible', *Sociologie du Travail* 3/3 (1993) pp.285–307.
27. Franco Bianchini and Michael Parkinson (eds.) *Cultural Policy and Urban Regeneration. The West European Experience* (Manchester UP 1993).
28. Philippe Urfalino, *L'invention de la politique culturelle* (Paris: Documentation Française 1997).
29. Cécile Bressat, 'Culture et autorité partisane: la politique de 'rééquilibrage' de la bibliothèque d'une municipalité FN. Orange 1995–1997', *Pôle Sud* 10 (1999) pp.75–92; Négrier (note 10).
30. Patrick Le Galès and Mark Thatcher (eds.) *Les réseaux de politique publique* (Paris: L'Harmattan 1995).
31. Patrick Hassenteufel, 'Do policy networks matter? Lifting descriptif et analyse de l'Etat en interaction', in Le Galès and Thatcher (note 30) pp.91–109.
32. Jurgen Grote, 'Réseaux de politique publique ou échange clientéliste: des métaphores à l'évaluation des relations Etat-société', *Pôle Sud* 3 (1995) pp.55–71.
33. Jean-Pierre Gaudin, 'Politiques urbaines et négociations territoriales: quelle légitimité pour les réseaux de politiques publiques?', *Revue Française de Science Politique* 45/1 (1995) pp.31–56.
34. Patrick Le Galès, 'Du gouvernement des villes à la gouvernance urbaine', *Revue Française de Science Politique* 45/1 (1995) pp.57–95.
35. Michael Keating and John Loughlin (eds.) *The Political Economy of Regionalism* (London: Frank Cass 1996).
36. Today a majority of French regions are obliged to reimburse the sums given to their own territory by the European Union within the framework of the Structural Funds (Midi-Pyrénées, Languedoc-Roussillon, Centre, Nord-Pas-de-Calais). Some of them (Haute-Normandie, Poitou-Charentes, Alsace), however, have so spent so much of their allowance that they canvass to increase it. See Emmanuel Négrier, 'Espaces urbains et sociétés de communication', *Espaces et Sociétés* 87 (1997) pp.59–91.

37. Jean-Yves Nevers, 'La relance de l'intercommunalité. Contextes et stratégies', in Balme *et al.* (note 23) pp.221–31.
38. Robert D. Putnam, *Making Democracy Work. Civic Traditions in Modern Italy* (Princeton UP 1993).
39. Emmanuel Négrier, 'Introduction', in Jouve and Négrier (note 20) pp.11–31.
40. Albert Mabileau, 'De la monarchie municipale à la française', *Pouvoirs* 73 (1995) pp.7–18.
41. Richard Balme, 'La participation aux associations et le pouvoir municipal. Capacités et limites de la mobilisation par les associations culturelles dans les communes de banlieue', *Revue Française de Sociologie* 28/4 (1987) pp.601–39.
42. Sarah Waters, 'Chambers of Commerce and Local Development in France: problems and constraints', *Government and Policy* 16 (1998) pp.591–604.
43. Xavier Piéchaczyk, 'Le rôle des commissaires-enquêteurs et l'intérêt général', *Politix* 42 (1998) pp.93–122; Cécile Blatrix, 'Vers une démocratie participative? Le cas de l'enquête publique', in CURAPP, *La gouvernabilité* (Paris, Presses Universitaires de France 1996) pp.299–314.
44. Olivier Nay, *La région, une institution. La représentation, le pouvoir et la règle dans l'espace régional* (Paris: L'Harmattan 1998).
45. Emmanuel Négrier, 'Une action publique sans coopération politique: le style languedocien de politique régionale', *Pôle Sud* 8 (1998) pp.41–54.
46. The proportion of *cumulards* in the French parliament was only 49 per cent in 1958. By 1988 it had grown steadily to 96 per cent and has now stabilized at 93 per cent. See Paul Alliès, 'Les effets du cumul des mandats sur le personnel politique', in CREAM, *Le cumul des mandats et des fonctions. Une réforme au coeur de la modernisation de la vie politique* (Paris: La Documentation Française 1998) pp.63–76.
47. Ibid. pp.63–76.
48. Philippe Garraud, *Profession: homme politique. La carrière politique des maires urbains* (Paris: L'Harmattan 1989).
49. Yves Mény, 'Le cumul républicain: la démocratie réduite aux acquets?', *Revue Politique et Parlementaire* 991 (1997) pp.5–12.
50. The law of 30 Dec. 1985 has made the office of member of parliament incompatible with more than one of the following office mandates member of the European Parliament, regional councillor, general councillor, mayor of a commune of more than 20,000 inhabitants or deputy mayor of a town of more than 100,000 inhabitants.
51. Marc Abelès, 'Le degré zéro de la politique. Réseaux de pouvoir et espace intercommunal dans le canton de Quarré-les-Tombes (Morvan)', *Études Rurales* 101–2 (1986) pp.231–71; Marc Abelès, *Jours tranquilles en 1989* (Paris: Odile Jacob 1989)
52. Bruno Dumons, Gilles Pollet and Pierre-Yves Saunier, *Pouvoirs locaux et élites municipales. Analyse comparée des villes de la France du Sud-Est* (Paris: Editions du CNRS 1997).

The Changing Dynamics of State-Society Relations in the Fifth Republic

VIVIEN A. SCHMIDT

The vision of state-society relations was clear at the inception of the Fifth Republic. The state would lead, society would follow. Guaranteeing this were the institutions, with a strong presidential model of parliamentary government to ensure against paralysis, as much as the men, with de Gaulle in the lead.[1] Forty years later, both the state and society have changed. The state is no longer so certain of its leadership capacity, even though it often still tries to operate autonomously, in the old 'heroic' leadership style. Society is no longer so willing to be led, despite the fact that it has not for the most part sufficiently organised itself to take the lead.

Change in state-society relations has been more pronounced in certain arenas than in others. Major transformation has occurred in particular in those arenas where the relationship between state and society has traditionally been closest, as in the relations between business and government. In other arenas, by contrast, the lack of change remains a serious problem, as in labour relations, in particular in the public sector. In such arenas, where the state has traditionally imposed on an often reluctant society, the relationship has remained difficult, and represents the greatest impediment to further positive development.

Generally, however, the state has modernised its societal relations, providing more efficient public services to the citizenry at large through a downsized bureaucracy, and liberalised them, allowing greater liberty to the individual, greater play to organised interests, and greater independence to business. The state has also loosened its control over the institutions that can serve as counterbalance to the executive, by allowing for the greater autonomy of sub-national authorities, by providing for the greater freedom of the press, and by establishing independent regulatory agencies in a wide range of areas. And yet, the technocratic nature of the state, with its domination by an administrative elite, remains, as does the periodic re-emergence of the old heroic policy style, in which the state formulates policy largely without significant input from societal interests, but then accommodates them in the implementation, or risks confrontation.

Increasingly in recent years, moreover, another major actor has interposed itself between French state and society. The European Union, with its own set of institutions and model of state-society relations, has increasingly served to alter the traditional balance in French state-society relations by allowing greater access and influence at the European level to French societal interests at the policy formulation stage and by reducing the flexibility of the state at the implementation stage.

STATE-SOCIETY RELATIONS IN FRANCE: AN OVERVIEW

France has long had a history of state centralisation and societal disorganisation, one in which the state structured its relationships with society, legitimating as it subordinated those groups with which it chose to deal, and ignoring the others, which found strength primarily in periodic moments of rebellion. This state-society relationship, in which the state acts and society reacts, and where the state is typically strong and assertive while society is weak and submissive, derives in large measure from France's centuries-old history of governmental centralisation and insulation from the political community.

The modern, democratic version of this relationship reached its pinnacle in the Fifth Republic, when the historical pattern was reinforced by institutions that ensured the state all the necessary instruments of government leadership and societal control by establishing a unitary state in which the executive, supported by an able technocratic elite, has tremendous powers over the legislature, judiciary, and sub-national units.[2]

Despite the changes that have occurred across the 40 years of the Fifth Republic, as the state divested itself of its powers in certain spheres, loosened its control over others, lost its capacity with regard to yet others, and generally liberalised, the relationship of stronger state to weaker society remains because the state retains sufficient institutional resources to impose on a society that is insufficiently self-organised.

In France, where the understanding of the role of the state is *Jacobin*, which means that elected governments are mandated to carry out the will of the people directly, without the mediation of other interests, organised interests are by their very nature suspect because they violate principles of democratic equality and electoral accountability. Unlike in pluralist or corporatist polities, where organised interests are seen to have a legitimate voice in policy formulation and a right to perform governing functions in a wide range of spheres,[3] in 'statist' France, the public good is seen as something above the pressures of interest. Interest group pressures on government are therefore generally regarded as illegitimate while comparatively few organised interests are granted self-governing functions.

This has a long history, beginning with the Le Chapelier Law of 1791, which outlawed all intermediary bodies, and was only rescinded in 1884. Yet even once interest groups were allowed to be formed without prior government authorisation, as of 1901, they continued to be viewed with some suspicion not only by government but even by the population at large. In consequence, France lacks not only the wide variety of self-organised, active interest groups with widespread support found in a pluralist polity like the United States. It also lacks the strong peak associations necessary to bargain as equals with government found in 'corporatist' polities such as the smaller European countries or Germany.[4]

Social protest movements, by contrast, which are quickly organised and as quickly dispersed, are much more the French model, with confrontation, whether by such protest movements or by organised interests unhappy with government decisions, considered a legitimate, and sometimes the only, way to be heard.[5] And this, in turn, is generally greeted either by government appeasement or repression.

The policy process that emerges from this state-society relationship is one in which the state acts, often by formulating policy unilaterally, without prior consultation with those interests most affected by the policy, and society reacts, as often as not by resisting the policies imposed by the state. In the face of societal resistance, moreover, the state may accommodate such interests, by developing common strategies for implementation, may be co-opted by such interests, by allowing those interests to devise their own implementation strategies, or may refuse to co-operate with those interests, and therefore risk confrontation. As a result, the state that appears strong with regard to society in policy formulation, as it announces 'heroic' policies with great fanfare, can appear weak in policy implementation, as it adjusts policies in response to societal concerns or even backs off policies in response to protest. Such weakness can sometimes also extend to policy formulation, in sectors where accommodation begins already at the formulation stage and societal interests hold sway, so much so that the heroic policies are replaced by 'everyday' policies.[6]

In policy formulation, certain policy sectors have traditionally been more subject to heroic policy making, such as industrial policy until the late 1980s and labour policy still today, than others, in particular those characterised by everyday policy making. In sectors such as education policy, agricultural policy from the early 1960s to the early 1980s, and local government policies up until the early 1980s, the periodic attempts at heroic policy making were for the most part doomed to failure because of the historical strength and cultural importance of well-organised interests. In these sectors, societal interests generally got their way through everyday policy making, whether by helping to shape government policies, as did the farmers between the late 1960s and early 1980s;[7] by blocking government policies, generally the pattern of the teachers;[8] or by co-opting government policies, the case of the complicitous relationship between prefects and local elected officials prior to the reforms of the 1980s;[9] and of the notaries public to this day.[10]

In sectors characterised by heroic policy making, by contrast, societal interests have had to wait until the implementation stage to get their way, since they have few ways into a formulation process centred on the top reaches of central ministries, if not in the prime minister's or president's office. And here, too, there are differences among sectors, with some having typically experienced greater accommodation than others. Thus, whereas in the industrial policy sector business generally benefited from accommodation with government, in large measure because of the traditional closeness of ties between big business and government, in the labour policy sectors, where the ties have traditionally been much more distant, confrontation has more often been the norm.

Even where there have been close ties and everyday policy making, however, confrontation may occur when highly organised interests no longer get their way, as the French farmers during the General Agreement on Tariffs and Trade (GATT) negotiations. Finally, confrontation is the only recourse for interests which have little ongoing organisation and minimal ties to government, as in social protest movements such as those that have periodically served to mobilise students against successive attempts to reform the university. Yet what this means is that sectors that are desperately in need of reform go wanting, because major reform initiatives are dropped time and again as government shows itself to be impotent in the face of protest.[11]

This overall pattern of policy making has been facilitated by the administrative state, in which state trained, elite civil servants not only elaborate the laws under government guidance and without necessarily consulting the most affected interests; they also implement them. And in the implementation process, these civil servants have tremendous administrative discretion – so much so that exceptions are granted as often as not.[12] In de Tocqueville's oft repeated phrase, 'The rules are rigid but the application flexible.' This is clearly in contrast to regulatory models of implementation such as those of the United States and the European Union, where exceptions are viewed as illegitimate.[13]

Yet even when civil servants are unwilling to grant exceptions, societal interests nevertheless often triumph, generally because they are able to take advantage of interministerial rivalries. The strong state, in other words, is not only weak because it capitulates to societal interests in the implementation but also because it is highly fragmented both between ministries involved in implementing major policies and within ministries.[14]

Over time, however, economic and institutional reforms have served to moderate or 'soften' this overall pattern of state-society relations, in particular through the decentralisation of executive power, functions, and financial resources to the benefit of the periphery; through the deregulation of government rules concerning business and the privatisation of nationalised enterprises; through the liberalisation of the regulations governing the media; and through the modernisation of state administration, the rise of independent regulatory agencies, and the growing independence of the judiciary. At the same time, moreover, society has changed, having become more organised and active, with the rise of associations; having come to expect more consultation and concertation; and therefore having become more restive in response to any state imposition. The restiveness is particularly evident in those areas where few economic and institutional reforms have been introduced or, having been introduced, have been unsuccessful, as in employment and social policy.

European integration has been an added source of disruption to the traditional pattern of state-society relations, by diminishing state autonomy in policy formulation and state flexibility in policy implementation.[15] At the formulation stage, the French state has lost autonomy not only because it is no longer the sole authority in the land, given the priority of EU law and institutions (in particular the EU Commission and the European Court of Justice), and that it is only one of 15 member-states in the Council of Ministers approving laws that apply to France, but also because the EU has allowed national societal interests into the European policy formulation process.

The openness of the EU to interest representation has enabled societal interests that were (and often still are) subordinated to government in national bargaining to become quasi-independent supranational actors that are most often partners with government in supranational bargaining, although they can even be adversaries. Big businesses in particular now find themselves partners rather than supplicants of French ministries in national lobbying efforts.[16]

Regional governments, moreover, which have themselves only recently gained significant powers of their own, have a direct relationship with the EU unmediated by the national government. Other interests, however, such as labour and consumer groups, which have been traditionally weak, have been slower to organise themselves effectively at the EU level, and have much less access or impact.

At the implementation stage, the French state has lost flexibility mainly because the European regulatory model, which demands that European laws apply equally to all and without exception, proscribes the administrative discretion that has been the state's way of responding to societal interests in the policy process. This closure to interest accommodation in the national implementation of European policies has effectively undermined the very way in which the state has traditionally managed interest representation.

For business and other interests which have access to and influence in European policy formulation, the loss of accommodation and co-optation at the implementation stage is not so serious. For those interests which for whatever reason lack access or influence at the European level, by contrast, the loss of accommodation and co-optation is likely to lead to increased confrontation with a state that no longer has the option to capitulate in response to protest. And because these are often (but not always, *viz.* the farmers in the GATT) also mainly the interests that have benefited the least from the economic and institutional reforms that have softened the hard edges of traditional state-society relations, European integration may exacerbate those very French state-society relations that have been most problematic.

Whatever the changes, for the better or the worse, the overall pattern of state-society relations for the most part remains, given a still centralised state served by an elite *corps* of civil servants that largely continues to seek to structure and control its relations with a still disorganised society that in many spheres continues to follow the pattern of submissiveness punctuated by explosions. Most importantly, perhaps, the economic and institutional changes have done only a little to dispel the suspicion with which governments have traditionally greeted societal interests, although this is more true of societal interests in certain arenas than others, and is often related to how close a relationship they have historically had with the state. For the closer the traditional relationship, the more willing the state has been to reform state-society relations through the transfer of state power to society.

This was the case for centre-periphery relations beginning in the early 1980s, where reforms beginning in the early 1980s transformed local government.[17] It has also largely been the case for business-government relations with the reforms beginning in the mid-1980s. But it has most definitely not been true for labour-government relations.

BUSINESS-GOVERNMENT RELATIONS

The state's general suspicion of societal interests, reflected in its concern to subordinate and control them in order to ensure the public good, has affected all areas of state-society relations, but for different reasons. As noted above, organised societal interests were outlawed until the 1880s, mainly for fear of sedition, and continued to be seen as illegitimate thereafter because they undermined *Jacobin* notions of democracy. Local authorities were held in tutelage by the state until the early 1980s, mainly because of fears that local liberty would constitute a threat to national unity.[18] Business was also subject to a virtual tutelage of the state until the reforms beginning in the mid-1980s. Here, state suspicion had less to do with the fear of sedition or of secession than of incompetence.

The experience of the Third Republic and the quick collapse of the country in the face of the Nazi onslaught at the beginning of the Second World War left the state convinced that it could not trust business to move the country and its economy forward. The modernising state of the post-war period felt that the only way to promote growth was for the state to lead, and business to follow. Thus, the state sought to lead business first through planning and later increasingly through industrial policy, as well as by way of a relatively large, well-developed nationalised sector. This *dirigiste* or directive role began during the Fourth Republic but it reached its apotheosis during the Fifth, in particular at the time of the nationalisations and interventionist industrial policies of the early 1980s.

By the mid-1980s, however, state *dirigisme* began its decline, the result of reforms related to deregulation and privatisation that, however *dirigiste* they were in policy style, nevertheless progressively took away the state's *dirigiste* capability. The state-society relationship with regard to business and government has really changed as a result of these reforms, with business now more independent of the state and interdependent such that business now leads itself more and the state directs it less.

This has not stopped the state from exhibiting *dirigiste* impulses, however, in the more limited sphere in which it still has impact, in particular with regard to enterprises in strategic areas or in trouble along with still-nationalised firms in the public service sector. And it has not rid business of state influence entirely. For although the state no longer has as much power over business through its policies, given deregulation and privatisation, its personnel continue to predominate as heads of business, given the move of career civil servants into top positions in top firms, private as much as public.

In the earliest years of the Fifth Republic, the industrial planning process, which had begun in the Fourth Republic, was the state's primary instrument of economic modernisation.[19] It involved a close business-government relationship that was characterised primarily by mutual accommodation: Government officials took the initiative in determining the overall objectives of the plan and in organising its implementation, set the goals and strategies in formal consultation with business, and implemented the resulting programmes in such a way that, while business benefited greatly through public investments, the planners had a variety of institutional mechanisms to ensure that business 'voluntarily' followed their recommendations.[20]

Over the course of the Fifth Republic, however, industrial policy increasingly became the state's preferred means for effecting economic change and influencing business, overshadowing planning which was proving less and less effective as it became more and more ambitious and politicised. Industrial policy was more 'heroic' than the planning process, since private interests had no formal part in the policy formulation process.

Under de Gaulle, planning was combined with a particularly heroic industrial policy that encouraged concentration among companies in order to create 'national champions'; established new public enterprises in strategic areas such as computers and aerospace; and instituted *grands projets*, some of which were successful, others of which were white elephants.

Under Giscard d'Estaing, planning was subordinated to the government's official industrial policy which sought to create leaders in particular sectors of the international economy, and to its unofficial policy of bailing out companies on the verge of bankruptcy.[21] All such industrial policies, however, were implemented in a manner that was just as accommodating as the national plans.

In fact, increasingly as this first part of the Fifth Republic drew to a close, government led less, and accommodation came to be replaced more and more by co-optation.[22] This was as much the case for national plans – in particular the Sixth Plan, in which the policy recommendations of the CNPF, the main employers' association, oriented the final product[23] as for the sectoral plans, especially in the case of the steel industry, characterised by a 'corporatist-style collusion'.[24] Even without this level of co-optation, however, other sectors of industry also got what they wanted, including the electronics industry, where the state took the risks while the enterprises disposed of the profits, and the oil companies. In these cases, as in many others such as nuclear energy, armaments, and aerospace, though, by contrast with steel, computers, and Concorde (in financial terms), although the relationship was also characterised by co-optation, it was for the most part effective in terms of policy outcomes.[25]

As a general rule, companies could basically do what they wanted as long as they did not need state funds.[26] Where they did need state funding, as in the case of monopolistic public firms in the transportation sector such as Air France and SNCF (national railway), they as often as not had to bow to government demands or suffer government delays on approval for new projects. This was also true of industries in less concentrated sectors facing economic downturn, such as textiles, machine tools, and computers, where the interventionism was also generally unsuccessful.[27] Only with the national champions that were already well established did industrial success go hand in hand with relative industry independence from government interference. And here, government policy makers had difficulty exerting control, lacking leverage by virtue of their size and their frequent lack of competitors.[28]

Accommodation and co-optation in the implementation of industrial policy and planning were facilitated by state fragmentation, which allowed businesses to play off one ministry against another, as well as by the personalistic nature of ministry-industry relations, where high-level government officials and top managers tended to negotiate on major firm-related issues. Because a majority of top managers shared with top officials old school ties, membership in a prestigious civil service *corps*, and government experience (CEOs were – and still are – as often as not themselves former top civil servants who moved over into top positions in business, public or private), CEOs in both public and private sectors had significant leverage.[29]

But even where shared state background and experience was not at issue, CEOs carried great weight as a result of their positions at the head of the relatively small number of large firms and of their technical expertise. By the same token, however, government officials also had great power to persuade, not simply by their elite status but also by their specialised knowledge; their institutional clout – administrative and financial; and their ability to appeal to business heads' patriotism, that is, their willingness to act in the public interest.

Little changed in the overall pattern of business-government relations with the advent of the socialists to power in 1981, even though heroic policy making returned full force with the nationalisation and restructuring of major firms. Nationalisation epitomised the return of *dirigisme*, since an extremely restricted group within the government determined the industries to nationalise and formulated the industrial policy which proposed a massive restructuring of the nationalised enterprises through vertical integration, recapitalisation, and streamlining of operations through the elimination of jobs and the closure of obsolete plants where necessary. And yet, even in the restructuring process for the nationalised industries, the state left internal decisions up to the firm while it exercised varying degrees of control over industry, with much accommodation even where there was a high degree of interventionism, as in the steel industry; some co-optation, in particular with regard to internationally competitive companies; and only the occasional confrontation, as in the cases of Saint Gobain and Rhône-Poulenc.

Moreover, by 1983 the Ministry of Industry returned to its traditional respect for the autonomy of public enterprises, with most internal management decisions left up to the firms themselves, and with the firm's goals and objectives and the state's commitments set by negotiated contracts between the state and the public enterprises.[30]

Privatisation under the neo-liberal government of 1986 to 1988 was as heroic as nationalisation, with the major outlines having been sketched out even before the right took office and with even less consultation than the socialists. But although privatisation involved minimal consultation on the choice of firms to be privatised and only somewhat more on the memberships in the *noyaux durs* ('hard core' investors who held up the 15 to 20 per cent of shares in a firm), most participant firms with only a few exceptions were satisfied with the outcomes, and therefore did not see the process as highly *dirigiste* as a result.[31] Privatisation itself, needless to say, altered the relationship between business and government significantly, since privatised firms were, for obvious reasons, no longer subject to the state's *tutelle* or to close ministerial scrutiny.

Deregulation, moreover, which had actually begun under the socialists but accelerated under the right, was also *dirigiste* in style, but anti-*dirigiste* in content, since it essentially stripped government of the policy instruments it had in the past used to gain business compliance, in particular through the opening of the financial markets, the lifting of price controls, the abrogation of barriers to competition, the easing of sectoral rules governing business, and so forth. The independent regulatory agencies that were set up in a range of deregulated areas only added to this, since they created intermediate bodies between government and business that were insulated from the state administration while they operated at arm's length from business.

For governments from 1988 forward, the direction of economic policy was set. Deregulation and privatisation, either officially or unofficially, remained the order of the day, pushed by the imperatives of European integration as well as the capital needs of firms. These had become everyday matters, however, as the heroic policies formulated without significant consultation gave way to ones that seemed to follow business much more than to lead it. In this period, ministry–industry relations became almost entirely ones of accommodation and co-optation. Succeeding governments for the most part either lacked the will or the means to impose decisions on business that looked less to the government for guidance, as business became increasingly subject to the imperatives of world competition, the constraints of the market, and the demands of technological advancement; or for support, given the growth of new, nongovernmental sources of financing in consequence of the liberalisation of the markets.

Most government actions came from the proposals of business, whether they involved the trading of shares in nationalised enterprises under Rocard, the trading of shares between nationalised and private firms under Cresson and Bérégovoy, or the outright privatisation of nationalised enterprises under Balladur and then Juppé.[32] And once the socialists returned to power in June 1997, although privatisation slowed, it did not stop by any means, and was still led by the desires of business and the pressures of international competition.

For all this, however, *dirigisme* is not entirely dead, although it is much more market-oriented and more circumscribed than in the past.[33] The French state continues to seek to influence business, primarily through a less directive method focused on strategic industries in the high-technology or defence sectors, on failing industries of major size and importance, and on the 'monopolistic' public sector enterprises that had generally been spared the often radical restructuring of the early to mid-1980s. It had hoped, moreover, to replace the interventionist industrial policy given up at the national level with European level industrial policy. However, this hope proved to be elusive, as early successes in instituting European industrial policy programmes (e.g., Esprit, Brite, Euram, Race, Eureka, and Jessi) were followed by failures (e.g., HDTV) or roadblocks (e.g., infrastructural programmes), mainly because of the Europe-wide absence of the institutional conditions and commitments necessary.[34] And in consequence, the French state concentrated on national level efforts.

These national efforts included encouraging mergers and acquisitions for industries of strategic importance to France and Europe in decent fiscal condition, in particular by creating new national champions prior to or even instead of European alliances. Such *meccano industriel*, however, has failed time and again, whether because of the resistance of one of the parties to the arranged marriage (e.g., the merger of Thomson and CEA, opposed by CEA), legal problems (e.g., the sale of Thomson to Lagardère), or political changes (i.e., the halt in the sale of Thomson once the Jospin government came to power). Interestingly enough, although the pace of privatisation has slowed with the Jospin government, the success rate initially went up – in part because of greater attention to industrial strategy, in part because of greater concertation with the employees in choice of acquirers (e.g., in the case of the bank CIC).

For companies in serious financial straits, moreover, the state has been much more rigorous in the conditions for state aid than in the past, given the constraints imposed by EU Competition Commission scrutiny and the new neo-liberal climate, and has made aid a one-shot deal contingent on a restructuring plan, a timetable for return to profitability and privatisation. The problems here relate to the fact that some firms have been unable to meet the requirements of the restructuring plan on the funds provided, and gone back to the state for more money (e.g., Bull, Air France, and, most egregiously, the Crédit Lyonnais, which has gone back at least four times, each time claiming it to be the last). Finally, for enterprises in monopolistic 'public service' sectors, the new market-oriented *dirigisme* sometimes contains echoes of the past statist pattern, with the state first seeking to impose but then retreating in the face of confrontation (e.g., with both Air France in 1993 and the SNCF in 1995).[35]

Outside of these more vulnerable sectors, most of business has become increasingly free from state interventionism. Interestingly enough, in a curious twist, as business has become more independent of the state, the state has become more dependent on business, at least with regard to the process of European integration. Because big businesses in particular find themselves the privileged interlocutors of the European Union Commission, the French state now needs them as allies in their efforts to influence the EU policy formulation process. As a result, from a system in which business had its say primarily at the national implementation stage, business has gone to one in which it also has input at the supranational formulation stage, an influence that is still largely denied it at the national level.[36]

In this supranational context, moreover, the state has tended to treat business as it traditionally has public enterprise, that is, as a defender of the interests of the French nation, and not as an enterprise which, whether public or private, has profitability as its main goal.[37]

This conviction that business acts in the public interest, in turn, can only have been enhanced because at the head of major business firms, as often as not, continue to be individuals whose education and career paths have been state-centred, and who landed in top management positions (although no longer immediately at the top) at a relatively early age after having had a high-flying career in the state civil service as well as, most often, having held a top post in a ministerial *cabinet*.[38] This recruitment pattern has, needless to say, made the transformation of the relationship between business and government relatively painless, as French administrative elites could be confident that the increasingly independent French businesses would be run as they might have run them themselves – or would run them themselves in the near future.[39]

The state-society relationship with regard to business was so readily transformed, in other words, because the state could now have confidence in the leaders of business in a way that they did not at the inception of the Fifth Republic. This was primarily because the state had largely populated the upper ranks of business. The retreat of the state, accomplished through the policies of deregulation and privatisation, was accompanied by the colonisation of business by the personnel of the state. Here, then, change in policies and processes was moderated by the lack of change in the players. A similar set of dynamics was operative in the case of the transformation in centre-periphery relations.[40] In other areas of state-society relations, by contrast, where relations have never been as close, change has been stymied, and instead of a transition to more everyday policy making, state heroism confronted by societal resistance remain the hallmarks of state-society relations.

LABOUR-GOVERNMENT RELATIONS

Unlike business-government relations or centre-periphery relations, where the closeness of relations has permitted a transfer of power from state to society, no such transfer has occurred with labour. The state still predominates, for good or ill, passing legislation affecting wages, social security, pensions, and work hours with little real consultation or participation by workers, whether considered as wage earners, social services recipients, or social security recipients. Time and again, therefore, when labour interests wish to be heard, their main recourse has been through confrontation. This was certainly the case in the years prior to the

1980s, and it remained true subsequently, despite various attempts to build stronger linkages between labour and business as well as government. More important for the overall reduction in labour militancy have been the changes in business related to privatisation and deregulation as well as the high unemployment rate, which have together meant that labour unrest has in recent years been limited primarily to public sector employees.

Part of the problem in the labour relations arena has surely been the relative lack of strength and organisation of labour relative to the state. To begin with, labour has traditionally been weak and has been getting weaker, having gone from approximately a 25 per cent unionisation rate in the early years of the Fifth Republic down to around 9 per cent in the early 1990s. The unions have always been highly fragmented and ideologically divided, although they have tended to be somewhat stronger in the public sector than in the private.

This weakness and fragmentation has prevented French unions from achieving the kind of legitimacy that enables strong, highly organised unions in corporatist countries to bargain as equals with government and business. In industrial policy, labour has been 'conspicuous by its absence'.[41] In collective bargaining, the unions have tended to play a minor role, with the government generally imposing its views in wage negotiations even under the socialists.[42]

At the plant level, labour has also been relatively impotent, before 1968 because it was not even allowed to have union locals. But even after 1982, once it had obtained the right to be present in all plants, its power did not increase. This was in part because the socialist reforms in the early 1980s intended to increase workplace democracy only further reduced the unions' power by allowing for direct dialogue between worker and management, although these did serve to ameliorate relations between management and labour.[43]

Workers, confronted with a situation in which their unions represent them neither fully nor effectively, as often as not have taken matters into their own hands. The biggest strikes tend to be spontaneous affairs, and often in response to general concerns about the social climate rather than about bread and butter issues, as in the United States. In consequence, labour unions tend to follow, rather than lead, worker protest, organising rallies after the fact, and taking the initiative for the most part only for the half-day or day-long strikes in general protest at social conditions or political measures. In the 1960s, bitter strikes in response to the deterioration of the labour market meant many workdays lost (about 6 million in 1963, 2.5 million in 1964, 1 million in 1965, 2.5 million in 1966,

4.2 in 1967), culminating in the events of May 1968, when workers joined the students in protest at government actions (with 150 million workdays lost).[44]

In this protest, as throughout the 1970s, autogestion became the battle-cry, as workers demanded the same kind of democratisation in the workplace that citizens were demanding of local government. Moreover, labour became more militant, as business–labour relations deteriorated along with the economic climate,[45] and more and more workdays were lost to strikes (in the early 1970s, 4 million on average; in the mid- to late-1970s, varying between a high of 5 million in 1976 and a low of 2.2 million in 1978).[46]

By the 1980s, the large-scale worker protests seemed to be over, and the number of strikes compared to previous decades decreased dramatically (with an average of only 1.4 million workdays lost per year).[47] In the first half of the 1980s, this was mainly because the socialists were in power. But even after, when the right came back in, the sporadic strike movements were smaller and less all-encompassing.[48] Privatisation played a major role in this, since it left more workers with fewer job protections, as did rising unemployment, which made workers generally fear for their jobs. By the 1990s, moreover, only public sector employees expressed their dissatisfaction with government measures through major walkouts, generally in response to fears of privatisation and the likely layoffs that would follow from it. Yet because these strikes affected mass transport and other public services, they had an impact way beyond the public sector firms involved.

Most telling, perhaps, in the growing gap between public and private sector labour organisation and action, is the fact that Balladur's 1993 private sector pension reform (extending the years needed to qualify for a pension) passed with nary a whisper from private sector employees, whereas when Juppé attempted to carry out similar reforms for the public sector in 1995 along with more general social security measures and an unpopular planning contract for SNCF, it resulted in an explosion of protest, the likes of which people had not seen since 1968 – or at least so it appeared, given the level of paralysis of Paris. But the strike spread from the railways solely to other public sectors employees, who claimed to be protesting social security reforms for the population at large although they were no less concerned with pending privatisation and rationalisation, particularly in the telecommunications and banking sectors in addition to the railroads. Private sector employees, although supportive of the strikes, took great pains to get to work, walking for hours to and fro if necessary.[49]

General public sympathy for the strikers, moreover, had as much to do with displeasure with the government's heroic style of policy making, that seemed outdated, as with the content. President Chirac's promise, immediately following the strike, to institute more 'dialogue and concertation', seemed empty, given the fact that the state has generally sought more to impose or to pacify (in the face of protest) than to engage in dialogue and concertation; and that the necessary intermediary bodies for such concertation are either weak or missing.

This is a result of the success of pre-1981 government actions focused on undermining unions and other alternative institutions and the failure of post-1981 policies to create intermediary bodies to substitute for direct state intervention as the government deregulated.[50]

The post-1981 reforms that introduced greater flexibility in employment did not, as intended, bring with them a new, German-style co-ordination system in which employers and unions would bargain as equals without the heavy hand of the state. And even though these reforms did serve to ameliorate labour–management relations and work conditions, they also liberalised hiring and firing, allowing unemployment to rise, and they did nothing to stem the erosion of union strength along with the number of workers and their pay. Moreover, one of the few vehicles for participation in socio-economic policy making, the system of union co-management with employers of social security, was eliminated by Juppé in favour of parliamentary oversight in his social security reform initiative.

Government response to the public sector strikes in 1995 followed a familiar pattern: in the face of confrontation, it sought to wait out the protest and, failing its early end, backed off its proposed reforms. This was the same pattern it had followed in 1986 in response to the strike of the SNCF against linking pay to merit rather than seniority, which then spread to much of the public sector, and in 1993 in response to the strike by Air France workers against a proposed restructuring plan. This pattern has continued through the late 1990s, delaying much needed changes in those public sector firms most exposed to European and global competition.

Nevertheless workers generally sense that theirs has become a losing battle, as European and global economic pressures force firms, public or private, to become more competitive. Most symbolic of this, perhaps, has been the closure of the Belgian Renault plant at Vilvoorde, which caused protest not only in Belgium by workers and government but also in France, but was nevertheless closed despite the pledges of a newly elected socialist government in June 1997.

This protest, moreover, suggests a new phase in worker mobilisation, one that sees the French labour market within the larger European context and that targets protest for maximum impact on Europe generally, and not just France. The 'Eurostrike' has become the wave of the future, and understandably so, given the increasing impact of EU-led deregulation on French workers.[51] The Renault strike is the first clear example of the Eurostrike, given the inter-European spread of protest and its impact on the EU Commission, which responded by calling for stronger workers' protections with regard to consultation requirements for European firms, though the Belgian-Renault plant workers themselves had no recourse.

Moreover, protests in other industries and industrial sectors also reflect a growing awareness of the importance of Europe. A case in point is the series of job actions in 1997 by truckers blocking major highways and border crossings in protest against European-instigated deregulation which leaves them in particular without protection and working long hours for little pay. French agricultural interests have been aware of the importance of Brussels much longer than French labour, since they have long been present in Brussels given the CAP (Common Agricultural Policy) that has Europeanised policy in the sector for decades, although they have become especially militant in EU-directed protest actions in the 1990s, in particular once policies went against them, as with the GATT negotiations.

The problem is that although these protests achieve part of their purpose, by embarrassing the French government, they cannot resolve the problem, because the French Government no longer has the kind of control it had in the past in the formulation of policies in these areas, given the primacy of EU decision-making, while in the implementation it no longer has the flexibility to bend, or not, in response to confrontation.

The most interesting recent development in France, however, has been the mobilisation of the least organised of labour groups: the unemployed. The occupation of state offices and even luxury restaurants, beginning over Christmas 1997 and continuing into the New Year, by unemployed workers protesting against low benefits and lack of jobs is perhaps the most significant new aspect of labour relations in France. It suggests not only that the traditionally most disorganised group has become highly organised and effective, at least in this moment of social protest, but also that the unemployed, in a climate of continuing over 12 per cent unemployment rates, are no longer willing to sit quietly as the employed remain quiescent. For the French government, with its expressed commitments both to social solidarity and to meeting the Maastricht criteria, this is a challenge to which it finds itself at a loss for a response.[52]

Labour–government relations, in sum, remain problematic. Unlike in business-government relations or centre-periphery relations, precious little transfer of power from state to society has occurred. The lack of significant change in this sphere, by comparison with either business-government or centre–periphery relations, has a lot to do with the fact that the state, whether led by the left or the right, has never trusted labour, and would not therefore entrust its leaders with responsibility for managing its relations with business autonomously. This lack of trust is at least in part related to the fact that labour leaders have never been close to government leaders, as have business leaders who have had the same career paths.

It is only very recently under the Jospin government that such trust would appear to be on the rise, given that business and labour have been given autonomous responsibility for the negotiation of work conditions, as in the 35-hour working week. But in the absence of the strong intermediary institutions which are the necessary preconditions to such an autonomous relationship, the negotiation still goes on 'in the shadow of the state', with the state itself ready to step in to coerce and control in order to ensure the success of its reform efforts.

Today, moreover, labour relations with government as well as management have become increasingly diverse in consequence of the degree of privatisation, deregulation, or international competition to which an industrial sector has been exposed. In the private sector, which has grown greatly as a result of privatisation, significant change has occurred, with business largely strengthened and labour weakened as a result of state reforms. Deregulation in the absence of intermediate labour institutions has led to the marketisation of labour relations, meaning that the state has left bargaining more and more to the market while firms can hire and fire with much greater freedom than in the past and with little fear of protest from its weakly unionised work-force.

In the public sector, that part sheltered from European or global competition, such as education, has changed relatively little, with its comparatively strong unions still able to block any deregulatory reform (and in the case of education, any other innovative reforms as well).

By contrast, that part of the public sector (along with parts of the private sector which formerly were heavily regulated, such as trucking) which is increasingly exposed to European and/or global competition and is in the process of privatisation and/or deregulation because of Europe-instigated reform is in flux. In this relatively large sector, labour still holds the state responsible for its fate, but the state has less and less control over the sector and less and less capacity to respond to labour demands, given European regulation and global and European competition, making the escalation of confrontation likely.

Changes have occurred in the labour relations arena as well, then, but they have not been greeted with the same level of approbation as in business-government relations. In the exposed part of the public sector, accelerating privatisation and deregulation has led to worker protests. In the sheltered part of the public sector, the lack of any forward movement has led to worker dissatisfaction. And in the private sector, the lack of job security and stagnating wages has led to worker insecurity. Add this to high unemployment and the recent general cutbacks in social security and pension benefits, and we have a picture of state-society relations that are in deep crisis rather than having been constructively transformed, as they have in business-government or centre-periphery relations.

RELATIONS WITH CIVIL SOCIETY

In government's more general relations with citizens, by contrast with relations with citizens as workers, transformation has occurred, mainly through a loosening of state control of civil society. The reforms, however, have focused less on the direct transfer of power from state to society, as it was with business-government relations or even centre-periphery relations, than from state to those professional groups or institutions that sit between state and society and/or serve to represent society as counter-powers to the state. Thus, the liberalisation of the rules governing the media, the rise of independent regulatory agencies, and the modernisation of state administration have brought about significant change in the relations between the state and its citizens, providing for greater transparency in state action and greater citizen insulation from the state. Direct citizen participation in policy making, however, has not improved.

The liberalisation of the media has perhaps represented the most significant of the reforms involving general state-society relations. Maintaining freedom of the press and electronic media has been a long struggle in France. The fact that the newspapers have since the liberation been subsidised by the state while the electronic media, that is, the major radio and television stations, were publicly held and financed monopolies until the privatisations and deregulation of the 1980s meant that the state could at least indirectly exert pressure over the media through financial means. It also had direct control through laws against publishing statements damaging to the president or other public authorities, which it used particularly frequently during the first half of the Fifth Republic to limit embarrassing media criticism of government action. And in the case of public audiovisual enterprises, the government exerted significant influence through its appointment of the heads of the radio and television stations.

Major change came as of the early 1980s, however, when the socialists liberalised the media, allowing for private radio and television stations to be regulated by an independent body in charge of the sector of information and communication as a whole, which was also to appoint the directors of publicly owned television, oversee the newly deregulated sector of radios, the content of television and radio programming, and so forth. When the right came in, moreover, it continued with liberalisation through privatisation of the symbol of government monopoly, TF1, although the regulatory body which it set up in place of the socialist one was attacked for being politically influenced. By the late 1980s, however, with yet another regulatory agency with slightly different powers from the previous, the independence of the media from politics was consecrated.[53]

The independent regulatory agency governing the media, just as the whole host of other new regulatory agencies that have followed from deregulatory reforms, have become intermediate institutions between state and society, mainly by replacing the 'administrations', in which top civil servants could choose to exercise their discretion in adapting laws to meet individual needs, with a system in which independent regulators must apply the law without discrimination or administrative discretion. The rise of independent regulatory agencies is tied not only to the economic reforms that have created greater distance between business and government but also to the administrative reforms that sought to provide greater transparency and openness to the public as well as to exercise oversight over private as well as public actors.

In the relations between citizen and public administration, a variety of commissions was established to ensure freedom of access to information, to control electronic eavesdropping, and to limit the arbitrary power of the tax authorities; in addition to an Ombudsman, with upwards of 23,000 complaints received and 22 reforms proposed in 1990. By 1990, moreover, there were almost 20 independent agencies that oversaw consumer protection, competition, and insurance. Most powerful, though, are the regulatory bodies in the financial sector, in particular the Stock Exchange Commission (the Commission des Opérations de Bourse), established in 1967 but not given concrete powers until 1989, in the wake of insider trading scandals, and the Council for Competition set up in 1986.[54]

Direct citizen participation in decision making, however, whether individually or in groups, has not improved much.[55] The statist pattern of policy making in which citizen input is left to the implementation stage remains the norm. The only recent legislative reform that purportedly increases citizen participation in the policy formulation process as a whole, a constitutional amendment passed at the end of July 1995 that enables the president to call referenda on a wider range of issues than in the past (e.g., on education, taxation, the diminution in the size of the welfare state, or privatisation), is one that does not necessarily ensure real participation, since the president would frame the question and set the terms of the debate, with a simple yes or no answer the only response possible. Moreover, although the project to 'reform the state', announced on 1 July 1996, was a step in the right direction, it is focused not on citizen participation but on state efficiency.[56]

There are other ways, of course, in which citizens' concerns are voiced. The courts have been increasingly active in pursuing administrative as well as business malfeasance, while the press has increased its investigative acumen. Both made the Juppé government uncomfortable enough that it sought to hamper the investigations of judiciary and media through a variety of means, including legal intimidation, and to question the legitimacy of the courts and the press within these contexts.[57]

By contrast, the Jospin government has sought to open up the policy-making process by consulting more on all reform initiatives at the formulation stage, mainly by using expert commissions to propose reforms on controversial issues (and choosing what to do based on public reaction); but this still suggests a more elite, rather than citizen, approach to policy making.

Moreover, there is little additional direct recourse for citizens at the European level, despite the fact that EU directives and the European court have in many instances served to promote citizen rights and protect citizens against government excess. The problem for French citizens with regard to the EU is that, outside of business interests, they have for the most part not been able to organise effectively enough to exercise influence. And EU processes offer little access to citizens *qua* citizens in policy formulation other than through individual appeals to parliament or through court cases. However, France's statist model ensures that citizens, whether organised in interest associations or not, have little impact on the formulation of national policies toward the EU.

CONCLUSION

Much has changed in state-society relations during the Fifth Republic. Deregulation and privatisation have reduced government power over business; decentralisation has diminished the centre's power over the periphery; liberalisation of the media has promoted greater state transparency; modernisation of state administration has brought it closer to those it serves; and the rise of independent regulatory agencies has enhanced citizen protections against the state.

In the labour relations arena, too, much has changed, in particular in the private sector and in that part of the public sector (or heavily regulated private sector) exposed for the first time to competition. However, in this arena, unlike in business-government relations or centre-periphery relations, the reforms have not led to a transfer of power from state to society, nor have they increased worker satisfaction, by contrast with reforms in state relations with civil society more generally that have indeed produced greater citizen satisfaction. Yet significant problems remain in this last sphere too, given that general citizen access and influence over national decision-making has not only not improved, it has even diminished in those areas affected by European integration, given that Europeanisation has decreased government autonomy and flexibility in decision making.

The remaining, overriding problem in state-society relations is that while the state has given up tremendous power through its deregulating, decentralising, liberalising, and Europeanising reforms, and thus has less capacity for action, it still perceives itself, and is perceived by society, as wholly responsible for what occurs within France. Moreover, at the same time that society expects state action, and has not as yet been able to organise itself to act autonomously, it is less willing to sit passively by as the state takes action.

The long-standing malaise in France, just as much as public sympathy for the protests of the unemployed and the strikes of public employees, has a lot to do with public disillusionment with state leaders, whom the public sees as a technocratic elite out of touch with everyday reality and stuck in the old, heroic patterns of action, where citizens are largely kept out of the decision-making process.

This has attenuated somewhat with the socialists' return to power, since Juppé's government was the lightning rod for such feelings. But even the socialists have not been as consultational as they had promised, the 35-hour work week being a case in point, since they announced the planned reform before much significant discussion had taken place, to much opposition from business and even from part of labour, although they have given business and labour time to work out their differences on the details before the reform takes effect.

In sum, even though state-society relations have been successfully reformed in a whole range of spheres, the French style of leadership remains problematic. Nevertheless, the Jospin government appears to have begun to address the problem. It has promoted more dialogue and concertation with societal interests when formulating policy. Its discourse seeks to moderate public expectations about the state's role. The government deliberately uses less heroic language to talk about its choices and actions in France, Europe and the world.

NOTES

1. Vivien A. Schmidt, *From State to Market? The Transformation of French Business and Government* (NY: CUP 1996) Ch.1; John T.S. Keeler, 'Patterns of Policymaking in the French Fifth Republic: Strong Governments, Cycles of Reform and Political Malaise', in Linda Miller and Michael Smith (eds.) *Ideas and Ideals: Essays on Politics in Honor of Stanley Hoffmann*, (Boulder, CO: Westview 1993); Stanley Hoffmann, 'The French Constitution of 1958: The Final Text and its Prospects', *American Political Science Review* 53/2 (1959) pp.332–57.
2. Schmidt (note 1) Chs 1, 2; John Zysman, *Political Strategies for Industrial Order: State, Market, and Industry in France* (Berkeley: Univ. of California Press 1977); David Wilsford, 'Tactical Advantages versus Administrative Heterogeneity: The Strengths and the Limits of the French State', *Comparative Political Studies* 21/1 (1988) pp.126–68; Jack Hayward, 'Mobilising Private Interests in the Service of Public Ambitions: The Salient Element of the Dual Policy Style', in Jeremy Richardson (ed.) *Policy Styles in Western Europe* (London: Allen & Unwin 1982) pp.111–40; Peter Hall, *Governing the Economy: The Politics of State Intervention in Britain and France* (Cambridge: Polity Press 1986) pp.165–6.
3. See Schmidt (note 1) Chs 1, 2.
4. Frank L. Wilson, 'French Interest Group Politics: Pluralist or Neo-Corporatist?', *American Political Science Review* 77/4 (1983) pp.895–910; John T. S. Keeler, 'Situating France on the Pluralism-Corporatism Continuum. A Critique of and an Alternative to the Wilson Perspective', *Comparative Politics* 17/2 (Jan. 1985) pp.229–49; Schmidt (note 1) Ch.1.
5. Wilsford (note 2) pp.152–6; Charles Tilly, *From Mobilization to Revolution* (Englewood Cliffs, NJ: Prentice-Hall 1978).
6. Schmidt (note 1) Ch.2.
7. John T.S. Keeler, *The Politics of Neo-corporatism in France* (Oxford: OUP 1987).
8. John Ambler, 'Neocorporatism and the Politics of French Education', *West European Politics* 8/3 (July 1985) pp.23–42.
9. Vivien A. Schmidt, *Democratizing France. The political and administrative history of decentralization* (Cambridge, CUP 1990).
10. Ezra N. Suleiman, *Private Power and Centralisation in France: The Notaires and the State* (Princeton UP 1987).
11. Denis Olivennes and Nicolas Baverez, *L'impuissance publique* (Paris: Calmann-Lévy 1989); Michel Crozier, *État modeste, État moderne. Stratégie pour un autre changement* (Paris: Fayard 1987).
12. François Dupuy and Jean-Claude Thoenig, *L'administration en miettes* (Paris: Fayard 1987).
13. Vivien A. Schmidt, 'European Integration and Democracy: The Differences among Member States', *Journal of European Public Policy* 4/1 (1997) pp.128–45.
14. Ezra N. Suleiman, *Politics, Power and Bureaucracy in France* (Princeton UP 1974) pp.137–54; Jean-Louis Quermonne, *L'appareil administratif de l'État* (Paris: Seuil 1991).
15. Schmidt (note 13); Vivien A. Schmidt, 'National Patterns of Governance under Siege: The Impact of European Integration', in Beate Kohler-Koch (ed.) *The Transformation of Governance in the European Union* (London: Routledge 1999).
16. Vivien A. Schmidt, 'Business, the State, and the End of Dirigisme', in John T.S. Keeler and Martin A. Schain (eds.) *Chirac's Challenge: Liberalization, Europeanization, and Malaise*

in France (NY: St Martin's Press 1996) pp.105–42.

17. See the essay by Emmanuel Négrier in this volume; and Schmidt (note 9).
18. Schmidt (note 9).
19. Hall (note 2); Schmidt (note 1) Chs 3, 9.
20. Andrew Shonfield, *Modern Capitalism: The Changing Balance of Public and Private Power* (Oxford: OUP 1965) pp.126, 145; Hall (note 2) pp.152–5; Schmidt (note 1) Ch.9.
21. Suzanne Berger, 'Lame Ducks and National Champions: Industrial Policy in the Fifth Republic', in William G. Andrews and Stanley Hoffmann (eds.) *The Impact of the Fifth Republic on France* (Albany: SUNY Press 1981) pp.160–78; Elie Cohen, *L'État brancardier, Politiques du déclin industriel (1974–1984)* (Paris: Calmann-Lévy 1989).
22. Schmidt (note 1) Ch.8.
23. Hall (note 2) pp.169–71.
24. Jack Hayward, *The State and the Market Economy: Industrial Patriotism and Economic Intervention in France* (NY UP 1986).
25. Michel Bauer and Elie Cohen. 'Le politique, l'administratif, et l'exercice du pouvoir industriel', *Sociologie du Travail* 27 (1985) pp.324–7.
26. Daniel Derivry, 'The Managers of Public Enterprises in France', in Mattei Dogan (ed.) *The Mandarins of Western Europe* (NY: Wiley 1975) pp.217–18.
27. Stephen S. Cohen, 'Informed bewilderment: French economic strategy and the crisis', in idem and Peter A. Gourevitch (eds.) *France in the Troubled World Economy* (London: Butterworth 1982) pp.21–48; Lynne Krieger Mytelka, 'In Search of a Partner: The State and the Textile Industry in France', in Cohen and Gourevitch, ibid. pp.132–50; Elie Cohen and Michel Bauer, *Les grandes manoeuvres industrielles* (Paris: Belford 1985).
28. Jonah D. Levy, *Tocqueville's Revenge: The Decline of Dirigisme and Evolution of France's Political Economy*, PhD Dissertation in Political Science, Massachusetts Institute of Technology (1993) pp.51–2.
29. Michel Bauer and Bénédicte Mourot, *Les 200: Comment devient-on un grand patron?* (Paris: Seuil 1987); Schmidt (note 1) Chs 11, 12.
30. Schmidt (note 1); Vivien A. Schmidt, 'The Decline of Traditional State *Dirigisme* in France: The Transformation of Political Economic Policies and Policymaking Processes', *Governance* 9/4 (1996) pp.375–405; Bauer and Cohen (note 25); Claude Durand, Michelle Durand and Monique VerVaeke, 'Dirigisme et libéralisme: l'État dans l'industrie', *Sociologie du Travail* 27 (1985); Jocelyne Barreau *et al.* (eds.) *L'État entrepreneur: nationalisation, gestions du secteur public concurrentiel, construction européenne (1982–1993)* (Paris: L'Harmattan 1990).
31. Schmidt (note 1) ch.4; Schmidt (note 30).
32. Vivien A. Schmidt, 'Running on Empty: The End of *Dirigisme* in French Economic Leadership', *Modern and Contemporary France* 5/2 (1997) pp.229–41; Schmidt (note 1) Chs 6, 13; Schmidt (note 30).
33. Schmidt (note 32).
34. Elie Cohen, *Le colbertisme 'high tech': Économie des télécom et du grand projet* (Paris: Pluriel 1992).
35. Schmidt (note 30).
36. Vivien A. Schmidt, 'Loosening the Ties that Bind: The Impact of European Integration on French Government and its Relationship to Business', *Journal of Common Market Studies* 34/2 (June 1996) pp.223–54.
37. Cohen (note 34) pp.217–18.
38. Bauer and Mourot (note 29).
39. Schmidt (note 30).
40. See the essay by Emmanuel Négrier in this volume.
41. Hayward (note 24) p.63.
42. George Ross, 'Labor and the Left in Power: Commissions, Omissions, and Unintended Consequences', in Patrick McCarthy (ed.) *The French Socialists in Power, 1981–1986* (NY: Greenwood Press 1987).
43. Mark Kesselman, 'The New Shape of French Industrial Relations: Ce n'est plus la même chose', in Paul Godt (ed.) *Policymaking in France: From de Gaulle to Mitterrand* (London:

Pinter 1989); W. Rand Smith, *Crisis in the French Labor Movement: A Grassroots Perspective* (NY: St Martin's Press 1988).

44. René Mouriaux, 'Trade Unions, Unemployment, and Regulation: 1962–1989', in James F. Hollifield and George Ross (eds.) *Searching for the New France* (NY: Routledge 1991) pp.175–6.

45. Mark Kesselman and Guy Groux (eds) *1968–1982: Le mouvement ouvrier français* (Paris, Editions Ouvrières 1984); George Ross, 'The Perils of Politics: French Unions and the Crisis of the 1970s', in Peter Lange (ed.) *Unions, Change and Crisis: French and Italian Union Strategy and the Political Economy, 1945–1980* (London: Allen & Unwin 1982)

46. Mouriaux (note 44) pp.179–84.

47. Ibid. p.186.

48. Chris Howell, *Regulating Labor: The State and Industrial Relations Reform in Postwar France* (Princeton UP 1992).

49. Vivien A. Schmidt, 'Economic Policy, Political Discourse, and Democracy in France', *French Politics and Society* 15/2 (1997) pp.37–48.

50. Jonah D. Levy, 'The Crisis of Identity of Post-Dirigiste France', *French Politics and Society* 14/1 (1996).

51. Doug Imig and Sidney Tarrow, *From Strike to Eurostrike: The Europeanisation of Social Movements and the Development of a Euro-Polity* (Working Paper no. 97-10, Weatherhead Center for Int. Affairs, Harvard U. 1997).

52. Schmidt (note 49); Schmidt (note 36).

53. See Jean-Noël Jeanneney, *Une histoire des medias: Des origines à nos jours* (Paris: Seuil 1996).

54. Marie-José Guédon, *Les autorités administratives indépendantes* (Paris: LGDJ 1991); Fabrice Demarigny, 'Independent Administrative Authorities in France and the Case of the French Council for Competition', in Giandomenico Majone (ed.) *Regulating Europe*, (London and NY: Routledge 1996); H. Dumez and A. Jeunemaître, *La concurrence en Europe: De nouvelles règles du jeu pour les entreprises* (Paris: Seuil 1990).

55. Alain-Gérard Slama, 'L'État sans citoyens', *Pouvoirs* 84 (1998) pp.89–98.

56. 'Repenser l'État?', *Revue Politique et Parlementaire* 982 (1996).

57. See *Le Monde*, 7–8 July 1996.

The *Service Public* Under Stress

ALISTAIR COLE

In his declaration of general policy in May 1995, President Chirac's first premier, Alain Juppé, called for a 'new republican pact' wherein 'French-style public services' would perform an essential cohesive role.[1] Two years later, Juppé slumped to defeat in the National Assembly elections, hoist upon the petard of a failed public service reform programme and by memories of the vast social protest movement of November–December 1995. This essay elucidates the various meanings of the elusive notion of *service public*. It then appraises European, national and sub-national challenges to traditional French understandings of the *service public*. Through observing examples of ideological and organisational resistance, the essay concludes that French policy makers have confronted the challenges to the *service public* in a way which is consistent with their political traditions.

WHAT IS THE FRENCH MODEL OF THE *SERVICE PUBLIC*?

There is no consensus over the notion of *service public*. It is an essentially contestable concept. The ambiguity of the notion is demonstrated by considering its various different interpretations and definitions. *Service public* appears in French law as a legal definition. In political discourse, *service public* has a powerful normative appeal to signify equality of opportunity and the neutrality of the French republican state. It is often understood in a generic sense as being synonymous with the public sector. Its most vigorous defenders are those for whom it provides a secure employment statute.

'Service Public' as a Legal Definition

Service public is first and foremost a legal definition.[2] As a legal definition, the principles of public service have varied according to the standards of the period concerned and the preferences of schools of legal thought. As defined in French jurisprudence, there are three primordial features of a public service.[3] It is delivered by a 'public person' (a public authority, or any organisation acting in a public capacity). It involves the delivery of a 'public service' benefiting the collectivity. It is protected by a special legal status: the regime of public service is subject to administrative law, when public persons engage in administrative acts. However, when public service agencies engage in commercial or industrial activities, they are subject to the civil law regime. The central problem lies in defining what constitutes a public service or an administrative activity.

This is essentially the preserve of the legislative, regulatory and quasi-judicial authorities. However, much as it has been refined in judicial terms, the decision to label an activity as a public service mission is a highly political one; politicians determine ultimately what constitutes a public service. There are obvious anomalies in French public law. Thus, until 1991 telecommunications were considered to be an administrative, rather than a commercial activity. As such, the telecommunications division (Direction générale des télécommunications) was a division of the PTT ministry, subjected to administrative rather than commercial law.

As it has developed, administrative jurisprudence has established that public service should respect certain principles: the continuity of service provision, the equality of access of all to public services and their adaptability to the evolution of society.[4] These principles often conflict. Defence of these principles underpinned the particular organisational style and structure of French public service utility firms. Public service operators had a monopoly of supply; there was a belief that natural monopolies (in gas, electricity, rail) were best organised by the public authorities. Public services were organised by monopoly state enterprises, whose workers benefited from the protection of the *fonction publique*.

Besides these core beliefs there were few formal rules. There were no independent regulatory organisations; rules were given by ministers. There was little financial transparency. The notion of public service was ambiguous and imprecise. If it meant anything, it implied a mission to serve in the general interest. This imposed certain constraints: a public utility firm had to charge the same fees to all consumers, irrespective of the cost of supply; cross-subsidies were permitted, notably from business users to ordinary consumers; public service firms had a non-profit-making mission; the Council of State insisted that they must not abuse their public sector monopoly.

As a counterpart, public sector actors were granted many privileges in French law, shielding them from the rigours of full competition. Public actors have rights of expropriation of private property, for example; these could be extended to non-public actors, such as chambers of commerce or mixed economy societies, when performing a 'public service' mission.

The legal definition of public service has given quasi-judicial actors an important role in defining the parameters of public service. The 1946 Constitution referred to the public ownership of economic monopolies as well as state provision of health, social assistance, social security and education. This gives the Constitutional Council a powerful claim to establish the parameters of what constitutes a public service, though the Council has never set out exactly which public services are enshrined in the Constitution. At the pinnacle of the French system of administrative law, the Council of State is an even more powerful actor. The Council of State lies at the very heart of the process of problem definition. Thus, the Council of State had always held firm to the principle that public services could not be created for financial gain – though profits might be made in the execution of any public service.

'Service Public' as a Mobilising Myth

Service public has been used – in a strongly normative manner – as a metaphor for the general interest.[5] It has been contrasted favourably with particularism or with the individualism underpinning Anglo-Saxon liberalism. The mobilising myth of social progress through public service has come to form part of modern French political culture.

Public service has become 'ideological, in the strong sense of the term'.[6] *Service public* is the embodiment of citizenship, the modern version of the social contract. For Christian Stoffaes, a director at Electricité de France (EDF), public service combined Republican values, the legacy of colbertism and the *fonction publique*.[7] This definition was the modern version of the doctrine refined by Léon Duguit at the beginning of the twentieth century.[8] Local and national public authorities should have a monopoly of certain types of service. They should decide alone how to implement public service. In return, they should be guaranteed certain privileges, and protected from the full rigours of civil law.

The equality and neutrality of the state forms an important part of the French republican tradition.[9] There is a widespread positive connotation of the state as an instrument of public service, as an agent of economic development and as a guarantor of equality between French citizens. The scope of the public sector is not static; it varies according to changing norms and domestic or international policy fashions.

After the discredit of the wartime Vichy regime, the state discovered new roles in the post-war period as an economic agent, and as provider of social welfare. The state became a first-rank economic actor in its own right. Though the importance of the five-year economic plans was often exaggerated, the state affirmed its presence as a key actor in the sphere of industrial policy, and its control over much financial investment. As in other Western European nations, the extension of the state's activity went beyond the economic sphere to encompass social protection and welfare.

The creation of a comprehensive social security system remains one of the achievements of the post-war tripartite government. French levels of social protection are among the highest in the world. Life expectancy, educational achievement, health standards have improved consistently.[10] These public services were won as social and political conquests. Safeguarding these public services is perceived as an electoral imperative – and not just by the left parties, as Juppé discovered to his cost.

'Service Public' and the Public Sector

An amalgamation is often made between public service and the public sector; this is misleading, in that, in accordance with French administrative law, private, professional, or associative actors can be invested with a public service mission. Public service is not synonymous with the state, or with the public sector. But the public sector forms a part of the public service. The scope of the public sector has varied according to prevailing norms. Certain public services are prescribed in constitutional documents. Thus, the Declaration of the Rights of Man imposed a police force, an army and an administration. The 1946 Constitution envisaged the public ownership of economic monopolies, as well as state provision of health, social assistance, social security and education. French administrative law distinguishes between services of protection and services of social progression.[11] In the former category (services of protection) there is national defence, police, justice, prison administration, fire fighting, civil protection. Social security and health care could also be placed in this category; these social rights had a constitutional status (they are referred to in the preamble of the 1946 Constitution). Services of social progression include education, research, culture, communication, and economic development. The latter services are not exclusively delivered by public sector actors but they are defined as lying within the public sphere of regulation.

'Service Public' as an Employment Category

At a rather different level, service public can be defined as an employment statute regulating the labour conditions of civil servants (*fonctionnaires*).

The French state directly employed 2,200,000 civil servants. In addition, 1,400,000 were employed by the local authorities, and 850,000 by the hospitals. A total of 9,000,000 people are treated in one capacity or another as servants of the state (including those on public sector pensions).[12] Staff costs accounted for 40 per cent of the total state budget. One in four French workers is employed by the state. A unified French civil service does not exist, however. There are 1,700 separate *corps*, each of which has its own methods of internal management, and promotions. It has proved impossible for the Finance Ministry or the Court of Accounts to control these *corps*. Though the French state had shrunk – through privatisations and decentralisation – the number of civil servants has actually increased.[13]

While identification of the exact nature of the *service public* is difficult to grasp, it is rather easier to identify challenges to this elusive being. In a rather schematic manner, we might identify challenges to the French model of *service public* as emanating from several internal and external sources, though in reality it is difficult to disentangle cause, effect and genealogy.

In the main body of this essay, we shall consider three separate challenges – with case studies – to the French notion of *service public*. The first two cases – Europeanisation and industrial privatisation – demonstrate how powerful features of the post-war French model of politics and policy have been challenged by combined exogenous and endogenous pressures. The third demonstrates the complexities of public service delivery, highlighting the important roles performed by private, associative and professional actors.

We conclude by arguing that, though the challenges to *service(s) public(s)* have been confronted in manners consistent with French political traditions, the French polity has mutated under the combined impact of internal and external pressures for change.

THE IMPACT OF EUROPEANISATION ON FRENCH PUBLIC SERVICES

As in other European countries, European integration has weighed increasingly heavily on the conduct of domestic French politics in the 1990s.[14] There is a growing literature on the impact of 'Europeanisation' upon the domestic political management of EU member states.[15] A good working definition of Europeanisation is that offered by Ladrech: 'Europeanisation is an incremental process reorienting the direction and shape of politics to the degree that EC political and economic dynamics become part of the organisational logic of national politics and policy-making.'[16]

National state traditions are inevitably weakened in the melting-pot of the EU policy process. The process of European integration has recast state administrations, introduced new spheres of EU policy intervention, and created new opportunities for variable coalitions of sub-national, national and EU actors. Even more than the role of specific political institutions, a certain idea of the state and a certain policy style have been called into question by the process of European integration. This can be demonstrated admirably by the public service notion and the extreme sensitivity with which this fragile edifice is defended.

Before the Single European Act (SEA) in 1987, the European Community had largely ignored public services. The Treaty of Rome clearly favours a common market over and above the safeguard of public services.[17] Thus, Articles 85 and 86 guarantee free competition between firms within the common market. These articles prevented firms from benefiting from unfair competitive advantages. Article 92 prohibits state aids to indigenous firms. Article 90-1 stipulates that public sector firms must operate under the same conditions as private sector ones. There was some reference in the Rome Treaty to public interest firms; Article 90-2 states that firms with a public interest mission might be exempted from the strict competition rules, if this was essential for the pursuit of their mission. On balance, the legal basis of the treaties is against state aids, public monopolies, and assisted sectors. In practice, however, until the mid-1980s the European Commission intervened only very rarely in national practices of industrial management.

Pressures for radical policy change came from the SEA, and the entrepreneurial action of the EC, in the form of the Competition Directorate (DG4) and the activism of individual commissioners. The specific regulations built into the SEA were the source of most tension. Strengthened by the tough competition regulations of the SEA, the Commission developed several mechanisms to break-up monopolies. The model was that of US anti-trust legislation, backed up by independent regulators. Favoured measures included privatisation, the strict regulation of state subsidies, the opening up of specific industrial sectors to competition and the creation of independent competition agencies. The harmonisation of national legislation as a prelude to opening the single market gave the Commission a large legal base to issue directives in specific sectors. These did not need the approval of the Council of Ministers or the European Parliament.

The role of policy entrepreneurs, such as Leon Brittan and Karel van Miert, and of bureaucratic turf wars in the activism of DG4 should be highlighted as agents of change.

As it emerged in the 1980s and 1990s, the EU regulatory framework was very different from the traditional French industrial model. The EU displayed its full potential as an arena of regulatory, rather than distributive politics.[18] Traditional French conceptions of public service – based on public sector monopolies and protection – went against the grain of EU competition policy. Though the reforming impetus was sparked by the SEA, the Treaty of Rome itself could be interpreted as forbidding restrictive practices. Thus, according to competition commissioner van Miert, 'if there is an amalgamation between French-style public service and public monopoly, then the former is contrary to the Treaty of Rome'.[19]

There was a strong belief that the EU model was incompatible with the French public service mission. French political and administrative elites held a negative representation of this unwelcome externality. Competition would challenge the role of natural monopolies. It would prevent cross-subsidies in favour of poorer consumers. It challenged the right of states to run loss-making public services, such as railways. Loss-making *grands projets* – so typical of the heroic French industrial policy style – would be difficult to sustain. Moreover, the privileged status of public sector employees appeared threatened.

In the sphere of public services as in others, however, the European 'constraint' was often used as a smoke screen to add intellectual weight to the argument in favour of modernising the French public service. Thus, Mark Thatcher considers that the EU provided a changed climate, more than a precise set of recommendations and regulations.[20] In practice, French elites dealt with the challenge to public service in manners consistent with French traditions. There remained a very strong determination not to go down the Thatcherite road of deregulation. The internal French constraint of mobilised public opinion – as illustrated by the 1995 strike movement – demonstrated very clearly the internal limits to public service reform.

The effective resistance of the French government proved a powerful obstacle in the way of the liberalising drive of the European Commission. The main Commission achievement was to open up the telecommunications market; from January 1998, there was a free market in this sphere. Air transport was also liberalised, despite French government opposition.

The deregulation of the energy sector met far stiffer resistance. After years of opposition, the French government finally accepted (from 19 February 1999) the limited opening of the electricity market to competition to meet the deadline of a December 1996 commission directive. Postal services provided an even greater obstacle. In November 1996, the French National Assembly adopted a resolution opposing the proposed EU directive on the liberalisation of postal services.[21]

In their text, the French deputies offered three principal arguments in favour of French style public service: as an instrument of territorial planning; as a source of social cohesion; and as a basis of European citizenship. As a result of fierce French pressure, postal services were to be exempted from liberalisation until 2003. France had managed to rally Germany to its position. Thus, the French government could claim some negotiating successes. But even where French resistance was stout, the direction of history was clear.

The case of the national electricity and gas company, EDF-GDF, was indicative of French resistance and the organisational defence of public sector monopolies. The Commission directive of 19 December 1996 was translated into French law on 19 February 1999. The French government waited until the very last minute and then adopted the minimal provision compatible with the directive. The French state worked hard to preserve EDF's situation; only one-third of the market was to be opened to public competition – and only 400 eligible clients would be able to shop around, clients defined by the state itself. The French government preserved the public service employment statute of EDF-GDF workers (a matter of critical political importance for the cohesion of the plural-left alliance) and imposed public service conditions on EDF's competitors.[22]

So much energy was dispensed in its favour because the EDF was the final bastion of technocratic state capitalism. Rather like the Communist Party in the 1960s, EDF was 'not a firm like the others'. It remained under the tight control of a ministry, which was at the same time the principal shareholder and *ministère de tutelle*. EDF workers continued to benefit from the status of *fonctionnaires*. The EDF model dated from the Liberation. It was the symbol of social-Colbertism, and a particular conception of French public service. It had relied on vast state resources to finance the visions of the narrow technocratic elite governing the EDF.[23] Quite apart from being an envied social model, EDF-GDF was the preserve of the Ponts et Chaussées *corps*, the most powerful of the technical *grands corps*.

The traffic was not all one-way. The Amsterdam Treaty of 1996 recognises the existence of 'general interest services, accorded a 'preponderant role' in the promotion of social and territorial cohesion within the Union.[24] This demonstrated the indirect influence of the French social protest movement of November–December 1995. The Amsterdam Treaty allows state aids to be granted for public service missions in certain specific circumstances, using Article 90-2 of the Treaty of Rome.[25]

The Amsterdam Treaty came on top of several European Court of Justice (ECJ) decisions tending to favour the French government's position.

In February 1997 the ECJ established that governments could assist public services in carrying out public service missions, on condition that the total of any aid was less than the cost of carrying out the mission. This judgment appeared to protect public services from the rigorous implementation of competition policy pursued by DG4. The February 1997 ruling by the Tribunal of First Instance appeared to back up French views of public service: it admitted that a public enterprise could be invested with a public service mission – and that this could allow state assistance in certain well defined circumstances.[26] Though public firms were to be treated in exactly the same manner as private ones when they acted as commercial organisations (i.e., no subsidies), they could receive state aid when fulfilling a public service mission.

To an extent French governments have been able to deal with the threat to public services in manners consistent with national traditions. On the other hand, we have observed how changing European regulatory norms have forced French governments to modify certain traditional industrial practices. The case of industrial privatisations demonstrates how French governments (of all complexions) have also proved adept at managing changing policy climates.

CHANGING POLICY FASHIONS: THE CASE OF INDUSTRIAL PRIVATISATIONS

The French model of politics and policy presupposed a rather different equilibrium between state and market than its neighbours.[27] There was more *dirigisme*. But there had always been two faces to French state activity. On the one hand, an interventionist state which actively promoted national champions and engaged in neo-protectionist practices.[28] On the other hand, Fifth Republic governments pursued a liberal macroeconomic policy based on sound money policies and international competitiveness.[29] The French economy thus developed under the dual impetus of state capitalism and classical liberalism.

State capitalism took the form of an interventionist industrial policy. As noted above, after 1945, the French state became a first-rank economic actor in its own right. The expansion of public service during the post-war period was built on the perceived incapacity of the private sphere to spearhead investment and reconstruction. After the 1946 nationalisation programme, the French state owned large tracts of French industry, notably in the sectors of transport, automobile, steel, and energy. With the nationalisations of 1946, the national public monopolies spearheaded the efforts of national reconstruction. Public service organisations were institutions whose existence was essential to make public service a reality. The socialists' nationalisation programme of 1981–82 added some leading industrial groups, and the bulk of the banking and financial sector to the state's portfolio.

Since 1986, French governments – albeit intermittently – have been busy privatising not only those firms nationalised in 1982, but also those in public ownership since 1946. If France has moved closer to the European norm, it remains committed to a larger measure of state economic interventionism than Anglo-Saxon or Germanic economic liberals consider appropriate. The nature of the French privatisation programme in 1986–88 illustrated this point: the French state preserved a powerful oversight role for itself, notably through the policy of creating a 'hard core' of institutional shareholders close to the state's economic interests.[30] This consistency with national traditions is demonstrated most effectively when considering the Jospin government, in office since June 1997.

The Jospin government has reinvented privatisation as a tool of industrial policy.[31] The left long resisted privatisation in any form. Even after accepting the economic 'conversion' in March 1983, the left had insisted upon a strong role for the French state: as provider of welfare, as economic regulator, as guarantor of employment. During the 1988–93 administration, the socialist government's position had been determined by Mitterrand's *ni-ni* policy: in his 1988 Letter to the French People, Mitterrand promised 'neither nationalisation, nor privatisation'. This led to a policy position based upon inertia. Consistent with their own partisan and statist traditions, in their 1997 manifesto, *Changeons d'avenir*, the French socialists categorically pledged to 'stop' the privatisations commenced under the Balladur and Juppé administrations.[32]

Once in power, the Jospin government was less categorical. Its responses have varied according to strategic interest and ideological preferences. Campaign promises notwithstanding, in July 1997 Jospin declared 'pragmatism' to be the guiding principle in its attitude towards privatisations: everything would depend upon the interests of the firm concerned, and the finances of the state.[33] There was a clear industrial strategy underpinning Jospin's 'privatisations'. In one or two instances, 'privatisation' was forced upon the French government by past commitments or by EU competition policy adjudications as in the case of GAN-CIC, and Crédit Lyonnais. These cases were relatively rare. Most 'privatisations' have been undertaken with a view to strengthening the strategic role of the state (or of firms close to the state) in an age of economic interdependence and globalisation. There have been three main forms: partial privatisations, designed to prepare state firms for competition; majority sell-offs, where the state retains an important blocking influence; and sell-offs strengthening the co-operative sector.

Partial Privatisations and Industrial Policy

The main justification for semi-, or partial, privatisations has been to allow leading French firms to build international alliances (the France-Télécom alliance with Deutsche Telekom and Sprint) by facilitating cross-shareholdings; and to encourage consolidation among competing French firms in a given sector (the case of Thomson-Alcatel, and Aerospatiale-Matra in the defence sector). Both France-Télécom and Thomson CSF were dealt with in a manner characteristic of French traditions. The opening up of 20 per cent of the capital of France Télécom in 1997 would encourage international alliances, assist the telecommunications giant to become a global player, and facilitate raising finance on the international money markets. Yet there was no question of outright privatisation. The public service mission of France Télécom was to remain. Moreover, the main institutional shareholders in France-Télécom were traditionally close to the French government: Bouygues, and Compagnie Générale des Eaux were two of the most important. A similar procedure was adopted for Air France in February 1999.

The defence sector provided specific challenges. The case of Thomson was another example of a controlled, or *dirigiste*, partial privatisation. A saga running since November 1996, the privatisation of Thomson was unfinished business from the previous government. Initially opposed to any privatisation, Jospin was persuaded that the *status quo* was not an option in the rapidly evolving defence world. There were too many medium-sized defence firms, not only in France, but in Europe as a whole. Rationalisation of this sector was essential, if the European defence industry was to survive the American challenge. While the Juppé government had favoured a strategic alliance between Thomson and the missile constructor Matra (itself in alliance with the German DASA and British Aerospace), Jospin arbitrated in favour of the rival firm Alcatel, in alliance with Aerospatiale and Dassault. Later on, in 1999, the Jospin government engineered the fusion between Aerospatiale and Matra. Given their dependence upon public procurement policies, even private defence firms could not resist the will of the French government in this sphere. The 'privatisation' of Thomson-CSF in reality involved the French state dictating an industrial alliance (cemented by cross-shareholdings) between Thomson-CSF, Alcatel-Alsthom, Dassault and Aerospatiale, as a prelude to a larger European-wide rationalisation.

The advantages of semi-privatisations were numerous. Partially private companies could raise money on the financial markets, while retaining state majority control. Workers could be associated with the company by becoming shareholders. In exchange, salary cuts could be demanded (as in the case of Air France, recently floated on the Paris stock exchange). Finally, opening up capital allowed for the research of industrial partners, while attempting to forestall hostile takeovers.

Covert Control Through Cross-Shareholdings

Even when the state lost a majority shareholding, it was often able to retain control. The *gré-à-gré* procedure was vital in this respect.[34] The influence of the government in drawing up the stable shareholding at the moment of privatisation was essential. Thus, in Thomson CSF the state's shareholding declined from 58 per cent to 43 per cent, but the other groups represented on the board (Alcatel, Dassault, Aerospatiale) were all close to the French state. Past experiences (such as that of the French insurer AGF, taken over by the German Allianz) demonstrated that such interventionist attempts to create stable shareholdings did not always work.

Financial Privatisations in Favour of the Mixed Economy

Wherever possible, the Jospin government attempted to make the associative and co-operative financial institutions the chief beneficiaries of privatisations in the financial sector.[35] Thus, the CIC was ceded to Crédit Mutuel. Thus, GAN was sold to Groupama. In both cases, the French state used the *gré-à-gré* procedure and favoured mutual banks over French and foreign commercial rivals. By ceding financial groups to mutual banks – with a public service mission – the government was strengthening the mixed sector of the economy.

In French law, the co-operative sector was vested with a public service mission – thereby subject to administrative law. The Finance Ministry had the right to block any decision taken by the co-operative sector that it considered against its interests. By giving this sector a public service mission, France hoped to escape from EU oversight. Paradoxically, in banking, privatisation strengthened the public service.

Innate resistance to forms of privatisation has faded in the face of changing global policy norms, ideological fashions and budgetary realism. These partial privatisations freed the French left from a taboo; privatisation was no longer off the agenda. There were few ideological defenders of nationalisation in France: even the communist Transport Minister was now willing to envisage forms of partial privatisation. For Jospin, privatisations were a new tool of industrial policy. Partial privatisation allowed strategic alliances to be formed and capital to be raised on the financial markets. Reinventing industrial policy compatible with globalisation lay at the heart of the Jospin government's strategy. The opening up of European and world markets was the driving force behind partial privatisations.

Thus far, we have considered two cases of internal and external challenge to the traditional French public service model. In both instances, we have observed how internal and external change has been managed in manners consistent with French political traditions. In the final case study, we pursue the theme of the ambiguity of the public service mission itself.

THE PRIVATE MANAGEMENT OF PUBLIC GOODS

Public service is a central notion of French administrative law. But there is no single form of public service. From the beginning of the twentieth century, the Council of State recognised the distinction between public management, and the private management of public services.[36] Pragmatism has underpinned this mixed economy policy style. It has manifested itself in various forms: by the granting of *concessions* to private operators, by profit-sharing government corporations, and through mixed economy societies. These various mechanisms have formed 'an acceptable compromise between the role of public authorities as guardians and the injection of the spirit of enterprise by private partners'.[37]

The mobilisation of private interests can take two related but distinctive forms. First, public firms often use private capital to finance public investments. French public firms such as the SNCF have for long used market instruments in pursuit of public service objectives, for instance raising capital on the markets to finance major new infrastructure developments. Such methods contributed to financing the ambitious TGV programme.[38] Second, public authorities can delegate management of public goods to private actors.[39] In the best known example, state authorities have granted *concessions* to private firms to construct and manage France's motorway network. Increasingly, public–private partnerships are being used for urban developments, such as inner-city toll roads, bridges, and tunnels.[40]

The involvement of private sector actors in service delivery highlights the essential ambiguity of the notion of *service public*. Public services can be administered by public actors, or they can be 'contracted-out' to other public or non-public authorities (such as mixed economy societies [SEMs], private firms, non-profit-making organisations [the '1901 associations'], public establishments, or individuals). The most common form of delegated public service is that of the *concession*. The public authority confers – through contract – the operation of a public service to an external party (the *concessionnaire*). After a stated period (usually from 25 to 75 years) during which time the *concessionnaire* recuperates the initial investment, the service resorts to the public sphere. The *concession* minimises the costs for the public authority. The *concessionnaire* recuperates the cost of the investment by levying charges. It also benefits from protection against competitors. As the private operators undertake a public service, normal competition rules do not apply. This explains why there have been major problems with the EU competition authorities, in particular over *concessions* to build and run motorways. The lack of transparency of these arrangements has often been criticised by the national Court of Accounts, as well as by the European Commission.

The *concession* allowed France to equip itself with modern infrastructure during the nineteenth and early twentieth centuries. This occurred, for instance, in the case of rail track, water distribution, gas and electricity. Most of these *concessions* were nationalised in 1946. The *concession* has made a comeback. Since 1970, French motorway construction and management has been delegated to private operators. Local transport services are often run by private companies – or mixed economy societies – on the basis of *concessions*. This is also the case for tunnels and toll-bridges. The Channel Tunnel was concluded on the basis of private sector *concessions* on both sides.

These mixed economy practices can best be demonstrated at the local level. As in the UK, most service delivery takes place at a local or infranational level. Local authorities (municipal councils, intercommunal authorities, departmental councils, regional councils) are required to deliver services in well-defined policy spheres.[41] The communal code outlines sanctions for recalcitrant authorities. Thus, communes have a responsibility to provide a funeral service, as well as the maintenance of public highways, waste disposal, preserving the communal archives and a range of other activities. These services are public services, though they can be managed by private actors. Apart from areas where they have statutory duties, local authorities can intervene in other areas in which they are not expressly forbidden from doing so. Thus, communes very often supply gas, central heating, local transport, and slaughterhouses.

New types of private involvement in service delivery have proved particularly attractive to local authorities since the decentralisation reforms.[42] With full control over urban planning since 1983, the demands placed on local authorities to deliver services have become acute.

Decentralisation did not strengthen local authorities structurally; they remained small, weak and dependent on external aid. No longer able to rely on central state assistance throughout the 1980s and 1990s, ambitious local authorities have turned to the private sector to build and manage public goods and services.[43]

Indeed, there is a long practice of communes 'contracting out' local services to private sector operators in spheres such as water, drainage, waste disposal, industrial heating and school canteens.[44] These practices preceded the decentralisation reforms, but they have extended their scope since then. 'Mobilising the private sector' in pursuit of public goods is a favoured tactic of ambitious mayors anxious to deliver election promises.[45] Such practices have become widespread. In its most complete form, this private sector penetration of French localities has led to the development of the *ensemblier* practice; this involves highly specialised and concentrated public utility firms (Vivendi, Lyonnaise des Eaux-Suez, Bouygues) offering a complete range of urban services to municipal authorities, allowing councils to overcome their own organisational and financial weaknesses.

These public utility firms comprise an oligopoly, with the power to define an urban product and to sell it to local authorities. Such strong and nationally present public utility firms benefit from economies of scale that local councils cannot match.

The French experience is, thus, entirely comparable with that of other European countries. In a way different to Britain, private sector operators have become essential actors in French governance. The closest French equivalent to a formal public–private partnership is the mixed economy society (SEM); this is a partnership between public and private partners, within which local authorities hold a majority of the capital.[46] SEMs are not new. They have existed since the Poincaré decree of 1926. They have always involved partnerships. Prior to the decentralisation reforms, however, they were closely supervised by the prefectures.

A new generation of SEMs were created by the 7 July 1983, decentralisation law. They are now easier to set up (the prefect no longer has to approve of their creation). They can have many objectives, rather than being created for a single purpose. Their operating modes were made far easier as they are allowed to set their own fees and draft their own constitutions.

In the 1980s, more SEMs became genuine public-private partnerships, with an influx of private capital. The range of activities undertaken by SEMs has increased dramatically, as has their number (a 100 per cent increase 1983–93). Apart from classic urban and industrial construction projects, the new generation of SEMs has allowed local authorities to become economic entrepreneurs in their own right. SEMs have been used for transport, museums, theatres, sports facilities, tourism, conference centres, even hotel chains. The advantage with the mixed economy formula is that it allows local authorities to maintain control over service delivery while attracting private capital. The flexible structure of a SEM is more suitable for economic development activities than the more rigid local authority bureaucracy. The SEM format can cover very high-risk economic development. Partnership allows risk to be spread among several partners.

Private sector influence in local public management has become pervasive. Partnerships have been stimulated by the weakness of local authorities and the complexity of normal administrative procedures; by the impact of decentralisation, which conferred new powers on mayors; and by the increasing complexity of urban development operations themselves, necessitating public and private resources. The rise of the SEMs and of new forms of private sector involvement indicates a new urban governance and the ambivalence of local public services.

CONTINUITY, CHANGE AND THE FRENCH MODEL OF SERVICE PUBLIC

The strikes of November–December 1995 were a major social movement in defence of French-style public service. They appeared to call into question the compatibility of public service à la française with the underlying norms of Maastricht Europe, essentially involving the free circulation of goods and services and untrammelled competition. These strikes were important well beyond France. The potency of mobilised public opinion as a powerful force was demonstrated within and beyond France. There is strong popular resistance to watering down public services.

French strikes – generally with a high level of public support – occur overwhelmingly in the sector of the service public; in public transport, education and health. The ability of public sector unions to mobilise support often contrasts with the general weakness of trade union movement in France and the experience of neighbouring countries.

This illustrates a strong residual attachment to the ideology of public service as political conquest and as a feature of republican political culture. And yet, this essay has highlighted the ambiguities involved in French conceptions of public service. Service public is an abstract legal doctrine whose central tenets have been challenged by the process of European integration. It is a set of normative values relating public activity to the pursuit of abstract goals of equality and the general interest. It refers to actual economic activities. It involves the defence of established positions.

Public service reform illustrated the complex interplay between the persistence of ingrained national traditions, and the strains produced by exogenous and endogenous policy change. Though the challenges to service(s) public(s) have been confronted in manners consistent with French political traditions, the French polity has mutated under the combined impact of internal and external pressures for change. Long a country which exported its model to others – within and beyond Europe – French elites have had to integrate many new ideas into their patterns of domestic government. Indeed, in certain respects, new external disciplines have been positively welcomed, as with the economic conservatives in the Trésor who applauded the discipline imposed by the Maastricht convergence criteria.[47]

This is less the case in service public, or in related areas such as employment, where a French social model is perceived to be under attack. Given the evidence presented in this article, we would argue on balance that the export market for French models of monopoly public services appears rather limited.

NOTES

1. M. Deger, 'Quand Bruxelles se rapproche de Paris...', La Tribune des fossés, 27 March 1996.
2. Gilles Gugliemi, Introduction au droit des services publics (Paris: LGDJ 1994); Jacques Chevallier, Le service public (Paris: PUF 1991).
3. Gugliemi (note 2) pp.27–9.
4. J.-L. Clergerie, 'L'Europe et l'avenir des services publics', La Croix, 5 Aug. 1997.
5. See Séverine Decreton, 'Introduction', in idem (ed.) Service public et lien social (Paris: L'Harmattan 1999) pp.13–29; P. Bauby, 'Une conception européenne des services publics', Témoignage Chrétien, 27 May 1994, p.9.
6. Elie Cohen, La tentation hexagonale (Paris: Fayard 1995) p.123.
7. Cited in M. Deger, 'La cohésion sociale, objectif principal des Quinze', La Tribune, 27 March 1998.
8. See Michel Hastings, 'Les constellations imaginaires du service public', in Decreton (note 5) pp.33–52.
9. See the essay by Vivien Schmidt in this volume.
10. Bernard Toulemonde, 'L'enseignement et la cohésion sociale', in Decreton (note 5) pp.77–97.
11. Gugliemi (note 2) pp.35–9.
12. P. de Jacquelot, 'Comment moderniser l'État?', Les Echos, 30–31 May 1997. See also 'Une gestion opaque', Le Monde, 27 June 1998, pp.14–15.
13. B. Perucca, 'Rendre l'État plus efficace: le diagnostic est posé, la dynamique à peine engagée', Les Echos, 21 March 1995.
14. Alistair Cole, French Politics and Society (Hemel Hempstead: Prentice-Hall 1998); Anne Stevens, The Government and Politics of France (London: Macmillan 1996); Roland Tiersky, France in the New Europe (Boulder, CO: Westview 1994).
15. See Kenneth Dyson, 'La France, l'Union économique et monétaire et la construction européenne: renforcer l'exécutif, transformer l'État', Politiques et Management Public 15/3

(1997) pp.57–77. See also Hussein Kassim and Anand Menon (eds.) *The European Union and National Industrial Policy* (London: Routledge 1996). See also Hussein Kassim, 'French autonomy and the European Union', *Modern and Contemporary France* 5/2 (1997) pp.167–80; Robert Ladrech, 'Europeanization of domestic politics and institutions: The case of France', *Journal of Common Market Studies* 32/1 (March 1994) pp.69–88; Christian Lequesne, *Paris-Bruxelles* (Paris: Presses de la FNSP 1993).

16. Ladrech (note 15) p.70.
17. Mark Thatcher, 'L'impact de la Communauté européenne sur la réglementation nationale: les services publics en France et en Grande-Bretagne', *Politiques et Management Public* 15/3 (1997) pp.141–68.
18. Gianfranco Majone, *Regulating Europe* (London: Routledge 1996).
19. Cited in F. Lemaître, 'L'Europe refuse l'amalgame entre 'services publics' et monopoles', *Le Monde*, 27 Dec. 1995.
20. Thatcher (note 17) p.141.
21. Clergerie (note 4).
22. C. Fabre and D. Gallois, 'L'ouverture d'EDF à la concurrence divise la majorité plurielle', *Le Monde*, 15 Jan. 1999.
23. E. Cohen, 'Les dinosaures meurent toujours', *La Croix*, 22 Sept. 1998.
24. Deger (note 1).
25. Ibid.
26. M. Durupty, 'Le service public consacré', *Les Echos*, 9 April 1997.
27. J. Barraux, 'L'État, acteur surdimensionné du nouveau jeu économique, *Les Echos*, 16 Nov. 1998.
28. Vivien A. Schmidt, *From State to Market? The Transformation of French Business and Government* (Cambridge: CUP 1996).
29. Kenneth Dyson and Kevin Featherstone, *The Road to Maastricht* (Oxford: OUP, forthcoming).
30. See, especially, Hervé Dumez and Alain Jeunemaitre, 'Les privatisations en France, 1986–1992', in Vincent Wright (ed.) *Les privatisations en Europe* (Paris: Actes Sud 1995) pp.105–32; also Mairi Maclean, 'Privatisation, *dirigisme*, and the global economy: An end to French exceptionalism', *Modern and Contemporary France* 5/2 (1997) pp.215–28.
31. M. Durupty, 'L'heure des privatisations en trompe-l'oeil', *Les Echos*, 6 May 1998; also Alistair Cole, 'French socialists in office: lessons from Mitterrand and Jospin', *Modern and Contemporary France* 7/1 (1999) pp.71–87.
32. Parti Socialiste, *Changeons d'avenir, changeons de majorité. Nos engagements pour la France* (Paris: Parti Socialiste 1997) p.11.
33. 'Que des mises sur le marché soient utiles, que des participations croisées puissent être réalisées, que des alliances soient nécessaires à la constitution d'un groupe de taille mondiale, que des actions soient distribuées au personnel, nous en sommes d'accord'. Interview with Jospin, *Le Monde* (16 Sept. 1997).
34. The *gré-à-gré* procedure allowed the French government to choose shareholders, without necessarily floating shares on the Paris Bourse.
35. Durupty (note 31).
36. Gugliemi (note 2) p.19.
37. Gilles Ribeill, 'Le développement à la française des réseaux techniques', *Metropolis* 73/74 (1986) p.84.
38. E.R. Powell, 'Public and private spheres in Britain and France: strict separation or blurred boundaries (1965–1993)?' (Paper presented to the Political Studies Assoc. conference, U. of Glasgow, March 1996) p.7.
39. Claude Martinaud (ed.) *L'expérience française du financement privé des investissements publics* (Paris: Economica 1993).
40. François Ascher, 'Le partenariat public-privé dans le (re)développement. Le cas de la France', in Werner Heinz (ed.) *Partenariats public-privé dans l'aménagement urbain* (Paris: L'Harmattan 1994) pp.197–247.
41. Cole (note 14) p.120.
42. Michael Keating, 'The politics of economic development. Political change and local

development policies in the US, Britain and France', *Urban Affairs Quarterly* 28/1 (1993) pp.73–96.

43. Dominique Lorrain, 'Après la décentralisation. L'action public flexible', *Sociologie du Travail* 3 (1993) pp.285–307.

44. Henri Coing, *Privatisation et régulation des services urbains, une étude comparative* (Paris: LATTS 1989); Jacques Caillose and Patrick Le Galès, *Les SEML dans la gouvernance urbaine* (Toulouse: PIRVILLE 1995).

45. François Ascher, *La République contre la ville: Essai sur l'avenir de la France urbaine* (Paris: Editions de l'Aube 1998).

46. Jean-Claude Mitchell, 'Des sociétés d'économie mixte locales à capitaux publics minoritaires: utopie, évolution ou révolution?', *Revue Française des Finances Publiques* 55 (1996) pp.117–29; Jean-François Bizet, 'Les SEM et la nouvelle conception de l'aménagement', *Droit Administratif*, 20 Sept. 1993, pp.594–601.

47. Dyson and Featherstone (note 29).

Restructuring Health Policy Networks: A French Policy Style?

STEVEN GRIGGS

Successive French governments, like indeed their West European counterparts, have sought to redesign health policy subsystems as the priorities of government have moved from expanding access in the initial post-war period through to imposing cost containment in the 1970s and 1980s and on to increasing efficiency in the 1990s. As to be expected, however, given the complex web of resource dependency in health policy making, not least that which ties the state to the medical profession, the results have been mixed. In the management of French public hospitals, we have witnessed, for example, major funding reforms, top-down organisational changes, new systems of health planning as well as the creation of new regional hospital agencies. These top-down changes in the regulation of the health policy subsystems have been matched by bottom-up changes in professional practices, changes in the balance of interest groups, and the emergence of new lobbies such as hospital directors.

Yet, despite the much trumpeted tactical advantages of the 'strong' French state, governments have lurched from funding crisis to funding crisis, with a long line of crisis plans carrying the names of such 'dignitaries' as Martine Aubry, Alain Juppé, Simone Veil, Philippe Séguin, Pierre Bérégovoy, and Jacques Barrot. Indeed, the Juppé Plan, having survived the widespread protests of the winter of 1995, was scuttled in less than five months, not by the organised resistance of the medical profession or by the absence of political will, but by the untimely failings of the French economy which reduced the contributions of employers and employees to the Social Security funds.[1]

These persistent attempts by French governments to impose cost containment demonstrate not only the intractable nature of certain policy problems, but also the often haphazard and unpredictable process of policy change. This essay examines this process of health policy change in France, analysing the dynamics of hospital management policy and the persistent attempts of the French state to restructure hospital management policy networks and renegotiate the state–medical profession compromise. It investigates how far we are able to identify a distinctly French pattern of policy change as characterised in the concept of a policy style. Recognising the cognitive and normative dimensions of public policies, it argues that policy styles should embody a prevailing policy frame or policy discourse.

However, it concludes that there is no specifically 'French' pattern of policy change and that there is, as such, no 'French' policy style. Policy making in France is little different from policy making in other West European states. It is erratic, driven by the 'demands' of politicians and proceeding more by trial-and-error than any rational response. The French state is neither 'strong' nor 'weak', but 'disoriented' with, as this essay argues, the different values and objectives imported into the management of health policy networks by successive sets of ministers and senior state officials driving the process of policy change.

The first part of this essay sets out the broad changes in the regulation of public hospitals from the initial moves towards cost containment in 1976 to the wide-sweeping changes to the management of public hospitals and the health sickness funds imposed by the Juppé Plan in 1995 and its accompanying ordinances in 1996. The second part examines the concept of policy styles, arguing that the quest for a 'French' policy style aids us little in our understanding of how politicians sought to renegotiate over time the regulation of public hospitals. The final part demonstrates both the erratic and contingent nature of this process of policy change, stressing the role played by politicians as the dominant selection mechanism within health policy making in France.

RENEGOTIATING THE STATE-MEDICAL PROFESSION COMPROMISE

In many aspects, the 'story' of hospital management reform in France is that of the reassertion of the state's central capacity to steer and guide actors in a policy subsystem where it had initially abdicated its managerial responsibilities. The state-medical profession compromise, concluded by the 1958 Debré ordinances, laid the framework of a health policy sub-system which was marked by weak centralisation and an absence of responsibility. First, control over both hospital funding and the delivery of services was firmly entrenched at the micro-level within public hospitals. The patient-day rate, a *per diem* payment made to hospitals for each day spent by patients in hospitals, gave control over budgets to public hospitals; with hospitals able to subsidise funding shortfalls by extending of patient stays in hospitals. The organisation of public hospitals as professional bureaucracies, characterised by a predominant professional operating core, also decentralised control over the delivery of services to doctors.

In addition, the weakness of the Health Ministry and its external services, blighted by its weak statistical support and inability to ward off the *Direction du Budget*, the budget division of the Finance Ministry, precluded its strategic intervention at the subnational level. In fact, administrative hierarchies were persistently short-circuited by local mayors who, as chairs of hospital boards of trustees, exploited their parallel political networks to advance specific hospital dossiers with one eye on their local electoral fortunes.

Second, the system operated without any clear gatekeepers and an absence of risk or responsibility attached to any individuals. The consumer sovereignty inherent in the French health care system reinforced competition between public hospitals and private clinics, and discouraged medical professionals from acting as gatekeepers (in the mould of GPs in the British NHS). Hospital doctors, entrenched in the operating core of public hospitals thereby installing a high degree of vertical dependency within the policy subsystem, were not prepared, or able, to enter into any corporatist arrangement with the Health Ministry. The social partners within the health sickness funds, the *Caisse Nationale de l'Assurance Maladie des Travailleurs Salariés* (CNAMTS), particularly the trade union confederation, Force Ouvrière (FO), which assumed the presidency of the funds from 1967 to 1996, were more concerned with protecting the rights of patients to access care than to manage the rising health care budgets. Equally, the employers' movement, the *Confédération Nationale du Patronat Français* (CNPF), although an advocate of cost containment, was weakened by its internal contradictions. Indeed, the health sickness funds failed to exploit the controls attributed to it by the Gaullist government in 1967. This impotence of the health sickness funds left the French state by default to occupy the regulatory space created by the absence of the medical profession or social partners.

However, with the imposition of top-down controls on investment and funding from 1976 onwards, the Barre government internalised policy formulation in the hands of ministers and state managers. This process culminated in the imposition of a *taux directeur*, a national-level increase in hospital budgets, as well as controls on investment. Indeed, at the end of September 1979, the Health Minister gained the right to close hospital beds against the wishes of local hospitals, although this right was not invoked. These top-down controls on health spending reached their zenith in the move to the global budget in 1983 which replaced the patient-day rate with a global monthly budget.

This policy change, which came amid the economic policy reversal of the Mauroy government in 1982–83, was associated with the appointment of Pierre Bérégovoy as Minister of Social Affairs after the profligate partnership of Jack Ralite at Health and Nicole Questiaux at Social Affairs. The global budget primarily closed significant loopholes in funding systems and formalised the system of the *taux directeur* whereby governments set annual increases in hospital budgets to be applied across the public hospital service. In short, it endowed the government with the possibility to block increases in the spending of public hospitals.

However, the application of across-the-board national increases froze inequalities between hospitals, leading to the progressive definition of departmental and regional envelopes within which adjustments could be made to the overall spending increases dictated at the national level. In fact, the global budget was, at implementation, perceived by the Directeur des Hôpitaux, Jean de Kervasdoué, as paving the way for the introduction of a programme of US-inspired diagnosis-related groups, the *Programme de Médicalisation des Systèmes d'Information* (PMSI), which was launched in 1982. Hampered by its technical complexities, as well as resistance from doctors and hospital directors and uncertainty concerning its use, the PMSI programme sought to provide a standard profile and cost for interventions in public hospitals thereby providing not only a funding tool, but also a database for the comparison of hospitals.

In 1989, the Health Ministry enforced the collection, from 1991 onwards, in all hospitals of individualised patient report cards summarising their treatment records, *résumés standardisées de sorties*, and created departments of medical information in public hospitals. In 1992, the Division of Hospitals and its collaborators drew up, from a study of some 50 hospitals, a series of relative costs for each diagnosis-related group, *groupes homogènes de malades* (GHM). These GHM were then attributed a points score on a synthetic activity index, the *indice synthetique d'activité* (ISA) thereby facilitating the identification of the case-mix of individual public hospitals and the comparison of case-mixes and production of hospitals with others. Indeed, from 1996, regional hospital authorities were able to exploit the ISA index both to gain an understanding of the regional case-mix of hospitals. They were also able to calculate, by dividing the regional budget by the total number of ISA points in the region, the value of an ISA point within the region. This value, multiplied by the number of ISA points per hospital, then enabled regional authorities to calculate hospital budgets (against the background of ISA regional value and the number of ISA points) to isolate areas of under or over-funding, thus facilitating the diminishing of regional inequalities.

While these top-down controls increased 'stress' in the system, politicians also introduced new institutional mechanisms to guide implementation structures and decision-making processes. The global budget introduced cost centres, *centres de responsabilités*, and the move towards departments tried to institute new managerial responsibilities for head doctors as well as new practices of accountability. This introduction of the more collectively-managed departments, in place of the traditional hospital services operated as the personal fiefdoms of head doctors, was fiercely resisted by the sections of the medical profession. Indeed, after a wave of strikes throughout 1983 and 1984 and mismanagement of the *dossier* by successive ministers in the Mauroy and Fabius governments, the 1986 Chirac government reversed the moves towards departmentalisation.

However, the return to services was not without its constraints on hospital doctors, since the Chirac government enshrined the penalisation of poor management. It reduced the tenure of head doctors to five years, with their reappointment dependent upon satisfactory reports on their management and their future plans for development.

In fact, the outcome power of hospital doctors led the state to foster the growth of hospital director-hospital doctor tandems as the strategic apex of public hospitals. The tandem of chair of the hospital medical commission and hospital director was progressively elevated in importance, while the influence of the mayor and the board of trustees was typically reduced (although Juppé reneged on the initial proposal to remove mayors from the presidency of hospital boards of trustees). This reinforcement of a reconfigured strategic apex was coupled with attempts both to fill in the middle-line of clinical managers, and to redefine collective medical responsibility (as seen in introducting departments and remodelling the hospital medical commission).

Consecutive reforms extended the consultative powers of the hospital medical commission to develop an overt decision-making role within the running of public hospitals. The 1987 Barzach Law sought to tie the hospital medical commission into discussions of medical treatments against the background of the budgetary constraints facing public hospitals. The 1991 Hospital Law gave it the role of preparing the strategic medical development plans for the hospital, the *projet médical*, upon which the director based the strategic plan of the hospital, the *projet d'établissement*. This was presented jointly by the director and the chair of the hospital medical commission to the board of trustees.

The development of this revised strategic apex within public hospitals underpinned the moves towards regionalisation and contractualisation within hospital planning. The planning ethos of the 1991 legislation saw politicians attempting to introduce a variant of managed competition as a mechanism to allocate resources within the hospital management system. Development contracts between hospitals and regional health authorities sealed the priorities of closures and opening of services. Indeed, hospitals were now obliged to produce strategic plans (see above) which, after submission to regional health boards, would be judged both alongside other proposals. These included the regional priorities for health care provision as defined in regional health organisation schemes and the health map of local services.

This mild competitive tendering or bidding process sat alongside attempts to devolve managerial decisions down to hospital directors, free to manage at the grassroots. This encouragement of entrepreneurial innovation sat uneasily, however, alongside the enhanced intervention of regional health boards, thereby reducing the local capacity to determine the overall pattern of service delivery. With the health sickness funds, the CNAMTS, quasi-excluded from negotiations, the managerial network was boosted by this legislation – which sought to foster the development of a cadre of regional health inspectors, nurse managers and the tandem of hospital directors and chairs of hospital medical commissions.

The regionalisation and contractualisation of the public hospital service was further embedded within the management of French public hospitals by the Juppé government. The Juppé Plan introduced 22 regional hospital agencies which brought together the external offices of the Ministry of Health and the offices of the health sickness funds in an effort to co-ordinate the provision of hospital services, both public and private. In many ways, it was a reaction to the difficulties of the first waves of health organisation schemes which saw a series of local protests against the closing of hospitals and maternities. As such, the regional hospital agencies were to be led by a 'super health prefect-director', appointed in the Council of Ministers and endowed with the capacity to set the health map, determine the budgets of hospitals, and force both co-operation between hospitals and necessary closures if possible. The board of trustees of these regional hospital agencies had no doctors or political representatives in an attempt to remove the embedded local lobbies allegedly opposed to change.

In short, the 22 heads of the regional agencies were expected to shake out the local inefficiencies of hospital provision. The development of the ISA point scale aided them in this process (see above) and went some way to reasserting market forces within public hospitals. The number of ISA points per intervention corresponded to a price mechanism.[2]

Alongside this primary axis, the Juppé Plan also implemented key reforms in the financing of the Social Security funds and its managerial attributions, the role of the National Assembly in health funding as well as encouraging moves towards evaluation and accreditation practices. Most importantly, outside the changes to funding from its reliance on employee and employer contributions and the aim of creating a single universal scheme of social insurance, three initiatives impacted upon hospital management.

First, the Juppé Plan invited parliament to set annually the national objective of spending for the health sickness funds during the vote on the funding of the Social Security funds. In fact, this involvement of parliament, which necessitated a reform of the Constitution, reasserted the state's involvement in funding as the representative of clients and the general interest over and beyond the social partners in the health sickness funds.

Second, the Juppé reforms put paid to election of representatives on Social Security funds and returned to parity representation thereby ending the tenure of FO over the CNAMTS. Indeed, the protests surrounding the Juppé Plan provided the window of opportunity for the Confédération Française Démocratique du Travail (CFDT) to cement its emergence as the managerialist 'support' of government within the health sickness funds in alliance with the CNPF.

Finally, the Juppé ordinances advanced the case of accreditation, revised by the 1991 Hospital Law, and given further enhancement in 1996. The ordinances created a National Agency for Accreditation and Evaluation in Health Care which in the original texts was concerned to audit the practices of hospitals, and to which all hospitals had to submit within five years.

Overall, therefore, the French state engaged from 1976 to 1996 in a far from unidimensional approach to health policy reform. Rather, it adopted a policy of 'tous azimuts' which applied multiple tools of network restructuring to incite change in professional practices. If overarching approach there was, it was to be found in the imposition of top-down controls on financial aggregates and the regionalisation, contractualisation and mild marketisation of public hospital services. This marketisation, however, was inherent in the French health care system by the privileged positions of consumers and the right of patients to choose the care of their choice.

Indeed, the regulatory mechanisms engaged by the French state were fraught with internal contradictions, not least the combination of top-down controls with the decentralisation and encouragement of competition in hospital planning. This 'return' of the French state also contrasts with the liberalisation and marketisation witnessed in other policy subsystems such as the media. Thus, the question arises as to how far there was anything typically French about this process of policy change. In analysing the process of health policy change, is it possible to identify a distinct 'French' policy style?

POLICY CHANGE IN FRANCE: A 'FRENCH' POLICY STYLE?

The search for a 'French' policy style seeks to identify a consistent and particular approach of the French government to problem-solving as well as distinctive relations between it and other actors in the policy process.[3] It is a search that has produced over time a somewhat 'hazy' consensus drawing together oft-contradictory 'French' policy-making characteristics such as the presence of an autonomous dynamic state, the recourse to sectoral corporatism à la française, techno-bureaucratic decision making, and the stalemate of a 'blocked society'.

Indeed, Hayward, in his identification of a 'dual' policy style in France, neatly displays the classical pillars which structure traditional studies of French policy change: reactive bureaucratic decision making unable to bring about change by negotiation allied to an assertive and pro-active decision making driven by the informal networks and concentrated power of the French executive.[4] Together, these two patterns of policy making produce an ambiguous policy style whereby state-led policy innovation is matched by mismanaged policy stalemates that can degenerate into short periods of crisis and rapid upheaval and change.

This crisis-ridden explanation of policy change permeates Crozier's influential study of France as a 'blocked society' whereby the cultural fear of face-to-face relations and hierarchical conception of authority in France mean that change comes through periodic crisis rather than incrementally.[5] It is mirrored in studies of health policy change by Wilsford who salutes the tactical advantages of the French state over wider societal groups while recognising the weakness of the state when faced with direct action.[6]

At first glance, such interpretations lend themselves to the understanding of the 'crisis' surrounding the formulation of the Juppé Plan in 1995 as well as the failure of the Mauroy and Fabius governments to negotiate the reorganisation of public hospitals between 1982 and 1986. In the case of the Juppé Plan, the internalisation of decision making during its formulation, particularly around Juppé and his advisers, coupled with the delays and *façade* of consultation with interest groups, amply demonstrates the assertive pro-active decision making and informal networks of the French core executive. Indeed, it is arguable that the autonomy of state-led decision making left trade unions with little choice but to take to the streets. As such, radical change is once again twinned with crisis and the failure to bring about change by negotiation.

However, the utility of the search for a 'French' policy style remains questionable, with even its originators recognising that exceptions to the dominant policy style will occur. Indeed, Richardson, Gustafsson and Jordan make no sweeping claims for the concept of a policy style, accepting that not all policies are dealt with in the same way, but arguing that 'policies are not so distinctive as to prevent them being accommodated in a basic simple typology of policy styles'.[7]

In fact, patterns of policy making vary both within and between policy subsystems, but also over time as state regulation of policy sectors responds to new challenges and evolving demands. This variation is amply demonstrated by the prolonged debates over the nature of interest group politics in France (see the discussions between Wilson and Keeler for example). Indeed, Mazey argues that there is no single model of interest intermediation in France, but rather an infinite variety of state–group relations from policy sector to policy sector.[8] Underpinning her claims is the recognition that the French government is not a cohesive body, but fragmented, and the French bureaucracy is not monolithic nor insulated from politics and self-interest. As such, the policy style approach deals poorly with the sectorisation and fragmentation of policy making inherent in the recognition that France, like other West European states, is a disaggregated polity. As Baumgartner is keen to point out, 'there is not and never has been a single "French" style of policy making. Many different styles of policy making coexist simultaneously in France, as they do in any complex country'.[9]

In the case of hospital management reform, there was over time a series of consolidations and expansions of decision-making networks as governments switched from policy style to policy style. With the imposition of top-down controls on financial aggregates, the Barre government assembled a loose linkaging of *Inspecteurs des Finances* within the ministerial divisions of health and social security and the administrative leadership of the health sickness funds, the CNAMTS, creating difficulties for most of the traditional partners of the Health Ministry as it opted out of the established relations with the regional teaching hospital elite and the public hospital lobby, the *Fédération Hospitalière de France* (FHF).[10]

This internalisation of policy making was exploited once again during the formulation of the global budget in 1983 where social partners and even hospital doctors were excluded from the decision-making process. Indeed, the exploitation by Bérégovoy, the then Minister of Social Affairs, of the decree powers open to the French government even bypassed the limited consultative arena of the National Assembly. These decree powers were also exploited by the Juppé government in 1996 when it implemented its wide-ranging reform of hospital management by recourse to ordinances. The formulation of this plan was internalised, led by a working party of four members, which was co-ordinated by Antoine Durrlemann, the social policy adviser of Juppé, and excluded the ministries of Health and Social Affairs. Neither the Social Security Division nor the CFDT and the FO were consulted. The consultation of the regional forums which ran in conjunction with the secret meetings of the Durrlemann working group were a 'diversion'.[11]

However, this strategy of top-down internalisation of policy formulation was not mirrored in the pursuit of organisational change in public hospitals. In the failed attempt at the departmentalisation of public hospitals, policy makers engaged in a series of consolidations and expansions of decision-making networks, particularly after the interventions in 1982 of the communist Health Minister, Jack Ralite, and, for that matter, his very appointment, broke the rules of consultation between the state and the medical profession and triggered the mobilisation of hospital doctor trade unions. This mobilisation of hospital doctors tied the Mauroy and Fabius governments into a series of consolidations and expansions of the membership of policy networks as they strove to broker agreements within the medical community. Uncertain of the support of hospital doctors, the PS government oscillated between answering the demands of modernising unions, alleged left-winger supporters and conservative trade unions and the elite hospital-doctor consultative bodies, the *conférences*.

This whole period of policy reversals and trial-and-error settlements culminated in the decision by the Fabius government to force through the implementation of departments only six months before the legislative election in March 1986 when the issue was already dead and just waiting for the re-election of the right.

After the crisis of relations between the PS and hospital doctors, the Chirac government awarded the traditional medical elite privileged access to the hospital policy-making process. Barzach's 1987 legislation mirrored the policy proposals put forward by the elite university-hospital consultative bodies. The right-wing government, eager to trade with the elite university hospital doctors, stood out against the influence of both the left-leaning pro-department doctors and the radical conservative wing of the elite mandarins.

Behind these essentially reactive ruptures of the opening and closing of access to different groups within the medical profession, politicians sought to construct and favour the resources of the more managerialist sections within the medical profession. Even the Chirac government's settlement refused to endorse a compromise acceptable to its vocal supporters behind Bernard Debré, leaving decisions to reorganise services in the hands of doctors themselves. That settlement acknowledged the principle of limited performance measurement (hampered in practice by the scarce resources at the disposal of the Health Ministry) and the obligation to attribute more responsibilities to junior doctors.

More importantly, at key stages of the moves towards department-alisation, the PS responded to the demands of the modernising *Intersyndicat National des Médecins Hospitaliers* (INMH), bringing its leader, Francis Peigné, into the core of decision makers, because he had access to the Elysée. Politicians' backing for Peigné continued under the Rocard government where he was brought into the policy-making process surrounding the 1991 Hospital Law by the then Minister of Solidarity, Health and Social Protection, Claude Evin, who tied him to the government's proposals. They commissioned him to report on the future of the public hospital service and appointing him to the Couty Commission which undertook a key role in the consultation surrounding the 1991 Hospital Law.

Thus, the PS continued the *barriste* attempts to construct an alternative policy network within the hospital management policy sub-system. It sought to create a 'partner' to negotiate with the financial 'community' of state managers who had invaded the management of hospital spending. Outside Peigné, the key beneficiary of this pro-active management of health policy networks was the *corps* of hospital directors which swept into pivotal positions within the decision making process surrounding the 1991 legislation, as Evin brought together a network of modernisers. This elevation of the *corps* was matched by improved working conditions and enhanced responsibilities for directors in public hospitals: it was the 'typical' French response to a policy dilemma.

Overall, this attempt to construct a policy network sat alongside the decline of the traditional partners of the Health Ministry (see above), confused periods of expansion and consolidation bringing rival unions in and out of decision-making forums as well as periods of policy internalisation where external groups were deliberately excluded. That these transformations might 'fit' within the alleged 'dual' policy style of French policy making says much about the generalised explanations of policy style approaches. In fact, the ultimate success of a search for a policy style depends upon its capacity to be more than the recognition that political opportunity structures or institutional frameworks constrain and facilitate different forms of political behaviour across political systems. Public policies are not simply a collection of institutional resources and carriers of rules and regulations, but operate at cognitive and normative as well as instrumental dimensions.[12]

Policy styles will thus have to embody a prevailing policy frame or policy discourse as portrayed in the concept of the *référentiel* pursued by Jobert and Muller.[13] They assume the existence within political systems of a global *référentiel*, 'the social image of all society' around which sectoral *référentiel* or policy discourses are constructed within policy sub-systems. Throughout the *trente glorieuses* of post-war economic growth, this dominant policy discourse in France was that of modernisation with French society conceiving of 'its relationship to the world through the action of the State'.[14] This distinctive community of values and assumptions was embedded over time within institutions, *grands projets*, the predominance of the elite civil service and the recourse to sectoral corporatism. It informed policy makers in their calculations of the constraints and opportunities facing them as well as the range of possible solutions available to them.

This recognition of dominant policy discourses can solidify the understanding of a distinct 'French' process of policy change, taking us beyond the mere acceptance of differing institutional frameworks. It elevates changing policy discourses or paradigms as the key variable in the definition of the prevailing policy style. In addition, it provides an explanation for changing policy styles which is not necessarily forthcoming in the approach of new institutionalism. The crisis of the 'French' policy style as defined by Muller thus corresponds to the emergence of a new paradigm based on the market.

However, the requirement to go beyond the lessons of institutional comparative politics, leads it into a misguided quest for a single dominant policy discourse. Indeed, Jobert and Muller both recognise that the *référentiel* should never be considered as a single over-determined frame dictating the actions of policy actors, and acknowledge that the global policy discourse will have to be articulated within each policy subsystem giving birth to different sectoral policy discourses. Thus, even here, the policy style approach risks sacrificing the depth of its analysis for breadth of its analysis.

In fact, the imposition of a specific policy style runs the risk of smoothing out, of 'softening' periods of policy change whereas these major policy changes often are a bit chaotic, with a good deal of tracking back and forward in short term 'wobbles'. They tend to ignore the role of random factors, contingency, and the unpredictability of the policy-making process. In the French context (and in Britain) powerful central government departments often tackle major long-run problems and the need for structural reforms by trying first one thing and then another. As such, policy evolves often through trial and error, learning from other developments or following examples set elsewhere.

The global budget was imposed upon public hospitals because it was a known quality which had worked in other areas, not least Canada. Equally, the PMSI programme was imported from the United States after field trips led by the then Director of Hospitals, Jean de Kervasdoué.

However, even accidental variations and mistakes can cause new ideas to emerge and become embedded within institutions.[15] The unforeseeable resignation of the first Health Minister in the Rocard government cannot be divorced from the emergence of hospital directors throughout the 1991 Hospital Law: Evin, who initially was to be somewhat distant from the direction of health policy, was integrated within the personal networks of hospital directors and his appointment thereby unexpectedly advantaged the *corps* of hospital directors. Neither can the prolonged negotiations surrounding the introduction of departments be divorced from the fact that the resignation of Mauroy in 1984 left the decree on departments unsigned on the ex-Prime Minister's desk thereby providing the opportunity for the renewal of negotiations under a new minister.

Indeed, the success of an accidental variation can encourage its replication by policy makers thereby encouraging path dependent policy making and longer-run dynamic of more coherent and consistent change. In this framework of analysis, as Kuhn argues, we should refer not so much to a weak or strong French state, but to a more disoriented French state.[16]

Overall, therefore, the concept of a distinct 'French' style of policy change aids us little in our understanding of health policy change. Rather, it fails to grasp the variety of policy making styles in existence and smoothes out the haphazard elements of an unpredictable policy process. Policy making in France is little different from that in other advanced liberal democratic societies. It is erratic proceeding often by trial and error in the search to a solution to an often intractable solution. The overriding task is not the issue of defining a single policy style, but rather that of isolating the selection mechanism which explains the shifts between different policy styles over time and across policy subsystems.

MINISTERS' SHIFTING AGENDAS: THE DOMINANT SELECTION MECHANISM?

Baumgartner conceptualises these shifts in policy styles in terms of changing agendas, as to whether issues are classified as high on the public agenda, defined as a 'political' question and open to partisan and public debate or are defined as 'technical' matters kept low on the agenda and confined to a small number of experts. His study of educational policy making argues that policy makers in France were strategic in seeking to define issues as low or high on the political agenda.[17] In health care, the diagnosis-related groups programme, the PMSI, was over time defined as a technical issue, confined to the working groups of the Health Ministry and its ultimate use deliberately kept vague so as to keep it off the agenda.

However, Baumgartner ultimately says little about which actor determines the agenda-status of issues and who controls the status of agendas. This selection mechanism, according to John, will vary over time and be subjected to success criteria, influenced by institutional design and be corrected over time if decision makers over-neglect one selection mechanism such as public opinion in favour of another: 'In some periods public opinion can be highly effective; in other times decision-makers believe they can ignore it.'[18]

More importantly, as the Juppé Plan demonstrates, there is not necessarily an overt relationship between agenda-status and the nature of decision-making practices. Despite the protests against the Juppé Plan, there was relatively little immediate action from the Juppé government to open the internalised decision-making mechanisms that characterised the formulation of the plan.

However, despite the shifting nature of the selection process, it is arguable that the predominant selection mechanism will be politicians. Politicians devote substantial time and effort to organising and reorganising policy arenas to support the formation and implementation of policies.[19] They are able to do so because governments possess legitimacy and greater opportunities for conditional and unconditional incentives than other actors: 'at the end of the day, the material power and legitimacy of elected government can ride roughshod over any policy community'.[20]

Rhodes attributes to government the capacity to manage access to policy networks, decide the rules of the game within policy networks and determine the scope and timing of consultation.[21] Smith contends that presidents and prime ministers can employ their despotic power to 'force new issues onto the agenda, ... take decisions themselves, ... give access to different groups, or ... change the institution which is responsible for making a decision'.[22] Indeed, the French President and Prime Minister excluded agricultural trade unions and high-ranking officials in the Agriculture Ministry from decision making during the 1991–93 GATT negotiations.[23]

In short, ministers can thus often choose between working alone or with policy communities.[24] Indeed, involvement within a policy network, even a consensual policy community, does not mean that core executives will necessarily develop policies in harmony with the interests of the wider membership of the network.

In fact, network restructuring in hospital management was driven by the different values and objectives imported into the management of health policy networks by successive sets of ministers and senior state officials, most notably the 'political' appointees within ministerial *cabinets*. Upon arrival in office, ministers did not necessarily share the entrenched rules and norms which governed relations within established health policy networks. Rather, they had their own distinct priorities which were formulated outside the network.[25] The concerns to impose cost containment, driven by Barre and his team of ministers and advisers, alienated ministers' traditional partners in the Division of Hospitals, the FHF, the medical elite in the regional teaching hospitals and even hospital directors. These distinct priorities, coupled with the turnover of ministerial chairs, meant that ministers could break the routine of policy network consultation.

Ralite and Questiaux relegated to the background concerns over health spending against the advice of senior bureaucrats, while Bérégovoy implemented the global budget. Blighted in the medical community by his communist affiliations, Ralite ignored the established rules of consultation even before he released for consultation the draft decree on departments.

Georgina Dufoix in 1984 reneged on the agreement on departments negotiated by her predecessor, Edmond Hervé, and began private negotiations with the leaders of the elite university hospital doctor consultative bodies.

Evin arrived in office with the expressed intention of revisiting the debate over departments and revising the system of hospital planning.

The centrist, Bruno Durieux, appointed as junior Minister of Health to gain the support of centrists and thus aid the passage of the 1991 Hospital Law through the National Assembly, intervened in the parliamentary negotiations of the 1991 Hospital Law to stamp his influence over the text.

Chirac and Juppé brought to a head the funding crisis facing the Social Security funds despite electoral pledges to do otherwise (although to be fair the Juppé government made the control of public spending one of its central preoccupations in its declaration of policy). So, ministers and senior state managers were often unpredictable policy actors.

In part, these interventions were designed to manage some short-term crisis or to achieve short-term payoffs for ministers. Jean Farge was appointed by Giscard to cap hospital spending by the presidential elections of 1981. His short-term mandate guided his use of network restructuring strategies, the internalisation of policy making, and his reluctance to launch the long-term implementation of the global budget.

The appointment in September 1986 by the Fabius government of Jean Terquem to push forward the introduction of departments, like previous hesitations by Hervé and Dufoix, was another attempt to achieve short-term payoffs (although Terquem was not a minister). The origins of the decision by Evin to rewrite the public hospital legislation lay in discussions with his *cabinet* about the best strategy to manage the 'crisis' that was mushrooming in public hospitals, particularly the discontent of nurses.

Finally, the Juppé Plan emerged from the acknowledgement of the rising deficits of the Social Security funds and the desire by Chirac and Juppé to meet the budgetary requirements of entry into the single European currency.

Ministers were also side-tracked by the desire to accommodate the demands of party clienteles. The primarily top-down emergence of the global budget contrasts with the bottom-up emergence of departments, which built upon the client groups of the French Socialist Party (PS), and the Gaullist Party (RPR). Political parties are not homogenous organisations, but are coalitions of interests embedded within networks of organisational interests and groups. These clienteles are sources of initiatives which do not fit within the rules and behaviour of the established policy community because they are intra-party processes and can have atypical dynamics. Where political parties have formal ties with interest groups or are 'captured' by a group, politicians are likely to engage in network structuring if their clienteles are closed out of the decision-making process. Such network restructuring is particularly likely to occur when partisan cleavages structure a fragmented professional group universe, as in the case of the differential support of hospital doctors for parties of the right.

The PS's few connections with hospital doctors, and its prolonged absence from office, acted as a source of dynamism within the policy subsector, paving the way for network restructuring strategies. In 1981, it brought into office individuals from *Santé et Socialisme* and elevated Peigné and his supporters.

However, these groups lost such privileged access once the RPR and the giscardian *Union pour la Démocratie Française* (UDF) returned to office and the Chirac government reinstated individuals from the *conférence* within ministerial *cabinets*. This inconclusive differential support promoted Evin to draw hospital directors into the ranks of decision makers as he sought to create an alliance of modernisers.

Elisabeth Hubert, appointed as junior Minister of Public Health and Health Insurance in the Juppé government, pursued a erratic stance towards the medical profession as she attempted to square the demands of cost containment with the desire to court her supporters within the medical profession.

However, ministers also took short-term actions which appeared to go against their chances of reelection. Debré and its more vocal supporters within the medical profession were ignored by the Chirac government. The PS minister, Georgina Dufoix, sought a negotiated compromise with elite hospital doctors, ignorant of the demands of Peigné and modernising left-leaning unions within the medical profession. The formulation of the global budget, by its very nature, provided only diffuse gains for potential beneficiaries outside the national state, while the costs to individuals were direct and its effects were highly visible and traceable to government leaders.

In addition, Chirac and Juppé by opening the Pandora's box of social security reform triggered the protests which ultimately contributed to the defeat of the right in 1997 – although it was the unfortunate inclusion of proposals to reform the pension rights of railway workers which led to the first wave of protests.

Health and Social Affairs ministers were also unable to insulate themselves from the broader policy concerns, particularly economic concerns, of senior core executive actors – expressed in interventions from the Finance Ministry, Matignon and the Elysée, who possessed a broader concern with policy dilemmas than health policy network actors. Senior core executive actors parachuted into Health like-minded individuals with externally defined agendas to control costs. Barre and Giscard imposed Farge. Mitterrand and Mauroy imposed Bérégovoy, who assembled a team of advisers led by the financial manager, Naouri.

However, Matignon and the Elysée intervened only sporadically in the implementation of departments, advancing the interests of doctors at various stages. Evin came up against the Budget Division as the 1991 Hospital Law became embroiled with internal PS battles and battles between the competing bureaucratic interests of ministries. More importantly, Juppé, acting in tandem with Chirac, removed not only the

Public Health Minister Hubert but also Codette Codaccioni, the Junior Minister for Solidarity between the Generations, from her post to facilitate the formulation of the proposals to reform the Social Security funds. They then, particularly Juppé, proceeded to centralise control of decision making outside the standard arenas of health and social affairs and, indeed, interministerial policy co-ordination.

However, ministers did not simply inject short-term concerns into the network restructuring of health policy networks. Neither should they be classified as non-strategic actors. There was policy learning by ministers and *cabinets*, as Evin and his advisers demonstrated in the formulation of the 1991 Hospital Law, an organisational reform which did not resurrect the spectre of departments. Indeed, the introduction of departments was never a priority of Matignon and the Elysée under the PS, and from 1987 the introduction of departments was a 'settled' issue. Likewise, although the launch of the global budget stuttered throughout the 1970s, the permanency of stringent controls on hospital spending was not questioned from the mid-1980s. Such policy learning supports conceptions of adaptive interventionism by ministers rather than knee-jerk reaction in non-strategic directions.

Ministers might not be dictated to by the norms of behaviour within policy networks, but there is a departmental history or conception of ideas to guide their actions. Reforms such as departments had been suggested and discussed long before the arrival in office of the French socialists. Most importantly, in health policy subsystems, both different governments and grassroots participants shared an interest in defining a workable compromise to regulate the delivery of services and allocation of resources. Much of the expansion and consolidation of networks and trial-and-error strategies engaged by politicians was a means of attempting to mediate and negotiate this workable compromise.

CONCLUSIONS

The reform of hospital management in France reveals the genuine and ineradicable difficulties confronted by top policy makers in making decisions with relatively poor information and foresight possible, and often confronting 'wicked' problems under conditions of severe constraints. There is no distinct 'French' policy style. Indeed, it is arguable that policy making in France is not significantly different from that of other advanced capitalist states.

First, it is erratic, driven not least by contingent responses, mistakes and the transfer of policy ideas.

Second, it is heavily politicised, with ministers and their policy advisers operating as the dominant selection mechanism. Indeed, a shifting cast of politicians and their assistant entrepreneurs and advisers scan for new ways of addressing intractable problems that fit with the politicians' own needs and orientations.

Interestingly, the development of PMSI, although delayed in its implementation, appears to have been protected from the vicissitudes of the policy-making process by its confinement to working groups in the Health Ministry and the avoidance of confrontation and the 'ownership' of the programme by politicians.

In fact, attractive solutions to politicians are those which seem to promise low transactions costs[26] by proposing as an agent institutions or groups whose interests are more congruent with legislators' interests than others; by allocating risks to social actors who can best insure against them; and by offering the prospect of a relatively long-lived and well-accepted solution, that will not simply be reversed in a few years' time by a new and different majority coalition of legislators or a differently-structured set of top policy elites.

In this world, actors whose solutions seem to work can command a higher price for their involvement in coalitions or networks. And, governments, French or otherwise, who pick up on such solutions will achieve some of their objectives, stabilising (if not actually solving) their problems in some dimensions.

NOTES

1. By the beginning of April 1996, the expected deficit for the Social Security funds for 1996 was put at 40 billion French Francs; far beyond the expected 17 billion estimated in the Juppé Plan. See *Le Monde*, 4 April 1996.
2. J-C. Moisdon, F. Engel and F. Kletz, 'Les volontés du savoir: transformations de la régulation du système hospitalier, *Revue Française d'Administration Publique* 76 (1995) pp.663–74.
3. Jeremy Richardson, Gunnel Gustafsson and Grant Jordan, 'The Concept of Policy Style', in idem (ed.) *Policy Styles in Western Europe* (London: Allen & Unwin 1982) pp.1–16.
4. Jack Hayward, 'Mobilising Private Interests in the Service of Public Ambitions: The Salient Element in the Dual French Policy Style?', in Richardson (note 3) pp.111–40.
5. Michel Crozier, *La société bloquée* (Paris: Seuil 1994).
6. David Wilsford, *Doctors and the State: The Politics of Health Care in France and the United States* (Durham, NC: Duke UP 1991).
7. Richardson *et al.* (note 3) p.5.
8. Sonia Mazey, 'Public Policy-making in France: The Art of the Possible', *West European Politics* 9/3 (July 1986) pp.412–18.
9. Frank R. Baumgartner, 'The Many Styles of Policymaking in France', in John T.S. Keeler and Martin A. Schain (eds.) *Chirac's Challenge: Liberalization, Europeanization and Malaise in France* (London: Macmillan 1996) p.97.

10. Bruno Jobert, *Le social en plan* (Paris: Éditions ouvrières 1981).
11. *Le Monde*, 17 May 1997; Patrick Hassenteufel, *Les médecins face à l'État: Une comparaison européenne* (Paris: Presses de Sciences Po 1997); David Howarth, 'Planning Le Plan Juppé: A Case Study of Centralised Co-ordination in the French Core Executive', paper presented at the Political Studies Association of the UK Annual Conference, University of Nottingham, 20 March 1999.
12. Bruno Jobert, 'The Normative Frameworks of Public Policy', *Political Studies* 37/3 (1989) pp.376–86.
13. Bruno Jobert and Pierre Muller, *L'État en action: Politiques publiques et corporatismes* (Paris: Presses Universitaires de France 1987).
14. Pierre Muller, 'Entre le local et l'Europe: La crise du modèle français de politiques publiques', *Revue Française de Science Politique* 42/2 (1992) p.280.
15. Peter John, 'Ideas and interests; agendas and implementation: an evolutionary explanation of policy change in British local government finance', *British Journal of Politics and International Relations* 1/1 (1999) pp.39–62.
16. Raymond Kuhn, 'The State and the Broadcasting Media: All Change?', in Mairi Maclean (ed.) *The Mitterrand Years: Legacy and Evaluation* (London: Macmillan 1998) pp.287–99.
17. Baumgartner (note 9) pp.85–101; Frank R. Baumgartner, *Conflict and Rhetoric in French Policymaking* (U. of Pittsburgh Press 1989).
18. John (note 15) p.45.
19. Geoff Dudley and Jeremy Richardson, 'Arenas Without Rules and the Policy Change Process: Outsider Groups and British Roads Policy', *Political Studies* 46/4 (1998) p.728.
20. Keith Dowding, 'Model or Metaphor? A Critical Review of the Policy Network Approach', *Political Studies* 43/1 (1995) p.144.
21. R.A.W. Rhodes, 'Power-dependence, policy communities and intergovernmental networks', *Essex Papers in Politics and Government* 30 (1985) p.9.
22. Martin J. Smith, *Pressure, Power and Policy. State Autonomy and Policy Networks in Britain and the United States* (London: Harvester Wheatsheaf 1993) p.96.
23. Paul J. Epstein, 'Beyond Policy Community: French Agriculture and the GATT', *Journal of European Public Policy* 4/3 (1997) pp.355–72.
24. Geoff Dudley and Jeremy Richardson, 'Promiscuous and Celibate Ministerial Styles: Policy Change, Policy Networks and British Roads Policy', *Parliamentary Affairs* 49/4 (1996) pp.565–83.
25. Ibid.
26. M. Horn, *The Political Economy of Public Administration* (Cambridge: CUP 1995).

The End of French Exceptionalism?

JILL LOVECY

Ten years ago the Bicentenary of the 1789 Revolution, falling immediately after the 40th anniversary of the founding of the Fifth Republic and in the wake of France's first 'cohabitation' experiment, provided the setting for a much publicised debate which spilled over from academia into the popular media. This centred on the claim that France was now experiencing *la fin de l'exception française.*[1] Today the same phrase still enjoys a strikingly widespread currency within and outside France, providing a recurrent *leitmotif* in newspaper headlines as well as academic writing.

This essay explores the literature of this period and examines how we can account for the prominence of this claim, and for the persistence with which it has been made. It does so primarily in respect of the Franco-French core of this debate, as it has developed in the field of political science and its sub-disciplines. Ultimately this is a debate centring on changes in French institutions, practices and *mentalités* and their relationship to those found elsewhere. A particular concern here will therefore be to link the terms of this Franco-French debate to an international (and, for the most part, English-language) literature of comparative political analysis.[2]

The discussion presented here is organised around three linked, but conceptually distinct, issues. For the usage of this deceptively simple formulation – *la fin de l'exception française* – masks fundamental differences in the literature of this period: as to what had previously been constitutive of France's 'uniqueness'; as to the causal factors and processes identified as promoting fundamental change in the contemporary period; and also – and not least – as to the characterisation of the new 'order of things' on to which, it is suggested, France is now being aligned. In unpacking the competing claims that this shared terminology has come to encompass, three central arguments will be developed.

The first of these arguments is concerned with distinguishing between two contrasting waves of discourse about the end of French exceptionalism within this period. What provided a unifying theme and focus for the first of these waves, which is confined to an earlier literature within this period, was its shared optimism: the conviction that the changes underway are indeed changes for the better.[3] This in turn is linked to these writings' common focus on what are essentially endogenous processes of causality. They thus portray the changes underway as deriving primarily, although not necessarily intentionally, from the efforts and behaviour of actors and agencies located in France. However this account of the demise of French exceptionalism proved to be short-lived. As these initial analyses encountered mounting difficulties in their empirical application, the same language came to be employed to establish a quite contrasting set of claims and counter-claims.

At the heart of this second set of claims lay the qualitatively different status which they conferred on exogenous factors and on externally situated models of society, economics and politics. By the mid-1990s the debate on *la fin de l'exception française* had largely been re-located around the twin processes of Europeanisation and globalisation, within which the French state and its domestic social and economic partners were now having to learn to operate. As a result, this second discourse on the demise of French exceptionalism came to be inextricably bound up with what have been conceptualised as a series of linked *contraintes extérieures*. And in much of this literature, the multifarious workings of such external constraints are portrayed as being imposed on France's citizenry, irrespective of their own perceived interests or of their democratically expressed preferences. These contrasting accounts of *la fin de l'exception française*, together with a selection of the variants found within each of them, provide the focus for the two main sections of this essay.

This discussion leads into a second argument, centred on the relationship between these new discourses and the underlying problematic on which they both draw: that of France's path-dependency over *la longue durée*, shaped by the Great Revolution and its Napoleonic and republican aftermaths. This problematic has informed a broad sweep of French social science and historical research, but it provides a framework within which several differing accounts of France's exceptionalism can be constructed. Certainly the predominant conceptualisation of French exceptionalism was one deriving from the intellectual traditions of French republicanism, and this has focused on the universalistic *exemplarité* of her democratic and egalitarian principles of citizenship.

France's republicanism had reconstructed national identity around a new conception of citizenship, symbolised in the triptych of the Revolution. For citizens to exercise their democratic freedoms – to have liberty – required that the state act as the guarantor of equality, by ensuring uniformity of rules throughout her territory and across all social groups, and of fraternity, by developing appropriate elements of social protection. This understanding of republican citizenship thus legitimised an activist role for the state: in managing her economy, her society and culture, and centre–periphery relations.

It also provided the framework for a particularistic account of France's role abroad as a colonial power and of her mode of 'integrating' immigrants at home.[4] And all of these, equally, could be projected as having universal appeal, and the potentiality for universal application.

Nevertheless, an alternative reading of this political path-dependency, of modern France as trapped within the flawed and problematical terms of the Great Revolution's settlement, has coexisted alongside that of her exemplarity. The writings on French government and politics, and on policies and the state, which have engaged with this 'second face of French exceptionalism',[5] have done so primarily by adopting a historical-comparativist methodology, focusing on patterns of continuity and change over time. In the field of constitutional law, with its strong institutional presence in France, Hauriou notably developed a much-cited model of cyclical political regime change. Similarly René Rémond's study of the political doctrines and organisational forms of the French right, an equally much-cited work, pointed to the persistence and cyclical renewal of what it identified as three distinct, historically embedded 'families'.[6]

More crucially, this 'second face' of France's exceptionalism has centred on a critical reading of France's 'strong state'. Patterns of state-society, state-economy and centre-periphery relations have thus been analysed as the creations of her *dirigiste* Jacobin and Napoleonic inheritance: the highly centralised and interventionist machinery of the French state. It was this reading of French history, which underpinned Michel Crozier's extraordinarily influential thesis on France's *société bloquée*. As an organisational – rather than a specifically political – sociologist, Crozier sought to explicate the distinctive dynamics of crisis and protest in France, themselves the products of hierarchical and centralised forms of organisation and leadership, but which by challenging them also thereby serve to reinforce these same patterns.[7] And it is just such an understanding of continuities sustained despite – or indeed because of – attempts at change that has been more familiarly encapsulated in the informal but ubiquitous idiom of *plus ça change*.

A variant of this 'second face' reading of the role of political crisis should also be noted here. For this third reading, or 'face', of French

exceptionalism has centred on the necessity of crisis in France as a
mechanism for achieving compromise. Crisis is thus depicted as being
'functional', but not in terms of it offering a safety-valve or acting as the
facilitator of a cyclical pattern of regime-progression. Rather the resort to
crisis makes possible what are ultimately more pragmatic and piecemeal
processes of policy and institutional change. This interpretation can be
found in the work of the French institutional analyst Pierre Avril, although
its classical exposition is in the detailed account of 'crisis and compromise'
under the Fourth Republic, by the British political historian Philip
Williams.[8] As will be seen, these three perspectives on France's
exceptionalism have by no means fallen from academic favour, but they
now contend with more insistent claims of rupture with the past which have
come to dominate the intellectual foreground.

Finally the third argument centres on the changing contours of French
political science in this period, which has enabled new analyses of the
particularistic contemporary outcomes of France's path-dependency to be
relocated within comparativist frameworks adopted more widely outside
France. Key strands of these Franco-French debates have, it is true, retained
resolutely Franco-centric preoccupations. Yet the vocabulary of *la fin de
l'exception française* and its implicitly comparativist frame of reference
(even where this is not clearly explicated – as is, indeed, often the case in
this literature) have brought a new impetus towards incorporating France's
contemporary experiences into broader typologies. Many of the trends
identified in the literature of this period are clearly ones affecting not only
France. With processes of globalisation now widely portrayed as having
produced a paradigm-shift in the operation and organisation of state-
economy and state-society relations, France may now be presented as one
of a variety of path-dependent models of capitalism. These are issues to
which we will return.

ESCAPING FROM FRENCH HISTORY? – *LA BANALISATION DE LA VIE
POLITIQUE* AND *L'ETAT DE DROIT*

The claims that initially emerged in the late 1980s centred on France
breaking with the conflictual and chequered constitutional history which
had resulted from persisting ideological and value-system fault-lines within
French society, dividing her citizenry. Two rather differently structured
arguments were developed at this time, in terms of the combinations of
independent and dependent variables they posited. Each drew, moreover,
upon an area of particular strength within the discipline of political science

as it had developed in France: political sociology and constitutional (and public) law. These analyses focused respectively on the alignment of French politics on to that found in other modernised states, *la banalisation de la vie politique française*, and on the reconstruction of France's system of governance as a law-bound state, *un État de droit*.

The work of Furet *et al.* and Mendras took up the first of these analyses,[9] exploring the impact of broadly sociological processes, and the way these were feeding into and reshaping party politics, electoral behaviour and, more generally, the operation of France's institutions of representative democracy. In Mendras' work this took the form of a thesis which was readily 'integratable' into an international literature on comparative political modernisation. This centred on France's 'second revolution' of urbanisation, declining religious practice, and cultural transformations along generational and gender dimensions. He portrayed this as *une révolution silencieuse*, nurtured within France's unprecedentedly long cycle of state-led economic expansion and modernisation from 1945, during *les trente glorieuses*.[10] Furet *et al.* focused their analysis more specifically on the changing landscape of party political discourse and party competition, with the emergence of new configurations of partisan identity blurring some of the more prominent and familiar features of left-right bipolarisation. They wrote following the French socialists' adoption in government, from 1984, of a discourse prioritising the competitiveness of France's economy and repositioning themselves as the managers of such a modernising project.

Both the socialists and the Gaullist right had by this time abandoned elements crucial to their state-centrist traditions. In government the former had implemented their 'new left' commitments to decentralisation (but had faced greater difficulties in respect of their other 'new left' acquisition: a pluralist conception of citizenship involving differentiated rights for women and immigrants). The Gaullists under Chirac had dramatically emerged as the champions of a neo-liberal strategy of privatisations.[11]

The second type of study focused instead on the constitutional innovations of 1958, assessing the impact of these on party politics, electoral behaviour and the working of representative democracy in France. Colas, Favoreu, Cohen-Tanugi and others now identified the Constitutional Council as the most critical of these innovations, entailing over time the subordination of electoral mandates and the politics of representation to legal norms and processes of law.[12] Moreover, they also portrayed this juridicisation of France's governmental system as integrating France into a broader trend: the rise of constitutionalism in Western democracies. As these writers emphasised, the new institutional arrangements created in France in this period had been reinforced by parallel developments at the supranational level in Europe. Both France's adherence to the European Convention of Human Rights and her membership of the European Economic Community (now European Union) had thus by now resulted in expanding areas of her legislation, and its implementation, being subject to challenge through these bodies' courts established, respectively, in Strasbourg and Luxembourg.

It should be noted, however, that neither of these two new bodies of writing was without significant forerunners. In particular, an earlier literature on the modernisation of French parties and her party system had included key writings on Gaullism and the new Socialist Party, which employed Kirchheimer's comparativist concept of 'catch-all parties'. In doing so, these studies had given due weight to his underlying thesis of economic, social and cultural modernisation from the 1950s 'unfreezing' the cleavage systems laid down in earlier historical periods.[13] Nevertheless, the designation of the Gaullist and Socialist parties as *partis attrappes-tout* had been portrayed in both these studies as contributing only one element towards their more distinctively French characterisation as *partis présidentialisés*. For these writings had also assimilated the analytic findings from institutional and constitutional studies of this earlier period. And these pointed to the central and path-breaking importance of the constitutional arrangements adopted during 1958–62 in reshaping electoral behaviour in France, the organisation of her parties and their interrelationships.

An especially substantial body of work in this latter area had sought to elucidate the distinctive character of the political regime established under France's Fifth Republic; and this, too, had entailed the adoption and development of comparativist typologies. Two main rival classificatory schemes had resulted, the one designating the Fifth Republic as a dualist, semi-presidential parliamentary democracy, the other as a presidentialist regime.[14] The former classification particularly emphasised the unusual, and unclear, distribution of executive powers between president and prime minister laid down in the 1958 text. The latter, in contrast, focused on the widely adopted political conventions which had supplemented – or supplanted – key constitutional provisions in the period until 1986, underpinning the practices of majoritarian presidentialism.[15] The former approach certainly underscored the extent to which 'cohabitation', when it finally occurred for the first time in 1986–88, would bring the textual provisions of the constitution centre-stage, along with what the newer writings on France's 'État de droit' had identified as the latter's core-mechanisms.

Nevertheless in one crucial respect the writers, who now proclaimed *la fin de l'exception française*, were indeed innovative. By directly linking the problematical and divisive outcomes of the revolutionary period back to the character of those events *qua* revolutionary project, their writings established a fundamentally revisionist reinterpretation of the 1789 Revolution. This produced a different and new reading of French exceptionalism: one that recast France's claimed *exemplarité* as an inherently and deeply flawed counter-model. This reconceptualisation of France's exceptionalism, popularised in Furet's co-edited work published on the eve of the 1989 Bicentenary, grew directly from his own specialist research as a historian on France's century of revolutions.[16]

France was thus portrayed as only now, two centuries later, emancipating herself from her costly resort to revolution and able, finally, to enter a new era of more pluralist and consensual democratic practice. For Cohen-Tanugi, trained as a lawyer and with direct personal experience of the American legal system, it was the contrasting relationship between legal and political processes in these two countries' periods of revolution, which provided the catalyst for analysing France as only now completing her democratic revolution.[17] This she had done by acquiring, with an 'activist' Constitutional Council, the crucial element whose previous absence had vitiated her democratic practice: 'an extraordinary machine for converting political problems into juridical equations, against the grain of our whole tradition ... a great regulatory mechanism for democracy'.[18]

Indeed what is striking, and almost paradoxical in retrospect, about these 'first wave' analyses of the demise of French exceptionalism is their tone of optimism, the high expectations they convey that France was now escaping from the hold of her previous history. And this involved the assigning of *exemplarité* to dominant practices and institutions established elsewhere (primarily in the USA and the UK), which are thus portrayed as offering a way forward for France. It is precisely this prognosis that would be radically reversed in the 'second wave' writings on *la fin de l'exception française*.

For writers of this 'first wave' such sociological, party-system and institutional changes had also been taken further by France's recent experiment with 'cohabitation'. This had not only conjured up new forms of institutional power sharing, having dislodged the presidency from its claimed primacy, but had also entailed an element of political power sharing between centre-right and centre-left that was new to the Fifth Republic. And this seemed not only to reflect, but also in turn to generate, increasing support for a more consensual and non-adversarial style of party politics – a development to which opinion polls of this period strongly testified.[19] The experience of 'cohabitation' thus gave credence to the judgement that the more broadly based sociological and cultural changes identified by Furet *et al.*, were indeed being appropriately matched by institutional arrangements deriving from the dualist and hybrid constitutional text that had been put together in the summer of 1958.

Nevertheless, as France entered the 1990s those within the sub-discipline of political sociology who remained unconvinced by the interpretative framework offered by these 'first wave' writings. They did not lack for ammunition to mobilise against a putative alignment of political behaviour in France on to less ideological or more pluralistic practices. This ammunition included significant levels of electoral support attracted, from 1984 onwards, to Le Pen's brand of populist racism.[20] The highly personalised, internecine disputes fuelling organisational fragmentation on both centre-right and the centre-left, and the cyclical, presidentialised character of these parties' electoral success. The drama of successive scandals focused on corrupt party-financing.[21] All this accumulating empirical evidence pointed to trends that were not readily assimilable into the thesis of *banalisation* but suggested, on the contrary, that contemporary France retained a crucially path-dependent distinctiveness, in line with a 'second face' reading of French exceptionalism.

Equally, constitutional and institutional analysts could point to a range of developments and practices in this period which could be taken to corroborate this latter reading of French history. Specialists in France's centre–periphery relations could argue that *le phénomène notabiliaire* and the distinctive practice of *cumul des mandats*, rooted in historically weak parties and an overweening state, had survived Defferre's decentralisation and regionalisation reforms, albeit in somewhat altered forms.[22] For political economists the neo-liberal discourse of 'more market and less state', which had clothed the right's privatisation programme, had not heralded the end of *dirigisme*. Instead it provided new opportunities for its practice: for example, in the Ministry of Finance's role in choosing core-shareholder groups for the privatised companies and appointing their chairmen.[23] Constitutional lawyers, too, could construct a less sanguine, and altogether more particularistic, account of the relationship between politics and law. Problematical issues here included the party-political ramifications of appointments to the Constitutional Council and of the procedures for referring legislation to it, and the constitutionally irresponsible status of a presidential office which retained scope for discretionary intervention even though it had been shorn of the more ambitious practices of its first four incumbents under the Fifth Republic.[24]

In these circumstances *la fin de l'exception française* could have proved an ephemeral intellectual commodity. In the event, its shelf-life was to be dramatically extended as the brand-mark was appropriated by what was, effectively, a rival product.

RECLAIMING FRENCH HISTORY – THE NEW CONTEXTS OF EUROPEANISATION AND GLOBALISATION

Where the 'first-wave' literature had transformed France's previously claimed *exemplarité* into a counter-model, the new discourse that took shape by the mid-1990s championed a resolutely 'first face' reading of French exceptionalism. In doing so, this 'second wave' discourse offered a reworking of the exemplary character of France's path-dependent institutions and political practices, as residing in a series of particularistic 'French models'. By 1994, *Le Monde*, in a publication entitled *Le modèle français en question*, could identify a whole set of such models. These ranged from social welfare, through 'national champion' firms; her assimilationist 'integration' of immigrants and state activism on the cultural front to *francophonie*; a foreign policy of *grandeur*, national defence based on an independent nuclear deterrent; and her *co-opération* framework in sub-Saharan Africa.[25] Yet equally intrinsic to this new discourse was its pessimistic assessment of the actors and forces ranged against, and threatening, these distinctive French achievements. The earlier benign vision, of an external world France should aspire to integrate into more fully, was now strikingly overturned by the perception of France as subordinate to external constraints. She had been drawn into a process of 'normalisation' – that is, of convergence around the 'dominant' model of a newly-emergent world order.[26]

The 'second wave' discourse on the demise of French exceptionalism was thus diametrically opposed in almost every respect to the analyses which writers such as Furet *et al.* and Cohen-Tanugi had previously presented. Its construction and popularisation could be read, essentially, as a response to the processes of Europeanisation and globalisation, which both came much more sharply into focus in the 1980s and especially the 1990s. In Europe successive negotiations saw France and her fellow member states committing themselves to a lengthening agenda of further political and economic integration. Her dramatic referendum in 1992, however, produced only the narrowest of majorities in support of the Maastricht Treaty.

France also joined in the world-wide deregulatory revolution in financial services (with her 'Little Big Bang' of 1989), while her 'national champion' firms became increasingly drawn into transnational production, cross-border joint ventures, mergers and, finally, hostile take-overs. At the international level in the protracted and acrimonious Uruguay Round of GATT negotiations on multilateral trade liberalisation there was drama, too, when France challenged the USA with her campaign for 'cultural preference' but failed to prevent the issue of Common Agricultural Policy reform from being taken from the EU into this external arena.

Throughout this period it was France's unprecedentedly high levels of unemployment – which were not to dip below 10 per cent at any point in these two decades – that provided an enduring 'second wave' symbol of external forces operating to constrain France's domestic preferences. But public perceptions of the external causalities at work shifted characteristically in this period. An initial focus on the OPEC countries' two oil-price hikes in the 1970s subsequently transferred to the role of 'Reaganomics' in exporting the costs of international recession from the USA to its trading partners. With the left's 1983 economic U-turn, however, attention turned more durably to the costs to France of the *franc fort* policy she now sustained in order to retain her membership of the European Monetary System. From the mid-1990s this was to be powerfully reinforced as France pursued further deflationary and budget-cutting measures in order to meet the Maastricht criteria for membership of EMU.

In this period the outside observer could have been forgiven for thinking that, in whichever policy sector one turned to look, yet another sector-specific 'French model' would materialise. From the perspective of comparative policy sector or 'policy community' analysis, such sectoral models could clearly lend themselves to a rather different, 'second face' reading. This centred on the French state's distinctive modes of, and capacity for, intervention as a 'strong state'.[27] Instead, the conceptual glue binding together these key discursive components of the new literature came from their claim to embody the combination of enduring rights and responsibilities, which France's project of republican citizenship conferred. This meant, in turn, that the longer-standing emphasis on her universalistic exemplarity was now demoted to being, at best, a residual feature.

In this revisiting of the 'first face' of French exemplarity, the value of each of these sectoral models for present and future generations in France did not just lie in their being the products of France's own national history, created by the democratic choices of French citizens. Even more crucial to this discourse was their role in sustaining the ambitions of republican citizenship. It was in this vein that Jacques Chirac, as President of the Republic, could exhort French firms to recognise the responsibilities incumbent on *l'entreprise citoyenne*.

However, equally crucial was the new discourse's identification of the external threats confronting this project. Indeed, among the reforms affecting the models commonly acknowledged as constituting the core of this reading of France's exceptionalism, only Defferre's remodelling of France's Jacobin framework for centre–periphery relations passed without exciting serious debate along these lines.[28] Yet this latter case scarcely lent itself to a causal explanation of the kind favoured by this 'second wave' discourse, centring on 'external constraints'.[29]

As in the case of 'first-wave' writings, there were evident forerunners for some of the arguments developed within this 'second wave' discourse. Most obviously, the designation of the US state and American firms as the major source of challenges to France's way of doing things was not new. This was a theme that had been popularised notably by de Gaulle and his supporters on the right and by the communists on the left, but it was by no means confined to these two ends of the party-political spectrum. What was perhaps the single most influential French polemic against US hegemony was, after all, the work of a leading figure of the radical centre in the mid-1960s.[30] As with the 'first-wave' writings, the claims associated with these 'French models' and their likely fate became the subject of a wide-ranging debate among academic specialists. For the most part the counter-claims drew on a 'second-face' reading of French exceptionalism. Critics thus focused on the contestable character of these models, as social and ideological constructs masking far more complex realities; and on the flawed and problematical nature of the French state's practices in each of these policy sectors, as in Elie Cohen's merciless depiction of France's *tentation héxagonale*.[31]

This academic debate from the outset also acquired a much more overtly politicised profile because in so many cases the models linked directly into policy issues that were now hotly disputed between and within France's parties. These policy issues provided the backdrop for a series of large-scale social mobilisations in this period. In challenging proposals to reforms established pension and health-care funding arrangements and the status of France's publicly-owned utilities, these movements invoked the republican citizenship themes of social protection and economic intervention to defend benefits. For which, it was claimed, these French ways of doing things conferred on her people as a whole, or on specific social categories within it. These developments were unlike anything associated with the 'first-wave' debate.

The discussion that follows concentrates on two of the models which featured especially prominently in the debates of this period: France's *dirigiste* model of state-led capitalism and her model for 'integrating' immigrants as citizens. These two cases illustrate some of the variety and contrasts present within this 'second-wave' discourse, and in its utilisation. In both these cases, moreover, the trends towards convergence and alignment on to 'dominant models', which this discourse points to, have been challenged by an expanding body of comparativist studies undertaken in France. By relocating and reconceptualising these French models as variants within a broad spectrum of sectoral policy management patterns to be found elsewhere, but especially in Western Europe, such writings have broken away from dualistic frameworks of analysis. The latter had informed much 'first' and 'second wave' writing on the demise of French exceptionalism. These studies have pointed instead to the likelihood of significant elements of national path-dependent divergences being sustained within the overarching processes of Europeanisation and globalisation.

If France's *dirigiste* model of capitalism since 1945 had come to serve as an archetype of French exceptionalism, the conceptualisation of its crucial characteristics had nevertheless changed over time. Where initially attention had been directed at the role of indicative planning in creating *une économie concertée*[32] (with de Gaulle declaring this to be *une ardente obligation* for the French nation), subsequent studies portrayed this as, essentially, a highly selective industrial policy. A mix of policy instruments could be identified, enabling the state to nurture 'national champion' firms, in both the public and the private sectors.[33] A core set of these instruments, covering selective capital injections and grants, fiscal and other exemptions, and the disbursement of medium- and long-term credit on advantageous terms, have all ultimately been under the aegis of the Treasury division of the Ministry of Finance. By contrast successive *grands projects* have largely fallen within the domain of presidential initiative, while state-to-state trading contracts and treaties have brought the Quai d'Orsay in as a key player.

Whatever the definitional problems associated with it, from the mid-1970s successive governments of the right and the left recognised that mounting problems required structural reforms to be made to the French model of capitalism. The left followed Giscard's limited shift towards liberalisation with their massive programme of nationalisations in 1981. The Gaullists, by now converted to a neo-liberal discourse, opting with their allies for an equally ambitious programme of privatisations in 1986–88 and 1993–97. Despite this adversarial zig-zagging, there was nevertheless evidence of significant continuities: both between left and right, with the left's early 'silent privatisations' and its later resort to partial privatisations between 1988 and 1993 and again from 1997. More continuities lay in the forms of familiarly *dirigiste* practices shaping the privatisation process and the management structures of the privatised companies.[34]

Two distinctive strands can be distinguished within the writings on the demise of France's model of capitalism that came to the fore in this period.[35] In the first of these, Michel Albert reconceptualised this French model, by integrating it into a wider 'Rhineland' model within a typology counterposing this to 'Atlantic' capitalism.[36] The variables Albert incorporated into this typology (including investment based on equity capital as against 'patient' capital sourced especially from long-term credit; conflictual as against co-operative management of labour markets and industrial relations; and differing funding principles and management mechanisms for welfare provision) brought this work closer to a longer-established Anglo-American body of comparative political economy. The latter included the pioneering work of Andrew Shonfield and John Zysman's typology of capital- and credit-based capitalisms.[37]

Despite his advocacy of the superior social and, in the longer-term, economic performance of the Rhineland model, Albert's underlying thesis concerned the advantages accruing to Atlantic capitalism by virtue of its organisation around realising shareholder value through short-term profitability. His variant on the dualism of a French model counterposed to a dominant 'other' nevertheless leads back into the familiar terrain of external constraints and the expectation of convergence – in this case, of other national capitalisms of the Rhineland-type, along with France's, on to the dominant Atlantic model.

An underlying element of dualism is also to be found in the writings of the Marxist economist François Chesnais, despite the very different theoretical and methodological concerns informing his work.[38] The US is portrayed here, too, as a dominant and privileged player within a new global finance-dominated accumulation regime. This approach again provides the basis for a pessimistic expectation of the convergent restructuring of French along with other national capitalisms, aligning them on to the behavioural characteristics and institutional logic of this new accumulation regime.

Other French specialists in this field have, however, developed analyses rejecting the dualism of 'second wave' writings on the demise of French exceptionalism. In the French 'École de la Régulation', these political economists had already written into their theoretical framework for analysing the 'Fordist' accumulation regime a concern with identifying national variations especially in respect of the social and political institutions regulating this accumulation regime.[39] As a result, in depicting what constitutes within this framework a paradigm-shift to 'post-Fordist' accumulation, writers from this school retained an emphasis on coexistence and competition between different national capitalisms as an inherent feature of capitalism as a world order.

This approach thus placed the French model of capitalism in a relativist perspective: of sharing with other national capitalisms a quality of being different, rather than exceptional. In the recent work of Robert Boyer, in particular, her state-led capitalism is placed alongside market-led, company-led, social-democratic and meso-corporatist models. These all undergo structural adaptations in an era of globalisation, but with no one system enjoying a dominance such that it could impose convergence via alignment on to its own model.[40] The work of Elie Cohen, in analysing the impact of Europeanisation and the new characteristic forms of globalisation on firms and on states, has similarly underlined the differing comparative advantages over time of national varieties of capitalism, rejecting the inevitability of convergence on to the American model.[41]

These writers' positive appreciations, on balance, of the advantages which French and other national capitalisms can draw from participation in the setting of EU-wide rules and regulatory regimes,[42] have also led them and other sectoral policy specialists in France to address the issues raised by multi-level governance in Europe in terms that reject the single logic of 'external constraint'.[43] At the same time the work of both these writers has been integrated within broader comparative edited collections, dealing with processes of convergence and the persistence of diversity within modern capitalism.[44] Such developments have led to an expanding French presence within what has been a key development in this field: growing networks of transnational academic collaboration and publication in major areas of comparative political and comparative policy analysis.[45] What was initiated primarily as a Franco-French debate has thus over time ensured that a notable body of French writing on France now both contributes to and is able to draw from wider comparative theorisation and analysis. That process focused on the advent of multi-level governance and the rise of the 'regulatory state', which are portrayed in this literature as offering new paradigms for the analysis of state-economy relations.[46]

French governments from the mid-1970s also faced mounting problems in managing their established framework for conferring French citizenship and for supervising short-term work and residency permits. France's distinctive, assimilationist model of *intégration* thus came under increasing challenges from parties on the left and the right, in rather the same way as the French model of capitalism had in this period.

On the left the socialists developed a new multi-culturalist discourse on *la France au pluriel*, breaking with the older equation between equality and uniformity of rules, and committed themselves to unhooking the traditional linkage between the political rights of citizenship and nationality status (at the least, by according the vote in local elections to immigrants without French nationality).[47]

On the extreme right Le Pen by the early 1980s was demanding that the automatic acquisition of nationality by young adults born in France of non-French parents should be replaced by a requirement of positive proof of (cultural) integration. A reform commitment along these lines was taken up within the mainstream right. Against these trends specialists nevertheless sought to reaffirm the validity of France's established approach, while in office the socialists lowered their sights. By 1990 it was they who established a new authority in this field, entitled the Haut Conseil à l'Intégration.[48]

In respect of this French model drawing on a 'first face' reading of republican citizenship, the presence of an 'external' threat challenging and perhaps hastening its demise was again brought into play. However, here the newer immigrant fluxes, whose religious and cultural practices were identified by some as precluding rapid assimilation into a secular citizenship, were actually located in France as part of her society and involved in political domestic interaction with the state and other social groups.[49] Yet another external threat, and one more closely parallel to those identified as operating in other policy sectors, could also be located in the presence of discursive counter-models of minority rights, multi-culturalism and affirmative action projected from the USA (and, to an altogether lesser extent, by the neighbouring UK) counter-models. These could be used to affirm cultural and other rights and oppose the French approach to citizenship-integration.

With the passage of time another version of this minority rights discourse as an external constraint also appeared at the European level. Both the Council of Europe and the Conference on Security and Co-operation in Europe sought, from the end of the 1980s, to incorporate into key texts formal statements on respect for minority rights; while at the United Nations similar moves also got underway.[50]

In this field, too, the simplifications involved in subsuming French policy and French practice within this integration model led a growing body of studies to develop critical accounts. These drew, to a greater or lesser extent, on a 'second face' reading of French exceptionalism. For example, Patrick Weil's careful analysis of developments in official policy and in policy-practice from the late 1930s underlined both the resource limitations and the presence of contradictory objectives (especially by way of state-to-state agreements with home-countries sourcing France's short-term labour market needs). These prevented this framework from effectively shaping important elements of official practice from 1945 on.[51] While concerned at the erosive impact of 'multi-cultural' practices on France's citizenship-basis for national identity, Weil also elucidates the longer-term dynamic interplay between the necessarily specific cultural baggage of successive waves of immigrants and the evolution of French identity and culture. He also notes the increasingly important role of the French state, not as *l'État acteur*, but as *l'État de droit*, in affirming basic rights of foreign residents and cultural rights of French minority-nationals, primarily through the Conseil d'État and on a case-by-case basis.

Other writers have offered a more radical, and essentially comparativist, re-reading of the French model of integration as it operated in earlier periods. In this mode Gérard Noiriel's analysis of *le creuset français* testified to the slow pace, stretched across several generations, of social and cultural integration (especially in terms of marrying out of the 'immigrant' community). This pattern is equally characteristic of immigrant communities operating in other countries with their quite different institutional and normative frameworks.[52]

A yet more fundamental, but again essentially comparativist, reconceptualisation of French policies and practices in relation to citizenship and immigration has also been developed in Michel Wieviorka's work. He uses the conceptual lens of racism to rethink (and relativise) France's claims to an exceptional and exemplary model of integration in this field.[53]

Thus, we find developments here paralleling those already noted in relation to the French model of capitalism: a renewed interest in placing France's policies in this sector in a non-dualist comparative perspective; the emergence of cross-national collaborative research and publications; the development of comparativist frameworks in which France's experience is portrayed as offering path-dependent differences rather than exceptionalism.[54]

CONCLUSION

The language of exceptionalism and national debates centring on such claims have certainly not been confined to France in the recent period. If we turn only to the USA and the UK, we find evidence of a resurgence of such intellectual preoccupations.[55] Yet the sheer insistence of such claims and the scale of the debate they have given rise to have been of a different order in France. Within much that has been written in France until quite recently, however, comparatively limited attention has been paid to portraying France's current experience of rupture and change as a variant on more widely-shared experiences of the reshaping of distinctively-structured national polities and national economies in the contemporary period.

This study has identified two contrasting problematics underlying the recent usage of this common claim – that France is experiencing *la fin de l'exception française*. It has argued that the Franco-French debate which developed around the second of these, portraying France as a victim of externally-driven processes of 'normalisation', has in turn contributed to a more focused placing of France. Her contemporary and earlier experiences are seen in comparative perspective, within a growing body of academic studies. Much of this newer work draws broadly on a historical-institutionalist approach in analysing the path-dependent character of France's modern state; the unusual configuration of her liberal democratic institutions; and the internal dynamics of her sectoral policy communities and the thematic issues around which these have been constructed.[56]

France has thus increasingly come to be portrayed as one of a variety of path-dependent liberal democracies and as one of a variety of path-dependent models of capitalism. Yet her path-dependency has been one in which the discourse of exceptionalism has itself played a central role – even while, as we have seen, her claims to exemplarity and exceptionalism have been subject to several contrasting readings. A range of research and writing in this vein may thus now point to France having been, and being likely to remain, different rather than exceptional. Nevertheless the embeddedness of the idea of French exceptionalism in the fabric of her modern history surely means that the language of French exceptionalism will retain its resonance and mobilising capacity within the realm of French politics.

NOTES

1. The seminal work which popularised this term was François Furet, Jacques Juillard and Pierre Rosanvallon, *La République au centre. La fin de l'exception française* (Paris: Calmann-Lévy 1988).
2. Jill Lovecy, 'Comparative Politics and the Fifth Republic. "La fin de l'exception française?"' *European Journal of Political Research* 21 (1992) pp.385–408.
3. This is notably the case of Laurent Cohen-Tanugi, *La métamorphose de la démocratie* (Paris: Odile Jacob 1989), and also of Furet *et al.* (note 1).
4. Raoul Girardet, *L'idée coloniale en France de 1871 à 1962* (Paris: La Table Ronde 1972).

5. By analogy with Tiersky's classical formulation of 'the four faces of French communism':
   Ronald Tiersky, *French Communism 1920–72* (Columbia UP 1974).
6. André Hauriou, *Précis de droit constitutionnel* (Paris: LGDJ 1929); André Hauriou and Jean
   Gicquel, *Droit constitutionnel et institutions politiques* (Paris: Montchrestien 1966); see also
   Olivier Duhamel, *Le pouvoir politique en France* (Paris: Presses Universitaires de France,
   hereafter PUF 1991) pp.8–15. René Rémond, *La droite en France de la Restauration à nos
   jours*, 1st ed. (Paris: Aubier 1954); idem, *Les droites en France*, 4th ed. (Paris: Aubier
   Montaigne 1982).
7. Michel Crozier, *La société bloquée* (Paris: Seuil 1970); idem and Erhard Friedberg (eds.) *Où
   va l'administration française?* (Paris: Editions de l'Organisation 1974). For an application of
   this approach to centre–periphery relations in France, see Pierre Grémion, *Le pouvoir
   périphérique: Notables et bureaucrates dans le système politique français* (Paris: Seuil
   1976). France's cyclical resort to 'charismatic' forms of strong leadership was analysed in
   Stanley Hoffman, 'Heroic Leadership: The Case of Modern France', in L.-J. Edinger (ed.)
   Political Leadership in Industrialised Countries (NY: Wiley 1967) pp.108–54.
8. Pierre Avril, *Politics in France* (London: Penguin 1969); Philip M. Williams, *Crisis and
   Compromise* (London: Longman 1958, 1964), translated into French as *La vie politique sous
   la IVe République* (Paris: Armand Colin 1971).
9. Furet *et al.* (note 1); Henri Mendras, *La seconde révolution française* (Paris: Gallimard
   1988), published in translation as Henri Mendras with Alistair Cole, *Social Change in
   France: Towards a Cultural Anthropology of the Fifth Republic* (Cambridge: CUP 1991).
10. Jean Fourastié, *Les trente glorieuses, ou la révolution invisible de 1946 à 1975* (Paris: Fayard
    1974).
11. Jean Baudoin, 'Gaullisme et chiraquisme', *Pouvoirs* 28 (1984) pp.53–66.
12. Dominique Colas, *L'État de droit* (Paris: PUF 1987); Louis Favoreu, *La politique saisie par
    le droit* (Paris: Economica 1988); Laurent Cohen-Tanugi (note 3). See also Léo Hamon, *Les
    juges de la loi. Naissance et rôle d'un contre-pouvoir: le Conseil Constitutionnel* (Paris:
    Fayard 1987); Jacques Chevalier, 'L'État de droit', *Revue du Droit Public* 3 (1988)
    pp.313–80; Pierre Avril, 'Une revanche du droit constitutionnel?', *Pouvoirs* 49 (1989)
    pp.5–13.
13. Jean Charlot, *Le phénomène gaulliste* (Paris: Fayard 1970); Hugues Portelli, *Le socialisme
    tel qu'il est* (Paris: Presses Universitaires de France 1980); Otto Kirchheimer, 'The
    Transformation of Western European Party Systems', in J. Lapalombara and M. Weiner
    (eds.) *Political Parties and Political Development* (Princeton UP 1966) pp.177–200. See
    also Hugues Portelli, 'La présidentialisation des partis', *Pouvoirs* 14 (1980) pp.97–107; Jean
    Charlot, 'Le président et le parti majoritaire: du gaullisme au socialisme', *Revue Politique et
    Parlementaire* 905 (1983) pp.27–42.
14. The first of these classificatory concepts was elaborated in Maurice Duverger, 'A new
    political system model: semi-presidential government', in *European Journal of Political
    Research* 8/2 (1980) pp.168–83; idem, *Les régimes semi-présidentiels* (Paris: Presses
    Universitaires de France 1986); Jean-Claude Colliard, *Les régimes parlementaires* (Paris:
    Presses de la FNSP 1987). On presidentialism, see Pierre Avril, 'Ce qui a changé dans la Ve
    République', *Pouvoirs* 9 (1979) pp.53–70; idem, *La Ve République. Histoire politique et
    constitutionnelle* (Paris: PUF 1987); and Jean Gicquel, *Droit constitutionnel et institutions
    politiques*, 10th ed. (Paris: Montchrestien 1980).
15. Jill Lovecy, 'Between "Majoritarian" and "Consensual" Democracy: The Case of the French
    Fifth Republic', in Geraint Parry and Michael Moran (eds.) *Democracy and Democratisation*
    (London: Routledge 1994) pp.224–7.
16. François Furet, *Penser la révolution* (Paris: Gallimard 1978); idem, *La révolution
    1770–1880. Histoire de la France, vol.1: 1770–1814; vol.2: 1814–1880* (Paris: Hachette
    1988, 1990).
17. Laurent Cohen-Tanugi, *Le droit sans l'État. Essai sur la démocratie en France et en
    Amérique* (Paris: PUF 1985); idem, 'From One Revolution to the Next: The Late Rise of
    Constitutionalism in France', *The Tocqueville Review* 12/1 (1991) pp.55–60.
18. Cohen-Tanugi (note 3) pp.24–6.
19. SOFRES, *L'État de l'opinion, Les clés pour 1986* (Paris: Gallimard 1986).

20. Nonna Mayer and Pascal Perrineau, *Le Front National à découvert* (Paris: Presses de la FNSP 1989); Guy Birenbaum, *Le Front National en politique* (Paris: Balland 1992); Gérard Le Gall, 'Le Front National à l'épreuve du temps', in Olivier Duhamel (ed.) *L'État de l'opinion 1998* (Paris: Seuil 1998) pp.49–83.

21. Yves Mény, *La corruption de la République* (Paris: Fayard 1992); Jean-Claude Masclet, 'Les règles du financement de la vie politique', *Problèmes Politiques et Sociaux*, 15–19 Nov. 1991, pp.667–8.

22. Albert Mabileau, 'Les héritiers des notables', *Pouvoirs* 49 (1989) pp.93–103; idem, *Le système local en France* (Paris: Montchrestien 1991) pp.83–118.

23. Michel Bauer, 'The Politics of State-Directed Privatisation: The Case of France, 1986–88', *West European Politics* 11/4 (Oct. 1989) pp.49–60.

24. Anne-Marie Cohendet, *La cohabitation. Leçons d'une expérience* (Paris: PUF 1993).

25. For an early survey of these models, see *Le Monde Diplomatique* (Aug. 1994).

26. Ibid. pp.96–7.

27. Bruno Jobert and Pierre Muller, *L'État en action. Politiques publiques et corporatismes* (Paris: PUF 1987); Yves Mény and Jean-Claude Thoenig, *Politiques publiques* (Paris: ibid 1989).

28. *Le Monde Diplomatique*, Aug. 1994, pp.6–7.

29. The 'second face' readings on the limits to these reforms have been previously noted.

30. This was an early critique of American multi-nationals, written by the editor of *L'Express* magazine (and later leader of the Radical Party), Jean-Jacques Servan-Schreiber, *Le défi américain* (Paris: Denoël 1967).

31. Elie Cohen, *La tentation héxagonale. La souveraineté à l'épreuve de la mondialisation* (Paris: Fayard 1996).

32. Pierre Massé, *Le plan ou l'anti-hasard* (Paris: Gallimard 1965).

33. Elie Cohen and Michel Bauer, *Les grandes manœuvres industrielles* (Paris: Belfond 1985); Elie Cohen, *Le colbertisme 'high tech'* (Paris: Hachette 1992).

34. See Bauer (note 23).

35. For a recent discussion see *Le Monde* (Dossiers et Documents, 274, March 1999), 'Le nouveau capitalisme français'.

36. The former of these encompassing the US and the UK along with much of the English-speaking world; the latter incorporating France along with Germany and also Sweden and Japan: Michel Albert, *Capitalisme contre capitalisme* (Paris: Seuil 1991).

37. Starting from Andrew Shonfield, *Modern Capitalism: The Changing Balance of Public and Private Power* (London: OUP 1965), and including notably John Zysman, *Governments, Markets and Growth: Financial Systems and the Politics of Industrial Change* (Ithaca, NY: Cornell UP 1983). On welfare provision, see G. Esping-Andersen, *The Three Worlds of Welfare Capitalism* (Princeton UP 1990).

38. François Chesnais, *La mondialisation du capital* (Paris: Syros 1997).

39. Michel Aglietta, *Régulation et crises du capitalisme* (Paris: Calmann-Lévy 1976); Robert Boyer, *La théorie de la régulation: une analyse critique* (Paris: La Découverte 1986).

40. Robert Boyer, 'The Variety of Capitalisms in the Era of Globalisation', paper presented to the International Symposium on Approaches to Varieties of Capitalism, University of Manchester, 12–13 March 1999; Bruno Amable, Rémi Barre and Robert Boyer, *Les systèmes d'innovation à l'ère de la globalisation* (Paris: Economica 1997) pp.185–263.

41. Cohen (note 31) pp.409–42.

42. Ibid. pp.439–53; Amable et al. (note 40) pp.290–94, 345–51.

43. For example, François d'Arcy and Luc Rouban (eds.) *De la Ve République à l'Europe. Mélanges en honneur de Jean-Louis Quermonne* (Paris: Presses de la FNSP 1996); Patrick Le Galès and Christian Lequesne (eds.) *Les paradoxes des régions en Europe* (Paris: La Découverte 1997), published in English as *The Paradoxes of Regions in Europe* (London: Routledge 1998); Patrick Le Galès and Jean-Claude Thoenig (eds.) *Les réseaux de politiques publiques* (Paris: L'Harmattan 1995); Yves Mény et al. (eds.) *Politiques publiques en Europe* (ibid. 1995); Joël Rideau (ed.) *Les états-membres de l'Union Européenne: adaptations, mutations, résistances* (Paris: LGDJ 1997).

44. Robert Boyer, 'French Statism at the Crossroads', in Colin Crouch and Wolfgang Streeck

(eds.) *Political Economy of Modern Capitalism: Mapping Convergence and Diversity* (London: Sage 1997), published in French as *Les capitalismes en Europe* (Paris: La Découverte 1996); Elie Cohen, 'France: National Champions in Search of a Mission', in J.E.S. Hayard (ed.) *Industrial Enterprise and European Integration: From National to European Champions* (Oxford: OUP 1995) pp.23–47.

45. Examples from this area of comparative political economy include: Robert Boyer and Daniel Drache (eds.) *States against Markets: The Limits of Globalisation* (London: Routledge 1996); Crouch and Streeck (see note 44); Hayward (note 44); Vincent Wright and Sabino Cassese (eds.) *La recomposition de l'État en Europe* (Paris: La Découverte 1998).

46. On the European regulatory state, see Giandomenico Majone, *Regulating Europe* (London: Routledge 1996), published in French as *La communauté européenne: un État régulateur* (Paris: Montchrestien 1996). See also Jacques Commaille and Bruno Jobert, *Les métamorphoses de la régulation politique* (Paris: LGDJ 1998).

47. Parti Socialiste, *La France au pluriel* (Paris: Entente 1981).

48. Dominique Schnapper, *La France de l'intégration* (Paris: Gallimard 1991); Catherine Wihtol de Wenden, *La citoyenneté* (Paris: Fondation Diderot/Eidilig 1988); see also Haut Conseil à l'Intégration, *Pour un modèle français d'intégration* (Paris: Documentation française 1991).

49. For a forceful critique of this analysis, underlining instead the cumulative social and other processes of integration underway, see Juliette Minces, *La génération suivante, Les enfants de l'immigration* (Paris: Flammarion 1986).

50. Norbert Rouland, 'Quel modèle d'intégration?', *Le Monde Diplomatique*, Aug. 1994, pp.46–7.

51. Patrick Weil, *La France et ses étrangers. L'aventure d'une politique de l'immigration 1938–1991* (Paris: Fondation Saint Simon/Calmann-Lévy 1991).

52. Gérard Noiriel, *Le creuset français, histoire de l'immigration XIXe, XXe siècle* (Paris: Seuil 1988).

53. Michel Wieviorka, *L'espace du racisme* (Paris: Seuil 1991), published in English as *The Arena of Racism* (London: Sage 1995).

54. For example, Dominique Schnapper, *L'Europe des immigrés* (Paris: F. Bourin 1992); Martin Bulmer-Edwards and Martin Schain (eds.) 'The Politics of Immigration in Western Europe', special edition of *West European Politics* 17/2 (April 1994); also book of same title from Frank Cass.

55. On the US, see Seymour Martin Lipset, *American Exceptionalism: A Double-Edged Sword* (NY: Norton 1996, 1997), and David K. Adams and Cornelius A. van Minnen (eds.) *Reflections on American Exceptionalism* (Keele: Ryburn 1994); on the UK see Linda Colley, *Britons: Forging the Nation* (New Haven, CT: Yale UP 1992) and idem, 'This Country Is Not So Special', *The New Statesman*, special issue, 1 May 1999.

56. André Faure, Gilles Polet and Philippe Warin (eds.) *La contribution du sens dans les politiques publiques: débats autour de la notion référentiel* (Paris: L'Harmattan 1995).

Abstracts

The Changing French Political System

ROBERT ELGIE

France is experiencing a period of economic, social and political change. Change has affected the politics of representation, incorporating political parties and civil society; the organisation of political institutions, encompassing areas such as the constitution, the judiciary and local government; and public policy making, including the role of the state and the creation of new policy networks. And yet, the current period of change needs to be placed in context. In particular, change should be seen as an ongoing process which has not simply resulted in the transition from one distinct model of French politics to another. Moreover, while the current period of change raises new issues concerning the nature of the French political process, older questions, such as the supposed exceptionalism of French politics, still need to be addressed.

The Parties of the French 'Plural Left': An Uneasy Complementarity

JOSEPH SZARKA

Focusing on the period June 1997 to April 1999, this essay considers the extent to which the 'plural left' coalition constituted an instance of party system change in France. It reviews ways of assessing party system change, analyses renewal within the individual parties of the *gauche plurielle* and probes the relationships between them. It concludes that although a distinct evolutionary stage emerged, allowing a new aggregation of electoral and social demands, a realignment of the French left did not take place.

The Right: Divisions and Cleavages in *fin de siècle* France

PAUL HAINSWORTH

In contrast to the initial 23 years of the French Fifth Republic, in recent decades the previously dominant right has had to alternate in power or even share power with the left. The 1995 presidential election saw the return of a (neo-)Gaullist, Jacques Chirac, to the presidency. Subsequently, though, the right has been characterised by division and conflict over personalities, leadership matters, policy orientation and strategy. As a result, the right remains fragile and the evolution towards a more consensual pluralistic right is still problematic.

The New Social Movement Phenomenon: Placing France in Comparative Perspective

ANDREW APPLETON

This essay examines the phenomenon of new social movements (NSMs) in contemporary France. It argues that NSMs in France can only be understood in a broader comparative perspective: moreover, it suggests that theoretical approaches developed more broadly in the social movement literature are applicable to the French case. The essay examines the first and second waves of social movement activity in contemporary France, noting that the differences between the two often cited in the literature are not perhaps as great as has been argued. Finally, it concludes that France cannot, and should not, be understood – in the realm of NSMs – from the perspective of exceptionalism, but that it is a good case for testing comparative theory.

Amendments to the French Constitution: One Surprise After Another

GUY CARCASSONNE

The Fifth Republic is a Republic of paradoxes and the theme of constitutional revision is no exception. On the one hand, the constitution of Fifth Republic has been amended more times than any other constitution that France has known. On the other hand, these amendments have, more often than not, been simple adaptations rather than real reforms, even though there is a desire for such reforms to be passed. Similarly, the sluggishness of the amendment process suggests that it can only be undertaken in favourable circumstances. However, the evidence shows that in recent times most revisions have occurred during periods of 'cohabitation'.

The Fifth Republic: From the *Droit de l'État* to the *État de droit*?

VINCENT WRIGHT

This essay examines the increasing interaction between law and politics in the Fifth Republic. Recent developments in this domain have led to the argument that France can now be characterised as an *État de Droit* – a state bound by and respectful towards the rule of law and due process. However, while the juridification of institutions, politics and public policy undoubtedly marks one of the main ways in which French political life has been transformed over the last two decades, there remain important limits to the processes of juridification. In short, the *État de Droit* in France is more incipient than fully realised.

The Changing Role of French Local Government

EMMANUEL NÉGRIER

Whatever their limits and internal contradictions, French decentralisation reforms forced a reconsideration of the concept of local government and how it is studied. New conceptualisations of public action emerged which were closer to those found in European scholarship than to the traditional French notion of 'cross-regulation'. The aim of this work was to account for the two main developments at the local level caused by the reforms: first, the rise of multi-level local empowerment, problems of co-ordination and the redefinition of the political capacity of the local state; and, second, the changing political dimension of local government, including the differentiated power structure between levels of local government and the nature of local political legitimacy. In this essay, the adaptation of French local government will be examined, concluding that in a European context the French system is now less exceptional than it was previously.

The Changing Dynamics of State-Society Relations in the Fifth Republic

VIVIEN A. SCHMIDT

The traditional relationship between state and society in France, where the state acts and society reacts, has been changing. Deregulation and privatisation of business, liberalisation of the media, modernisation of state administration, decentralisation of local government, and European integration have all served to alter state-society relations. The state is no longer so certain of its leadership and society is no longer so willing to be led. The transformations have been more dramatic in those areas where the relationship has been traditionally closest, as in business-government relationship, than in those where is has traditionally been distant, as in labour-government relations. Whereas for business, there has been a significant transfer of power from state to society, for labour no such transfer has occurred, and relations continue to be problematic. Moreover, although relations with civil society have generally improved through a loosening of state control and an increase in state efficiency and transparency, these have little affected citizen participation and access to decision making.

The *Service Public* Under Stress

ALISTAIR COLE

This essay elucidates the various meanings of the elusive notion of *service public*. *Service public* is an abstract legal doctrine, a set of normative values, a category of public employment and a form of economic activity. The main body of the essay appraises European, national and sub-national challenges to traditional French understandings of the *service public*. Through observing examples of ideological and organisational resistance, the essay concludes that, though French policy makers have confronted the challenges to the *service public* in a manner consistent with their political traditions, the French polity has mutated under the combined impact of internal and external pressures for change.

Restructuring Health Policy Networks:
A French Policy Style?

STEVEN GRIGGS

Successive French governments have sought to redesign health policy subsystems as the priorities of government have moved from expanding access to health care to imposing cost containment and increasing efficiency in the delivery of health services. This essay investigates how far we are able to identify a distinctly French pattern of policy change as characterised in the concept of a policy style. Recognising the cognitive and normative dimensions of public policies, it argues that policy styles should embody a prevailing policy frame or policy discourse. However, it concludes that there is no specifically 'French' pattern of policy change and that there is, as such, no 'French' policy style. Policy making in France is little different from policy making in other West European states. It is erratic, driven by the 'demands' of politicians, and proceeds more by trial-and-error than any rational response. The French state is neither 'strong' nor 'weak', but 'disoriented' with, as this essay argues, the different values and objectives imported into the management of health policy networks by successive sets of ministers and senior state officials driving the process of policy change.

The End of French Exceptionalism?

JILL LOVECY

This essay argues that two successive, and contrasting, discourses on the end of French exceptionalism need to be distinguished over the last decade, if we are to account for both the prominence and the persistence of the claim to French exceptionalism. This claim masks fundamental differences as to what had previously constituted France's 'uniqueness'; as well as causal factors promoting change in the contemporary period. Not least, it hides the characterisation of the new 'order of things' on to which France is now being aligned. The exceptionally widespread resort in France to this deceptively simple formulation has nevertheless provided an impetus towards incorporating her contemporary politics within broader comparativist typologies. France is seen as one of a variety of path-dependent liberal democracies and one of a variety of path-dependent models of capitalism.

About the Contributors

Andrew Appleton is currently Associate Professor at Washington State University, where he teaches courses in political parties, participation and comparative politics. He has published articles on France in *Comparative Politics*, *West European Politics*, *Party Politics* and other journals. He is currently working on the role of local party organisations in working-class communities.

Guy Carcassonne is Professor of Public Law at the University of Paris X – Nanterre. He is a regular contributor to *Le Point*. He is also the author of many publications, most recently the third edition of *La Constitution*, 3rd edition (Paris, Seuil 1999).

Alistair Cole is Professorial Research Fellow at Cardiff University. He has published extensively in the sphere of French and European politics. His most recent book is *French Politics and Society* (Hemel Hempstead: Prentice-Hall 1998).

Robert Elgie is Senior Lecturer in European Politics at the University of Nottingham. His publications are in the fields of French and comparative politics. They include *The Role of the Prime Minister in France* (London, Macmillan 1993), *French Politics: Debates and Controversies*, with Steven Griggs (London, Routledge forthcoming), *The Politics of Central Banks*, with Helen Thompson (London, Routledge 1998) and *Semi-Presidentialism in Europe*, as editor (Oxford: OUP 1999).

Steven Griggs is Senior Lecturer in Public Policy in the Field of Political Studies at Staffordshire University. His doctoral research examined the mobilisation and professionalisation of hospital managers and health policy change in France. He has published on French politics and health policy, and has recently completed a book with Robert Elgie, *French Politics: Debates and Controversies*, to be published by Routledge in 2000.

Paul Hainsworth is Senior Lecturer in Politics at the University of Ulster at Jordanstown. He has published widely on French and European politics in books, journals and chapter formats. He is the co-editor of *Regional and Federal Studies*.

Jill Lovecy is Lecturer in Government at the University of Manchester. She has published essays and articles on comparative and French politics and public policy and, more recently, on issues relating to professional regulation in the European Union, France and the UK.

Emmanuel Négrier is CNRS researcher in the Centre Comparatif d'Étude des Politiques Publiques et les Espaces Locaux (CEPEL) at the University of Montpellier I. He has worked extensively on European territorial politics and policy, cultural policy and the politics of private territorial interests. His publications include *Que gouvernent les régions d'Europe* (Paris, L'Harmattan, 1998) edited with Bernard Jouve, as well as articles in *International Journal of Urban and Regional Research*, *European Planning Studies* and *Pôle Sud*.

Vivien A. Schmidt is Professor of International Relations at Boston University. She has published widely in European political economy and public policy, including *From State to Market? The Transformation of French Business and Government* (Cambridge: CUP 1996) and *Democratizing France* (ibid. 1990). Recent articles have appeared in *Daedalus, Governance, Journal of European Public Policy, Journal of Common Market Studies*, and *Comparative Politics*. Currently, Professor Schmidt is completing a book on the impact of European integration and globalization on economics, institutions, and discourse in France, Britain, and Germany. She is also co-directing a project at the Max Planck Institute for the Study of Society (Cologne) on the adjustment of the welfare state to international economic pressures.

Joseph Szarka is Senior Lecturer in the Department of European Studies, University of Bath. He has published widely on a range of economic and electoral issues. He is currently working on environmental politics and policies in France and Britain.

Vincent Wright was the joint editor of *West European Politics* from its creation in 1977 until his death in July 1999. He has written books on French government and politics, most notably on French prefects and on the Conseil d'État, and has edited or co-edited several volumes on government and administration in Western Europe. He co-directed a major comparative project on core executive policy co-ordination in Western Europe.

Index

BOOKS OF RELATED INTEREST

Politics and Policy in Democratic Spain
No Longer Different?
Paul Heywood, University of Nottingham (Ed)

'A set of enormously rich and in-depth analyses from a wide array of important yet underresearched topics in Spanish public policy and political processes. Some individual chapters present an excellent mixture of theoretical and empirical analysis ... Very good essays ... Many excellent chapters.'

Choice

'Spain is different' was a favourite tourist board slogan of the Franco dictatorship. But is Spain still different? Spain's 1978 Constitution marked the formal establishment of democracy, following nearly 40 years of dictatorial rule, but what shape has Spanish democracy taken? This volume provides an original series of analyses of the development of politics in Spain since the remarkable success of the transition to democracy. Drawing on the latest research by both established and younger scholars, most of them Spanish, the book offers an up-to-date assessment of democracy in the least studied of Europe's major states. It will be essential reading for those who want to understand politics in contemporary Spain.

248 pages 1999
0 7146 4910 4 cloth £37.50/$52.50
0 7146 4467 6 paper £16.50/$24.50
A special issue of the journal West European Politics

Compounded Representation in West European Federations
Joanne Bay Brzinski, **Thomas D Lancaster** and **Christian Tuschhoff**, all at Emory University, Georgia, USA

For two years, the three Editors have collaborated on a research project entitled 'Federalism and Compounded Representation in Western Europe'. It took a fresh approach to scholarly exchange and brought together scholars from America, Canada and Europe in three separate workshops. Substantively, the eight selected essays address a key issue of European integration bringing together two separate fields in comparative politics: federalism and political representation. The question posed is 'How does federalism affect institutions and methods of representation?' Federalism and representation deal with similar issues such as problems of societal diversity and cohesion, and the separation and aggregation of power. Despite their conceptual commonality, scholarly literatures tend to treat them separately. Compounded Representation as a term will be one of the important contributions this volume makes in its overlapping of the literatures on federalism and representation.

200 pages 1999
0 7146 4997 X cloth £37.50/$54.50
0 7146 8058 3 paper £16.50/$24.50
A special issue of the journal West European Politics

FRANK CASS PUBLISHERS
Newbury House, 900 Eastern Avenue, Newbury Park, Ilford, Essex IG2 7HH
Tel: +44 (0)20 8599 8866 Fax: +44 (0)20 8599 0984 E-mail: info@frankcass.com
NORTH AMERICA
5804 NE Hassalo Street, Portland, OR 97213 3644, USA
Tel: 800 944 6190 Fax: 503 280 8832 E-mail cass@isbs.com
Website: www.frankcass.com

Britain in the Nineties

The Politics of Paradox

Hugh Berrington, Emeritus Professor of Politics, University of Newcastle upon Tyne (Ed)

'This is a fascinating collection of essays which, taken as a whole, ask (and answer) vital questions regarding contemporary British political life'.

Contemporary Review

This volume looks at the striking changes in British politics and government since the accession of Mrs Thatcher and in particular at the last six or seven years. Its aim is to explore some of these recent changes and to emphasise the recurring paradoxes in the political developments of the last 20 years, for example, the changes of sides by the main parties on Europe.

240 pages 1998
0 7146 4880 9 cloth £35.00/$49.50
0 7146 4434 X paper £16.50/$24.50
A special issue of the journal West European Politics

Crisis and Transition in Italian Politics

Martin Rhodes and **Martin Bull**, European University Institute, Florence (Eds)

'Indispensable to students of Italian Politics.'
Contemporary Politics

This book seeks to analyse the last decade and a half of Italian political development through the prism of the changes of the early 1990s. The authors identify the deep trends of political change in Italy's transition beneath the ephemera of day-to-day political life – the focus of much current analysis. They reveal a political system that is both dynamic and sclerotic, adaptable and blocked, and with a surprising degree of flexibility alongside institutional inertia.

256 pages 31 tables, 8 figs 1997
0 7146 4816 7 cloth £32.50/$45.00
0 7146 4366 1 paper £16.50/$22.50
A special issue of the journal West European Politics

FRANK CASS PUBLISHERS
Newbury House, 900 Eastern Avenue, Newbury Park, Ilford, Essex IG2 7HH
Tel: +44 (0)20 8599 8866 Fax: +44 (0)20 8599 0984 E-mail: info@frankcass.com
NORTH AMERICA
5804 NE Hassalo Street, Portland, OR 97213 3644, USA
Tel: 800 944 6190 Fax: 503 280 8832 E-mail cass@isbs.com
Website: www.frankcass.com